EVERYMAN, I will go with thee,
and be thy guide,
In thy most need to go by thy side

WACE and LAYAMON

Arthurian Chronicles

Translated by Eugene Mason

Introduction by Gwyn Jones

Dent: London and Melbourne
EVERYMAN'S LIBRARY

© Introduction, J. M. Dent & Sons Ltd, 1962

Made in Great Britain by
Guernsey Press Co. Ltd, Guernsey, C.I. for
J. M. Dent & Sons Ltd
Aldine House, 33 Welbeck Street, London W1M 8LX

This edition was first published in
Everyman's Library in 1912
Last reprinted 1986

No 1578   Paperback ISBN 0 460 11578 2

INTRODUCTION

'THE nature of a preface', said Dryden, 'is rambling, never wholly out of the way, nor in it.' The pronouncements of a thousand oracles contain no more of truth for him who writes of Arthur. Let him rear as high as he likes he will keep one hoof in the rut; let him be grave, soft and circumspect and he will crash through safe hedgerows to the dubious verges of truth.

Luckily the two works now to be introduced to new readers do not involve us too deeply in the problem of Arthurian origins. The origins of Layamon are to be sought mainly in Wace, and the origins of Wace mainly in Geoffrey of Monmouth, and at Geoffrey (a Monmouthshire man is speaking) we can draw the line.

Geoffrey completed his *Historia Regum Britanniæ* about 1135–7, and it is simple and true to call it a major contribution to the Arthurian legend. It is an important part, that is to say, of that immense literature in a score of languages which pays tribute to one of the foremost figures and symbols ever to enchant the human imagination. To begin with, let us listen to yet another twelfth-century writer and share his amazement at what had happened to the fame of Arthur as early as the 1170's. The testimony occurs in the commentary on Geoffrey's *Prophetia Merlini*, long but erroneously attributed to Alanus de Insulis:

What place is there within the bounds of the empire of Christendom to which the winged praise of Arthur the Briton has not extended? Who is there, I ask, who does not speak of Arthur the Briton, since he is but little less known to the peoples of Asia than to the Bretons, as we are informed by our palmers who return from the countries of the East? The Eastern peoples speak of him as do the Western, though

separated by the breadth of the whole earth. Egypt speaks of
him, and the Bosphorus is not silent. Rome, queen of cities,
sings his deeds, and his wars are not unknown to her former
rival Carthage. Antioch, Armenia and Palestine celebrate his
feats.

This sounds like the language of rhapsody, but the facts
are not hard to arrive at, and these make it clear that the
spread of the Arthurian legend during the course of the
twelfth century is one of the most remarkable phenomena in
literary history. The outstanding names in that diffusion
are those of the Welshman or Breton, Geoffrey of Monmouth, and the Frenchman, Chrétien de Troyes. Geoffrey
was early branded as 'the father of lies', and there have been
few critical readers during the last eight hundred years to
quarrel with the description. But that he told lies (that is,
refashioned material and invented authorities) is a circum-
stance relevant to the diffusion of the Arthurian legend only
in so far as it was helpful to that diffusion. There is a kind
of truth which simply does not matter, as *Ossian* was to
demonstrate so powerfully six and a half centuries later.
Who now reads William of Newburgh? As Burke said of
Bolingbroke: 'Who ever read him through?' But Geoffrey
is within sight of a millenium, with his eight hundred and
twenty years of readers and influence. Even before he wrote
his *Historia*, stories about Arthur and certain of his knights
were much the fashion in western Europe. Geoffrey in no
sense created this fashion, but he exploited it, he made the
most of it, and in doing so gave it still greater vogue. His
book was exceedingly popular and has survived in a great
number of manuscripts, almost fifty of them from the
twelfth century alone. It was popular not so much because
it was new, or because it was lies, but because it was what
everyone wanted to read and be informed about, and
because it had the desired aura of history.

Of Chrétien de Troyes it is enough to say that his is the
most important name in the history of Arthurian romance,
and that this is so for three main reasons: his merits as a

poet and story-teller, his personal contribution to, and his influence upon, the *genre*. With Chrétien (he wrote his Arthurian poems about 1160–85) and after him the story is clearer and the evidence fuller, and it is not hard to see the Arthurian legend grow into our common European heritage. But our more modest task now is to look briefly at two Arthurian poets, one of whom preceded the illustrious Chrétien (and may have helped to fashion him), the other, the Englishman Layamon, who came after him but, most curiously, entirely escaped his influence.

First, Wace. Where does he stand in the story? The little we know of him is of his own telling. In the *Roman de Rou* (i.e. Rollo), his verse chronicle concerning the dukes of Normandy, he says:

> If any one should ask who said this, who put this history into the Romance tongue, I say and will say to him that I am Wace of the island of Jersey, which lies westward in the sea, and is part of the fief of Normandy. In the island of Jersey was I born, and to Caen I was taken when a little lad, where I was put to the study of letters. Thereafter I studied long in [the Île de] France; and after I returned from France I lived a long time at Caen. I busied myself with making books in Romance; many of them I wrote, and many of them I made.

He describes himself further as a *clerc lisant*, but what kind of 'reading clerk' that means is hard to determine. The title he most fancied was *Maistre*, which may denote that he was a teacher; but whatever the nature of his official employment posterity sees in him (and one suspects he saw in himself) a professional author and literary man. He wrote extensively, translations, romans, serventeis or duty-poems, chronicles and saints' lives. Above all he rendered Geoffrey's *Historia* into French verse, by 1155.

Not that he was the first or only one to do so. The Anglo-Norman Gaimar had produced a metrical translation of the *Historia* called *Estorie des Bretons* during the 1140's, and there are almost a dozen fragments of other, for the most part unidentifiable, translations still extant, though this

emphatically does not mean that there were a dozen translations of Geoffrey into French. But Wace with his *Roman
de Brut* (i.e. Brutus, the eponymous founder of the British
race and history) seems to have cleared them all from the
field. For one thing, he had royal patronage—the *Roman de
Brut* was written to please King Henry II; for another, he
knew his business and was a good poet.

Thus he was too good a poet to reproduce Geoffrey as
literally as he could in verse. His 15,000 lines follow Geoffrey
closely as to order and substance, but there are marked
differences of tone, style and emphasis. He had a native
caution and common sense which sharply distinguish him
from his high-flying predecessor, while the very act of
running his tale into the quick and vigorous French octo-
syllabic couplet produces effects different from Geoffrey's
ornate and resounding Latin prose. Like the self-respecting
professional he was he had mastered the conventions of
metrical chronicle and romance; he was well up in rhetoric,
especially the devices of parallelism, balance, repetition and
sententia or gnomic sayings; and if, like most medieval poets,
he could be garrulous, he was sparingly so. Again, he had
learned the art of stylized description, and added to it what
is sometimes more pleasing to the modern reader, a visual
quality of his own. The favourite example is also the best:
When Arthur begins his Roman campaign Geoffrey whips
him aboard in a twinkling, but Wace gives us such a scene
of embarkation and departure as thrills and delights even
now. In brief, he is in command of his poem, and not under
orders from the ingenious Geoffrey. Further, he was
addressing himself to a society which was learning *courtoisie*.
With Chrétien to come, we must be careful not to exaggerate,
but clearly Wace's Arthur is more courtly and less *farouche*
than Geoffrey's, who in turn is more chivalric than the rude,
savage, primitive and protective folk-hero Arthur of the
earliest Welsh sources. All this is exactly what we should
expect of a French poet in the second half of the twelfth
century.

Finally, he had access to sources of information other than Geoffrey. He was of an inquiring turn of mind, with, for his day, a scholarly and sceptical approach to lais, marvellous tales and fables. He rejects the Prophecies of Merlin which Geoffrey had incorporated into the *Historia*, and sifts the other evidence. 'Not all lies, nor all true, all foolishness, nor all sense. So much have the story-tellers told, and so much have the makers of fables fabled to embellish their stories, that they have made all seem fable.' With it all he sharpened Geoffrey's take-it-or-leave-it hints about Arthur as 'the hope of Britain' who will return to his anxious people in their hour of trial; and he is the first to mention the famous Round Table.

Our second author, Layamon, was as English, that is to say Anglo-Saxon, as Wace was Norman-French. We cannot be sure when he composed the poem now conveniently known as his *Brut*, but it was probably completed not long after 1190. This is his own endearing account of himself and his undertaking:

There was a priest among the people who was named Layamon. He was son of Leovenath—the Lord be good to him!—and lived at Areley at a noble church on Severn's bank —pleasant he found it there—near Redstone, where he read books [or his Mass or Bible]. It came into his mind, a happy thought, that he would tell the noble deeds of the English, what they were named and whence they came who first possessed the English land. . . . Layamon travelled widely throughout this nation and procured those excellent books which he took as his model. He took the English book which Saint Bede made; another he took in Latin which Saint Albin made and the fair Augustine who introduced baptism here; the third book he took and laid in their midst which a French clerk made, whose name was Wace and was most skilled at writing; and he [i.e. Wace] gave it [dedicated it?] to the noble Eleanor, who was Henry the high king's queen. These books Layamon laid before him and turned over the leaves; lovingly he beheld them—the Lord be good to him!—seized pen with fingers and wrote on vellum, set true words together and condensed the three books into one.

The first two of these books were the English and Latin
versions of Bede's *Ecclesiastical History*, and he was sparing
indeed in his use of them. For Layamon it was Wace first
and the rest of the field nowhere—and the rest included
Geoffrey, Wace's original. But just as the *Roman de Brut*
was no hand-tied translation of the *Historia Regum Britanniæ*, so Layamon's *Brut* was a free rendering of the
Roman de Brut. Once more there is a close correspondence as
to order and substance, but Wace's 15,000 octosyllabics
have become what can be described either as some 16,000
alliterative long lines or 32,000 short irregular lines. It is
assumed by some scholars that there were two kinds of Old
English verse, the 'classical' (with which we are familiar:
the verse of *Beowulf*, for example), conforming to strict
rules, and the 'popular', written either in ignorance or in
disregard of these rules, and that Layamon is in direct line
of descent from this popular verse, with the two halves of
his long line often linked not only by alliteration but by
assonance or rhyme, and so sounding like couplets variously
organized, or at times, it must be admitted, variously dis-
organized. On the other hand, it is an equally reasonable
assumption that Layamon's verse is the foreseeable outcome
of the modification of Old English classical verse in the
tenth and eleventh centuries. In any case, the insecurity and
roughness of his metre are not fatal to him; like Wace he
was a good poet and like Wace he is worthy of the honour
which both close readers and distant admirers have joined
in according him.

In the *Brut* Arthur, hero and emperor, makes his first
appearance in English vernacular literature. The 'historia
Britonum' very properly starts with the flight of Aeneas
from Troy and continues till the departure of Cadwalader
to Rome and the dispersal of the Britons, henceforth to be
called the Welsh, among 'the rocks and cliffs, the churches
and monasteries, the woods and mountains', which they
love so well. But with Geoffrey, Wace and Layamon it is the
Arthurian part of the story which receives pride of place. It

is this abundant presentation of our national hero to the English reader, together with Layamon's many poetical merits, which has led to estimates of the poem ranging from Dorothy Everett's 'the most considerable and by far the best of the early Middle English alliterative poems' to Tatlock's 'the nearest thing we have to a traditional racial epic'.

Layamon was an intensely English poet. His subject was British history; his hero of heroes a British king who banged the English up hill and down dale and hammered the Alemain race from Iceland to Lombardy; his source-book was Norman-French; but his spirit, mood and manner were English, in the sense that *Beowulf* and *Brunanburh* were English. Even the British Arthur becomes an Englishman, a Germanic hero, brave, daring and open-handed. We are in a world of feasts and vaunting speeches, flytings and lusty battles, fierce deeds and bloody humour, with the Fiend, the Adversary of Man, always round the next corner. Even the pithy formulas, 'the doomed men fell', 'woe came upon the people' and the like, so regularly repeated, are remembrancers from the Germanic past. But Layamon's Englishry is national rather than provincial; one assumes that he rejected French influence because his interests lay elsewhere, and because he was the willing heir of an older, more native, tradition.

He has considerably expanded his original, in part by the use of new material, in part by the elaboration of what he borrowed. Thus Layamon gives us a much fuller account of the founding of the Round Table than does Wace; it is Layamon who tells of the elves that attended on the infant Arthur and endowed him with gifts and qualities; and in a passage of remarkable beauty he launched as upon a great river flowing towards posterity the story of how Arthur after his last battle was carried away by two maidens in a boat, to Argante in Avallon, to be healed of his wounds. 'And afterwards I will return to my kingdom and dwell among the Britons with great joy.' These things are new, and qualitatively hardly to be measured; but in the bulk of Layamon's

expansions they do not weigh heavily against the additions
that arise from the poet's temperament and methods. The
feasts, the armings, the similes, the oratory account for far
more lines, his descriptions of natural background, like that
of Loch Lomond (where we would not be surprised to find
Grendel's mother bathing among the monsters), and above
all his zest for scenes of rapid and warlike action. The
account of Arthur's wars against Colgrim, Baldulf and
Childric is brilliantly done. The images of the hunted fox,
the harassed crane, the steel fishes in the flood are in his
most enthusiastic and powerful vein; the folk-tale ferocity
of Arthur, the exultation in warlike deeds of this boast-
uttering, boast-performing, hostage-hanging king, are made
as exciting to us as to Layamon himself. Like many a quiet-
living man before and since, our poet liked to imbrue his
literary hands with blood and snuff destruction. But he was
not limited to these strong effects. How delightful his sketch
of the four queens at the Whitsuntide service at Caerleon:
'Four chosen queens; each bore in her left hand a jewel of
red gold, and three snow-white doves sate on their shoulders.'
How elegiac and beautiful his account of the passing of
Arthur. He had a brave poetic imagination which he
exercised on a variety of transmutable material, and for the
most part transmuted it for good.

The literary history of the Arthurian legend in the twelfth
century is distinguished above all by Geoffrey's flair for
exploiting an opportunity and Chrétien's ability to enrich
and enhance it. With these two, on a lower but most
honourable plane, stand Wace and Layamon, poets and
chroniclers and pillars bearing up our British story.

GWYN JONES.

1962.

SELECT BIBLIOGRAPHY

Wace, *Le Roman de Brut*, ed. I. Arnold, 2 vols., Paris 1938–40; Layamon, *Brut*, ed. F. Madden, 3 vols., London 1847; *Selections from Layamon's Brut*, ed. J. Hall, Oxford, 1924; *Layamon*, ed. G. L. Brook and R. F. Leslie, for the Early English Text Society, Vol. 1, 1963; Vol. II, 1978.

For the Arthurian legend in general see R. S. Loomis, *Arthurian Tradition and Chrétien de Troyes*, Oxford, 1949; J. S. P. Tatlock, *The Legendary History of Britain*, Berkeley and Los Angeles, 1950 (with chapters on Wace and Layamon and extensive bibliographical reference); R. S. Loomis (ed.), *Arthurian Literature in the Middle Ages*, Oxford, 1959 (a chapter on Wace by C. Foulon and on Layamon by the editor. This is the best Arthurian survey available). M. Houck, *Sources of the Roman de Brut of Wace*, Berkeley, 1941, and D. Everett, 'Layamon and the Earliest Middle English Verse', in *Essays on Middle English Literature*, Oxford, 1955, are rewarding. Thomas Jones, 'The Early Evolution of the Legend of Arthur', in *Nottingham Medieval Studies*, VIII, 1964; R. L. Brengle, *Arthur King of Britain* (contains an essay on Wace by R. H. Fletcher, and on Layamon by H. C. Wyld), Appleton-Century, Crofts, 1964; R. Barber, *King Arthur in Legend and History*, Boydell, 1974; *The Arthurian Legends*, Boydell, 1979.

CONTENTS

WACE'S ROMAN DE BRUT

WACE'S ROMAN DE BRUT

CONSTANTINE came to Totnes, and many a stout knight with him—there was not one but was worthy of the kingship. The host set forth towards London, and sent messages in every part, bidding the Britons to their aid, for as yet they were too fearful to come from their secret places. When the Britons heard these tidings they drew, thick as rain, from the woodlands and the mountain, and came before the host in troops and companies. To make short a long matter, these marched so far and wrought such deeds that in the end they altogether discomfited those evil men who had done such sore mischief to the land. After these things they held a great council at Cirencester, commanding thereto all the lords and barons of the realm. In that place they chose Constantine as their king, with no long tarrying, none being so bold as to say him nay. So when they had ordained him king, they set the crown on his head with marvellous joy, and owned themselves as his men. Afterwards, by their counsel, Constantine took to wife a dame who was come of gentle Roman blood. On this lady he begat three sons. The eldest—whom the king named Constant—he caused to be nourished at Winchester, and there he made him to be vowed a monk. The second son was called Aurelius, and his surname Ambrosius. Lastly was born Uther, and it was he whose days were longest in the land. These two varlets were held in ward by Gosselyn, the archbishop.

So long as Constantine lived the realm had rest and peace; but he died before his time had come, for he reigned but twelve short years. There was a certain Pict of his household, a traitor, a foul felon, who for a great while had been about his person. I cannot tell the reason why he bore the king so mortal a grudge. This Pict took the king aside privily in an orchard, as though he would speak to him of some hidden matter. The king had no thought to keep himself from this false felon, who whilst he made seeming to speak in his master's ear, drew forth a knife and smote him therewith so shrewdly that he died. Then he fled forth from the garden. But many a time have I heard tell that it was Vortigern who caused Constantine to be slain. Great was the sorrow the lords and all honest people made above their king, for the realm had now no prince, save only those children of so tender an age. They laid him in his tomb, but in no wise put him from remembrance. The whole realm assembled together that they might make to themselves a king. They doubted sorely which of the two young children they should choose, for of them they knew neither good nor ill, seeing they were but small and frail, and yet in their warden's charge. As to Constant, the eldest son, who was of more fitting years, they dared not to pluck the habit from his back, since all men deemed it shame and folly to hale him forth from his abbey. The council would have ordained one of the two children to be king had it not been for Vortigern, who arose before them all. This Vortigern came from Wales, and was earl in his own land. He was a strong knight of his body, exceeding rich in goods and kin. Very courteous was he of speech; right prudent in counsel; and long since had made straight the road that he coveted to tread. "What reason is here," said he, "for doubtfulness? There is nought else to do but to make this monk, Constant, our king. He is the rightful heir; his brothers are not long from the breast; neither is it fitting that the crown should be placed upon a stranger's head. Let us strip the gown boldly from his shoulders. I charge the sin upon my own soul. My hand alone shall draw him from the abbey, and set him before you as your king." But all the lords of the council kept silence, for a horrible thing it seemed in their eyes that a monk should wear the mantle of a king. Vortigern, purposing evil in his heart, took horse, and rode swiftly to Winchester. He sought Constant at the abbey, praying the prior of his courtesy that he might speak with him in the parlour. "Constant," said he, "thy father is dead, and men seek to bestow his throne upon thy brothers. Such honour is not seemly, for thine is the crown and seat. If thou bearest me love and affiance, and for thy part wilt promise to make richer all the riches that are mine, on my part I will free thee from these sullen rags and array thee in the purple and ermine of a king. Choose now between this monastery and the heritage that is thine own." Very desirous was Constant of the lordship, and little love had he for his abbey. Right weary was he of choir and psalter, and lightly and easily he made him ready to be gone. He pledged oath and faith to

all that Vortigern required, and after he had so done Vortigern
took him with a strong hand from the monastery, none daring
to gainsay his deed. When Vortigern was assured of his fealty,
he caused Constant to put off the monk's serge, and clothe him
in furs and rich raiment. He carried him to London, and sat
him in his father's chair, though not with the voice and welcome
of the people. The archbishop who should have anointed the
king with oil was dead, neither was any bishop found to give
him unction, or to put his hand to the business. It was Vortigern alone who took the crown and set it on his head. This
king had no unction nor blessing, save from the hand of Vortigern
alone.

Constant reigned in his father's stead. He who had betrayed
the commandment of God, was not one to hold his realm in
surety; and thus he came to an evil end. Sorrow not thereat.
The man who sells his master with a kiss may not hope to spend
the wages of his sin. Vortigern held Constant and his senarchy
in the hollow of his hand. The king did all according to his
pleasure, and granted freely to his every need. Very quickly,
by reason of divers matters, Vortigern perceived that the king
knew but little of the world, since he was nourished in a cloister.
He remembered that the two princes were of tender age. He
saw that the mighty lords of the realm were dead, that the
people were in sore trouble and unrest, and judged that the
place and time were come. Mark now the cunning craft with
which he set about to take his seisin of the realm. " Sire,"
said he, " I have learned and would bring to your knowledge
that the sea folk are gathered together from Norway, and from
the country of the Danes. Since our knights are few in number,
and because of the weakness of the land, they purpose to
descend upon the kingdom, and ravish and spoil your cities.
Draw now together thy men, to guard the realm and thee. Set
food within the strong places, and keep well thy towers. Above
all, have such fear of traitors that thy castles are held of none
save those true men who will hold them to the death. If you
act not after this counsel right speedily there must reign another
king." " I have granted," answered Constant, " everything
to thy hand, and have done all according to thy will. Take
now this fresh burthen upon thee, for thou art wiser than I.
I give you all the realm to thy keeping, so that none shall ravage
it or burn. Cities and manors; goods and treasure; they are
thine as constable. Thy will is my pleasure. Do swiftly that
which it is seemly should be done." Vortigern was very subtle.

None knew better how to hide away his greed. After he had taken the strong towers, the treasure, and the riches to himself, he went again before the king. "Sire," said he, "if it seem good to the king, my counsel would be that he should send to the Picts of Scotland to seek of them horsemen and sergeants to have with him about his household. In that place where the battle is perilous we can call them to our aid. Through these Picts and their kindred we shall hear the talk of the outland men. They will parley between us and these Danes, and serve as embassy between us and our foes." "Do," replied the king, "at thy pleasure. Bring of these Picts as many as you wish. Grant them as guerdon what you deem befits. Do all which it is seemly should be done."

When Vortigern had taken to himself the walled cities, and gathered together the treasure, he sent such messages to the Picts as he desired, so that they came according to his will. Vortigern received them with much honour, giving them greatly to drink, so that they lived in mirth and in solace, altogether drunken and content. Of his bounty Vortigern granted such wages, and spoke so sweetly in the ear of each, that there was not one amongst them who did not cry loudly in the hearing of any who would hearken, that Vortigern was more courteous and of higher valiance than the king—yea, that he was worthy to sit upon the king's throne, or in a richer chair than his. Vortigern rejoiced greatly at these words. He made much of his Picts, and honoured them more sweetly than ever before. On a day when they had sat long at their cups, and all were well drunken, Vortigern came amongst them in the hall. He saluted them sadly, showing the semblance of a woeful man. "Right dear are you to my heart;" said he, "very willingly have I served you, and right gladly would I serve you still, if but the wealth were mine. But this realm belongs altogether to the king. Nought can I bestow, nothing is mine to spend, save only that I render him account of every doit. So little revenue is mine of this land, that it becomes me to seek my fortune beyond the sea. I have set my whole intent to serve my king to the utmost of my might, and for recompense have of him such estate that I can maintain scarce forty sergeants to my household. If all goes well with me we may meet again, for I commend me to your goodwill. This weighs heavily upon me that I must leave you now. But, beggar as I am, I can do no other; only I entreat you this, that if you hear my business has come to a fair end, you will of a surety seek my love again." For all his piteous speech Vortigern was false, and had falsely spoken, but those who had well drunken gave faith to his words. They held for gospel truth what this vile traitor had told them. They murmured together amongst themselves: "What then shall become of us, since we lose so generous a lord! Let us rather slay this mad king, this shaveling, and raise Vortigern to his seat. Worthy is he of crown and kingdom; so on him we will cast the lot. Too long already have we suffered this renegade monk, whom now we serve." Forthwith they entered in the king's chamber, and laying hands upon him, slew him where he stood. They smote the head from off his shoulders, and bare it to Vortigern in his lodging, crying, "Look now, and see by what bands we bind you to this realm. The king is dead, and we forbid you to go from amongst us. Take now the crown, and become our king." Vortigern knew again the head of his lord. He made semblance of bitter sorrow, but rejoiced privily in his heart, though of his cunning he hid his gladness from the eyes of men. To cover his falseness the deeper, Vortigern called the Romans together in council. He struck the heads from off those traitors, leaving not one to escape alive. But many a citizen was persuaded, and some said openly, that these murderers would not have laid hands upon the king, neither looked evilly upon him, nor thought to do him mischief, had not Vortigern required of them such deed.

When the death of the king was told to them who held the two brothers in ordinance, they were assured that he who slew the king would not scruple to serve the princes in the self-same fashion. For fear of Vortigern they took Aurelius and Uther, and fled beyond the sea to Little Britain, commending themselves to the pity of Budes, the king. Since they were of his kin King Budes welcomed them right courteously. He received them to his table with great honour, and bestowed upon them many rich gifts. Now having taken to himself the strong places, the castles, and the cities of the kingdom, Vortigern proclaimed him to be king with marvellous pride. His joy was the less because the realm was harassed by the Picts, who would avenge their kindred, whom he had slain with the sword. Moreover he was sorely troubled, since it was noised abroad that the two princes were gathering a company together, purposing in a short space to return to their own land. The rumour ran that the barons were resolved to join this great host, and to own the brothers as their lords, so that in a while Vortigern would be utterly destroyed. Many there were who told of such things.

Whilst men talked thus, there came to a haven in Kent three galleys, bearing a strange people to the land. These folk were fair of face and comely of person. They owned as lords Hengist and Horsa, two brethren of mighty stature, and of outland speech. The tidings came to Vortigern at Canterbury, where he abode that day, that a foreign folk from a far country had drawn to the realm in ships. The king sent messages of peace and goodwill to these strangers, praying that be they whom they might, they would come quickly and speak with him in his palace, and return swiftly to their own place. When they received his commandment they sought him with the more surety. They came into the king's presence and did reverence, with a proud bearing. Vortigern looked closely upon the brethren. Shapely were they of body, bright of visage, taller and more comely than any youth he knew. "From what land have you come," inquired the king, "and on what errand? Tell me now the place of your birth." The elder and the mightier of the brethren, called Hengist, made answer in the name of all his fellows. "We be of a country called Saxony," said he, "there were we born and there we abode. If thou wilt learn the chance we seek upon the sea, I will answer truly, if so it be according to thy will." "Say on," said the king, "and hide nothing. No harm shall come to thee of this." "Fair king," answered Hengist, "gentle sire, I know not if I can make it plain. Our race is of a fertile stock, more quick and abounding than any other you may know, or whereof you have heard speak. Our folk are marvellously fruitful, and the tale of the children is beyond measure. Women and men are more in number than the sand, for the greater sorrow of those amongst us who are here. When our people are so many that the land may not sustain nor suffice them, then the princes who rule the realm assemble before them all the young men of the age of fifteen years and upwards, for such is our use and custom. From out of these they choose the most valiant and the most strong, and, casting lots, send them forth from the country, so that they may travel into divers lands, seeking fiefs and houses of their own. Go out they must, since the earth cannot contain them; for the children came more thickly than the beasts which pasture in the fields. Because of the lot that fell upon us we have bidden farewell to our homes, and putting our trust in Mercury, the god has led us to your realm." When the king heard the name of Mercury as the god of their governance, he inquired what manner of men these were, and of the god in whom they believed. "We have," answered Hengist, "gods a many, to whom it is our bounden duty to raise altars. These gods have to name Phœbus and Saturn, Jupiter and Mercury. Many another god we worship, according to the wont of our country, and as our fathers have told us. But above all gods we keep in chiefest honour Mercury, who in our own tongue is called Woden. Our fathers held this god in such reverence that they devoted the fourth day of the week to his service. Because of their hope in Woden they called his feast Wednesday, and yet it bears his name. By the side of this god of whom I have spoken, we set our goddess Freya, who is held in worship of us all. To show forth their love, our fathers consecrated the sixth day to her service, and on the high authority of the past we call Friday by Freya's name." "Ill is your faith," replied the king, "and in an evil god you put your trust. This thing is grievous to me, but nevertheless I welcome your coming right gladly. You are valiant men, as I deem, accustomed to harness, and so you will be my servants, very willingly will I make you of my household, and of wealth you shall find no lack. Certain thieves from Scotland torment me grievously at this time, burning my land and preying on my cities. So it be God's pleasure, your coming may turn to my rich profit, for by His aid and yours, I look to destroy these same Picts and Scots. For from that land come and return these thieves who so harass and damage my realm. You shall find me no grudging master, and when I am avenged upon them, you will have no complaint to find with bounty or wages or gifts." In this manner the Saxons came from out their ships, and the king's court was strengthened by a mighty company. Now in no long time afterwards the Picts entered the king's realm, with a great host, burning, wasting, and pilling at their will. When they would have passed the Humber, the king, who was told thereof, hastened to meet them with his lords, the Britons, and these Saxons. The hosts came together, and the battle was grim and lasting, for many were discomfited to death that day. The Picts, doubting nothing but that they would gain the victory as they had done before, carried themselves hardily, and struck fiercely with the sword. They fought thus stoutly, and endured so painfully, since they were shamed to do less than was their wont. But their evil custom was broken, for the Saxons gained possession of the field. Since by these Saxons, and their aid, Vortigern was delivered of this peril, he gave them their wages, and added thereto of his bounty.

On Hengist he bestowed fair manors, and goods, and great riches, so that love lasted between them for a long space.

When Hengist saw that the king might in no wise pass him by, he sought to turn this to his own profit, as was his undoubted right. He knew well how to flatter the king to his own advantage by specious words. On a day when the king's heart was merry, Hengist opened out what was in his mind. " Thou hast given me many honours," said he, " and bestowed on me plenteously of thy wealth. I am not ungrateful, but am thy servant and will remain thy servant, striving to serve thee better in the future even than I have striven in the past. But the longer I am about the king's person, and the more closely I know his court, the more clearly I see and hear and am assured that thou hast not the love of one only baron of thy realm. Each bears thee hate; each nurses his own grudge. I cannot speak, since nothing I know, of those children who have stolen away the love of thine own house. They are the lawful lords of thy barons, and these are but loyal to the sons of their king. Within a little they will come from over sea, and spoil thee of this realm. Not one of thy men but purposes to do thee a mischief. Evil they wish thee, and evil they hope will be thine end. Horribly art thou abhorred; horribly art thou menaced; for evil is on thy track, and evil purposes shortly to pull thee down. I have considered how best I may help thee in this peril. If it pleases the king to bring my wife and children and all that is mine from my own land, the sweeter hostages will be his, and the more faithful will be my service. So diligently will I keep my trust that no foe, however bold, shall spoil thee of one foot of thy heritage. Moreover, sire, it is now a great while since I became thy servant, and many bear malice against me by reason of thy love. Because of their wrath I dare not tarry at night outside my house, nor go beyond the walls. For this cause, sire, so it may please thee, it would become thy honour to grant me some town or tower or strong place, where I may lie in peace of nights, when I am wearied in the king's quarrels. When thy enemies mark the generosity of the king, they will cease to annoy so large a lord." " As to the folk of thine house," made answer the king, " send thou at thy pleasure, and receive them with all worship. The cost of their sustenance shall be mine. For the rest thou art not of the faith. Pagan thou art, and no Christian man. Men, therefore, will deem that I do very wrongfully should I grant thee the other gift you require." " Sire," replied Hengist, " I would of thy bounty a certain

manor. I pray thee of thy courtesy to add thereto so much land—I seek no more—as I may cover with a hide, and as may be compassed therewith. It will be but the hide of a bull, but for the gift's sake I shall go the more surely." Vortigern granted the boon, and Hengist thanked his master. He made ready his messenger, and sent for his kindred from oversea. He took the hide of a bull, and cutting it as small as he might, made one thong of the whole skin. With this thong he compassed a great spoil of land, and gathering good masons together, built thereon a fair castle. In his own tongue he called this place Vancaster, which being interpreted means Thong Castle, forasmuch as the place was compassed by a thong. Now it is hight by many Lancaster, and of these there are few who remember why it was first called after this name.

When Vancaster was well builded there drew near eighteen war galleys, bearing to land Hengist's kindred, together with knights and footmen. With these came Hengist's daughter, Rowena by name, a maiden yet unwed, and most marvellously fair. After all things were made ready Hengist prayed the king to lodge with him awhile, that he might delight himself with meat and drink, and view the new folk of his household, and the castle that he had builded. And the king was pleased to hearken unto his prayer. The king rode to Vancaster with a mean company, since he would not have it noised about the land. He marked the castle and its towers, which were both strong and fair, and much he praised the work. The knights who were freshly come from sea he took to his service, and gave of his bounty. At the feast that day men ate and drank so greatly that for the most part they were drunken. Then came forth from her chamber Rowena, Hengist's daughter, sweetly arrayed and right dainty to see, bearing in her hand a brimming cup of wine. She kneeled before Vortigern very simply, and saluted him courteously after the fashion of her land, saying, "Washael, lord king." The king, who knew nothing of her language, sought the meaning of the maiden's words. This was made plain to him by Redic, the Breton, a fair scholar, who—as it is related—was the first to become apt in the Saxon tongue. He answered swiftly, "The maiden saluted thee courteously, calling thee lord. It is the wont of her people, sire, that when friend drinks with friend, he who proffers the cup cries, 'Washael,' and that he who receives answers in turn, 'Drinkhael.' Then drinks he the half of this loving cup, and for joy and for friendship of him who set it in his hand, kisses the giver with all fair fellowship." When he had learned this thing, the king said " Drinkhael," and smiled upon the damsel. Rowena tasted of the cup, and placed it in the king's hand, and in taking it from the maiden the king kissed her sweetly. By the Saxon were we first taught in this land to greet, saying, " Washael," and afterwards to answer, " Drinkhael; " to drain the cup in full measure, or to share it with one other; to kiss together when the cup was passed. The custom was commenced as I have shown you, and we observe this ritual yet, as well I know, in the rich feasts of our country.

Now the maiden was gracious of body, and passing fair of face; dainty and tall, and plump of her person. She stood before the king in a web of fine raiment, and ravished his eyes beyond measure. She filled the king's cup willingly, and was altogether according to his wish. So merry was the king, so well had he drunken, that he desired the damsel in his heart. The devil, who has led many a man astray, snared Vortigern with such sorcery, that he became mad with love to possess Hengist's daughter. He was so fast in the devil's net that he saw neither shame nor sin in this love. He denied not his hope, though the maid was of pagans born. Vortigern prayed Hengist that he would grant him the maid in marriage, and Hengist accorded her with goodwill. But first he took counsel with his brother and his friends. These praised the marriage, but counselled Hengist to give the damsel only on such covenant that the king should deliver him Kent as her dowry. The king coveted the maiden so greatly, he doted so dearly, that he made her his queen. She was a pagan woman, and became his wife according to the rites of the paynim. No priest blessed that marriage, there was neither Mass nor prayer. So hot was the king's love that he espoused her the same evening, and bestowed on Hengist Kent as her dowry.

Hengist went into Kent, and seized all the country into his hand. He drove forth Garagon, the governor, who had heard no word of the business. Vortigern showed more credence and love to the heathen than to christened men; so that these gave him again his malice, and abandoned his counsel. His own sons held him in hatred, forsaking his fellowship because of the pagans. For this Vortigern had married a wife, who long was dead and at peace. On this first wife he had begotten three sons, these only. The first was named Vortimer, the second Passent, and the third Vortiger. Hated was this king by all the barons of his realm, and of all his neighbours. His very kindred held him in abhorrence. He came to an evil end, for he died in his shame, and the pagans he befriended with him. "Sire," said Hengist to the king, "men hold thee in hatred by reason of me; and because of thy love they bear me malice also. I am thy father, and thou my son, since thou wert pleased to ask my daughter for thy wife. It is my privilege to counsel my king, and he should hearken to my counsel, and aid me to his power. If thou wilt make sure thy throne, and grieve those who use thee despitefully, send now for Octa my son, and for my cousin Ebissa. There are not two more cunning captains than these, nor two champions to excel them in battle. Give these captains of thy land towards Scotland, for from thence comes all the mischief. They will deal with thy foes in such fashion that never more shall they take of thy realm; but for the rest of thy days we shall live in peace beyond the Humber." Then answered the king, "Do what you will, and send messages for such men as it is good for us to have." At the king's word Hengist sent messages to his son and nephew, who hastened to his help with a fleet of three hundred galleys. There was not a knight of their land, who would serve for guerdon, but they carried him across the water. After these captains were come, in their turn, from day to day, came many another; this one with four vessels, this other with five, or six, or seven, or eight, or nine, or ten. So thickly did the heathen wend, and so closely did they mingle with the Christians, that you might scarcely know who was a christened man and who was not. The Britons were sorely troubled at this matter, and prayed the king not to put such affiance in the outland folk, for they wrought much mischief. They complained that already were too many pagans in the land, working great shame and villainy to the people. "Separate thyself from amongst them," they said, "at whatever cost, and send all, or as many as may be, from the realm." Vortigern made answer that he might not do this thing. He had entreated the Saxons to the land, and they served him as true men. So when the barons hearkened to his words they went their way to Vortimer.

The Britons assembled themselves together, and taking the road to London, chose Vortimer—the eldest of the king's three sons—to be their lord. The king, who was assotted on his wife, clave to her kindred, and would not forsake the heathen. Vortimer defied the Saxons, and drove them from the walled cities, chasing and tormenting them very grievously. He was

a skilful captain, and the strife was right sore between Vortimer
and the Britons, against his father and the Saxons. Four times
the hosts met together, and four times Vortimer vanquished his
foe. The first battle was fought upon the banks of the Darent.
The second time the hosts strove together was upon the ford
near Aylesford. In this place Vortiger, the king's son, and
Horsa the Saxon, contended so fiercely in combat, body to body,
that each did the other to death, according to his desire. The
other battle was arrayed on the sea shore in Kent. Passing
grim was this third battle, for the ships fought together upon
the water. The Saxons withdrew before the Britons, so that
from beyond the Humber even to Kent they were deceived
in their hope. The heathen fled in their galleys to an islet
called Thanet. The Britons assailed them in this fastness, and
so long as it was day, harassed them with arrows and quarrels,
with ships and with barges. They rejoiced loudly, for the pagans
were caught in a corner, and those not slain by the sword were
fain to die of hunger. For this reason, the Britons raised a
mighty tumult and shouting, when they trapped their enemy
in the Isle of Thanet. When the Saxons were assured that
worse would befall them, save they departed from the realm,
they prayed Vortigern to go in embassy to Vortimer his son,
persuading him to give them safe conduct from the land, and
not to do them further mischief. Vortigern, who was in their
company and would in no wise depart from their fellowship,
went to his son to procure such truce as the Saxons required.
Whilst he was about this business the Saxons entered in their
galleys, and with sail and oar put out to sea as swiftly as they
were able. Such was their haste to escape that they left their
wives and sons with the Britons, returning to their own country
in exceeding fear. After the Saxons had all forsaken the realm,
and the Britons were assured of peace, Vortimer gave again to
every man that of which the heathen had spoiled him. To
build anew the churches, and to declare the law of God, which
had fallen into disuse amongst the people because of Hengist
and his heathendom, St. Germanus came to Britain, sent by
St. Romanus, the Apostle of Rome. With him came St. Louis
of Troyes. These two fair bishops, Germanus of Auxerre and
Louis of Troyes, crossed the sea to prepare the way of the Lord.
By them were the tables of the law redelivered, and men con-
verted again to the faith. They brought many a man to
salvation; many a miracle, many a virtue, did God show in
their persons, and many a country was the sweeter for their lives.

When the law of God was restored, and Britain made again a Christian land, hearken now what foul work was done by treason and by envy. Rowena, that evil stepmother, caused Vortimer, her husband's son, to be poisoned, by reason of the hatred she bore him, since he chased Hengist from the realm. After Vortimer was certified that he must die, and that no physician might cure him of his hurt, he called together all his barons, and delivered unto them the treasure which he had greatly gathered. Listen well to that he prayed his friends. "Knights," said he, "take into your service warriors not a few, and grudge not the sergeant his wages. Hold one to another, and maintain the land against these Saxons. That my work may not be wasted, and avenged upon those who live, do this thing for their terror. Take my body, and bury it upon the shore. Raise above me such a tomb, so large and lasting, that it may be seen from far by all who voyage on the sea. To that coast where my body is buried, living or dead, they shall not dare to come." Having spoken in this fashion the gentle king died, finishing his course. His body was borne to London, and in London he was lain to his rest. The barons raised no barrow upon the shore, as with his dying speech he had bidden them.

After Vortimer's death, the Britons made Vortigern their king, even as he had been in days before. At the entreaties of his wife he sent messages to his father-in-law, Hengist. Him he prayed to return to the kingdom, but with a small company, so that the Britons should not give heed to the matter; for since Vortimer his son was dead, there was no need of a host. Hengist took ship gladly, but with him he carried three hundred thousand men in mail. For dread of the Britons, he made him ready as never he had done before. When the king learned that Hengist drew to land with so mighty a host, he was altogether fearful, and knew no word to say. The Britons assembled together in great wrath, promising amongst themselves that they would join them in battle, and throw the heathen from the realm. Hengist was cunning and felon of heart. He sent false messages to the king, praying for a truce and love-day to be granted, that they might speak together as friend with friend. Peace above all he desired; peace he ensued; peace was his love, and he sought her with tears. Nothing was further from his wish than war, and he would rather be banished from the realm than remain by force of arms. It was for the Britons to elect those whom they willed to stay, and for the others they would return whence they came.

The Britons granted the love-day, and the two peoples took
pledges, one of the other; but who can trust the oath of a liar?
A time was appointed when this council should be holden. The
king sent messages to Hengist that he must come with few
companions; and Hengist plighted troth right willingly.
Moreover, it was commanded that none should bear weapons
at the council, for fear that men should pass from words to
blows. The two parties met together near the Abbey of Ambresbury, on the great Salisbury plain. The day was the
kalends of May. Hengist had taught his comrades, and warned
them privily, that they should come each with a sharp, two-
edged knife hidden in his hose. He bade them to sit in this
Parliament, and hearken to the talk; but when he cried, "Nimad
covre seax" (which being interpreted means "Pluck forth your
knives," and would not be understanded of the Britons), they
were to snatch out their daggers and make each a dead man of
his neighbour. Now when the council was met, and men were
mingled together, the naked Briton near by the false heathen,
Hengist cried loudly, "Nimad covre seax." The Saxons, at his
word, drew forth the knives from their hose, and slew that man
sitting at their side. Hengist was seated very close the king.
He held the king fast by his mantle, so that this murder passed
him by. But those who gripped the knives thrust the keen
blades through cloak and mantle, breast and bowels, till there
lay upon back or belly in that place nigh upon four hundred
and sixty men of the richest and most valiant lords of the
kingdom. Yet some won out and escaped with their lives,
though they had nought to defend their bodies save the stones.

Eldof, Earl of Gloucester, got a great club in his right hand,
which he found lying at his feet, though little he recked who
had carried it to the council. He defended his body stoutly
with this mighty staff, striking and smiting down, till he had
slain fully sixty and ten of the pagan. A mighty champion
was he, and of rich worth. He clave a path through the press,
without taking a wound; for all the knives which were flung
at his body he escaped with not a hurt to the flesh. He won at
the end to his horse, which was right strong and speedy, and
riding swiftly to Gloucester, shut himself fast in his city and
victualled tower. As to Vortigern, the Saxons would have
slain him with his barons, but Hengist stood between them,
crying, "Harm not the king, for nothing but good have I
received at his hand, and much has he toiled for my profit.
How then shall I suffer my daughter's lord to die such a death!

Rather let us hold him to ransom, and take freely of his cities and walled places, in return for his life." They, therefore, slew not the king, but binding him fast with fetters of iron, kept him close in bonds for so long a space that he swore to render them all that they would. In quittance of his ransom, and to come forth from prison, Vortigern granted Sussex, Essex, and Middlesex to Hengist as his fief, besides that earldom of Kent which he had held before. To remember this foul treason, knives were long hight seax amongst the English; but names alter as the world moves on, and men recall no more the meaning of the past. In the beginning the word was used to rebuke the treason that was done. When the story of the seax was forgotten, men spoke again of their knives, and gave no further thought to the shame of their forefathers.

When Vortigern was a naked man he fled beyond the Severn, and passing deeply into Wales, dwelt there, taking counsel with his friends. He caused his wise clerks and magicians to be summoned, inquiring of them in what fashion he should maintain his right, and what they would counsel him to do, were he assailed of a mightier than himself. This he asked because he feared greatly the two brothers of Constant, who were yet living, and knew not how to keep him from their hate. These sorcerers bade him to build so mighty a tower, that never at any time might it be taken by force, nor beaten down by any engine devised by the wit of man. When this strong castle was furnished and made ready, he should shut himself within, and abide secure from the malice of his foes. This pleased the king, who searched throughout the land to make choice of a fitting place to raise so strong a keep. Such a place he met, altogether according to his mind, on mount Erir.[1] He brought masons together, the best that might be found, and set them to the work as quickly as they were able. The masons began to build, getting stones ready and making them fast with mortar, but all the work that the builders raised by day, adown it fell to the ground by night. They laboured therefore with the more diligence, but the higher they builded the tower the greater was its fall, to the very foundations they had digged. So it chanced for many days, till not one stone remained upon another. When the king knew this marvel, and perceived that his travail came in nowise to an end, he took counsel of his wizards. " By my faith," said he, " I wonder sorely what may be amiss with my tower, since the earth will not endure it.

[1] Snowdon.

Search and inquire the reason of this thing; and how these
foundations shall be made sure." Then the magicians by their
lots and divinations—though, for that matter, it may well be
that they lied—devised that the king should seek a man born
of no earthly father; him he must slay, and taking of his blood,
slake and temper therewith the mortar of the work, so that the
foundations should be made fast, and the castle might endure.
Thereat the king sent messengers throughout all the land to
seek such a man, and commanded that immediately he were
found he should be carried to the court. These messengers
went two by two upon their errand. They passed to and fro
about the realm, and entered into divers countries, inquiring of
all people, at the king's bidding, where he might be hid. But
for all their labour and diligence they learned nothing. Now
it came to pass that two of the king's embassy went their
road until they came together to the town called Caermerdin.[1]
A great company of youths and children was gathered before
the gate at the entrance to the city, and the messengers stayed
awhile to mark their play. Amongst those who disported
themselves at this gate were two varlets, named Merlin and
Dinabus. Presently the two youths began to chide and jangle,
and were passing wroth the one with the other. One of the
twain spake ill of his fellow, reproaching him because of his
birth. "Hold thy peace, Merlin," said Dinabus, "it becomes
you not to strive with me, whose race is so much better than
thine own. Be heedful; for I know of such an evil matter that
it were well not to tempt me beyond my power. Speak then
no more against my lineage. For my part I am come from
earls and kings; but if you set out to tell over your kindred,
you could not name even your father's name. You know it
not, nor shall learn it ever; for how may a son tell his father's
name when a father he has never had?" Now the king's
messengers, who were in quest of such a sireless man, when they
heard this bitter jibe of the varlet, asked of those around concerning the youth who had never seen his sire. The neighbours
answered that the lad's father was known of none; yea, that
the very mother who had borne him in her womb, knew nothing
of the husbandman who had sown the seed. But if his father
was hidden, all the world knew of the mother who nourished
him. Daughter was she to that King of Dimetia, now gone
from Wales. Nun she was of her state, a gentlewoman of right
holy life, and lodged in a convent within the walls of their city.

[1] Carmarthen.

When the messengers heard these tidings, they went swiftly to the warden of the city, adjuring him, by the king's will, to lay hands upon Merlin—that sireless man—and carry him straightway to the king, together with the lady, his mother. The warden durst not deny their commandment. He delivered Merlin and his mother to the embassy, who led them before the king. The king welcomed the twain with much honour, and spoke kindly unto them. "Lady," said he, "answer me truly. By none, save by thee, can I know who was the father of Merlin, thy son." The nun bowed her head. After she had pondered for a little, she made reply, "So God have me in His keeping, as I know nothing and saw nothing of him who begat this varlet upon me. Never have I heard, never may I tell, if he were verily man by whom I had my child. But this I know for truth, and to its truth will I pledge my oath. At that time when I was a maid growing tall, I cannot tell whether it was a ghostly man, but something came often to my chamber, and kissed me very close. By night and by day this presence sought me, ever alone; but always in such fashion as not to be perceived. As a man he spake soft words in my ear; as a man he dealt with me. But though many a time he had speech with me, ever he kept himself close. He came so often about me, so long were his kisses on my mouth, that he had his way, and I conceived; but whether he were man in no wise have I known. I had of him this varlet; but more I know not, and more I will not say."

Now the king had a certain clerk, named Malgantius, whom he held for very wise. He sent for this learned clerk, and told over to him the whole matter, that he might be assured whether things could chance as this woman had said. The clerk made answer, "In books I have found it written that a certain order of spirit ranges between the moon and our earth. If you seek to learn of the nature of these spirits, they are of the nature partly of man, and partly of a loftier being. These demons are called incubi. Their home and region is the air, but this warm world is their resort. It is not in their power to deal man great evil, and they can do little more mischief than to trick and to annoy. However they know well how to clothe themselves in human shape, for their nature lends itself marvellously to the deceit. Many a maid has been their sport, and in this guise has been deceived. It may well be that Merlin was begotten by such a being, and perchance is of a demon born." "King," cried Merlin suddenly, "you brought me here; tell me now

what you would, and wherefore you have sent after me."
" Merlin," answered the king, " know it you shall. Hearken
diligently, so shall you learn of all. I commenced to build a
high tower, and got mortar together, and masons to set one
stone upon another; but all the work that the builders raised
by day, adown it fell to the ground, and was swallowed up of
night. I know not if you have heard tell thereof. The day
has not so many hours to labour, as the night has hours to
destroy; and greatly has my substance been wasted in this
toil. My councillors tell me that my tower may never stand
tall, unless its stones and lime are slaked with thy blood—the
blood of a fatherless man." " Lord God," cried Merlin, " believe
not that my blood will bind your tower together. I hold them
for liars who told over such a gab. Bring these prophets before
me who prophesy so glibly of my blood; and liars as they are,
liars I will prove them to be." The king sent for his sorcerers,
and set them before Merlin. After Merlin had regarded them
curiously, one by one, " Masters," said he, " and mighty magicians, tell us now I pray you the reason why the king's work
faileth and may not stand. If you may not show me why the
tower is swallowed up of the earth, how can your divinations
declare to you that my blood will cause it to endure! Make
plain to us now what troubles the foundation, so that the walls
tumble so often to the ground; and when you have certified
this thing, show to us clearly how the mischief may be cured.
If you are not willing to declare who labours secretly to make
the house to fall, how shall it be credited that my blood will
bind the stones fast? Point out this troubler to the king, and
then cry the remedy." But all the wizards kept silence, and
answered Merlin never a word. When Merlin saw them abashed
before him, he spake to the king, and said, " Sire, give ear to
me. Beneath the foundations of your tower there lies a pool,
both great and deep, and by reason of this water your building
falleth to the ground. Right easily may this be assured. Bid
your men to delve. You will then see why the tower was
swallowed up, and the truth will be proven." The king bade
therefore that the earth should be digged, and the pool was
revealed as Merlin had established. " Masters and great magicians," cried Merlin, " hearken once more. You who sought
to mix your mortar with my blood, say what is hidden in this
pond." But all the enchanters kept silence and were dumb;
yea, for good or ill they made answer never a word. Merlin
turned him again to the king. He beckoned with his hand to

the king's servants, saying, " Dig now trenches, to draw off the water from this pool. At the bottom shall be found two hollow stones, and two dragons sleeping in the stones. One of these dragons is white, and his fellow, crimson as blood." Thereat the king marvelled greatly, and the trenches were digged as Merlin had commanded. When the water was carried about the fields, and stood low in the pool, two dragons got them on their feet, and envisaged each the other very proudly. Passing eager was their contention, and they strove together right grievously. Well might be seen the foam within their mouths, and the flames that issued from their jaws. The king seated himself upon the bank of the pool. He prayed Merlin to show him the interpretation of these dragons which met together so furiously. Merlin told the king what these matters betokened, as you have oft-times heard. These dragons prophesied of kings to come, who would yet hold the realm in their charge. I say no more, for I fear to translate Merlin's Prophecies, when I cannot be sure of the interpretation thereof. It is good to keep my lips from speech, since the issue of events may make my gloss a lie.

The king praised Merlin greatly, and esteemed him for a true prophet. He inquired of the youth in what hour he should die, and by what means he would come to his end. For this king was marvellously fearful of death. " Beware," said Merlin, " beware of the sons of Constantine. By them you shall taste of death. Already have they left Armorica with high hearts, and even now are upon the sea. Be certified of this, that their fleet of fourteen galleys comes to land on the morrow. Much evil hast thou done to them; much evil will they do to thee, and avenge them of their wrongs. In an ill day you betrayed their brother to his death: in an ill day you set the crown on your head; in an ill day, to your own most bitter loss, you entreated this Saxon heathenry to your help. You are as a man against whom arrows are loosed, both this side and that; and I know not whether your shield should be arrayed to left or to right. On the one road the Saxon host draws near, eager to do you a mischief. Along this other comes the rightful heirs, to pluck the realm from your hand, the crown from your head, and to exact the price of their brother's blood. If you yet may flee, escape quickly; for the brethren approach, and that speedily. Of these brethren Aurelius shall first be king, but shall also die the first, by poison. Uther Pendragon, his brother, will sit within his chair. He will hold the realm in peace; but he, too, will fall sick before his time, and die, by reason of the brewage of his friends. Then Arthur of Cornwall, his son, like to a boar grim in battle, will utterly devour these false traitors, and destroy thy kinsfolk from the land. A right valiant knight, and a courteous, shall he be, and all his enemies shall he set beneath his feet." When Merlin had come to an end, he departed from Vortigern, and went his way. On the morrow, with no longer tarrying, the navy of the brethren arrived at Totnes, and therein a great host of knights in their harness. The Britons assembled themselves together, and joined them to the host. They came forth from the lurking places whence they had fled, at that time Hengist harried them by mount and by dale, after he had slain the lords by felony, and destroyed their castles. At a great council the Britons did homage to Aurelius as their king. These tidings came to Vortigern in Wales, and he prepared to set his house in order. He fled to a strong castle, called Generth,[1] and there made him ready, taking with him the most valiant of his men. This tower was on the banks of a fair running water, called by the folk of that country the Wye. It stood high upon Mount Droac, in the land of Hergin, as testify the people of these parts. Vortigern furnished his fortress with a plenteous store of arms and engines, of food and sergeants. To keep himself the surer from his foes, he garnished the tower with all that wit might devise. The lords of the country, having joined themselves to the brethren, sought so diligently for King Vortigern, that in the end they arrayed them before the castle where he lay. They cast stones from their engines, and were ever about the gates, paining themselves grievously to take it, for they hated him beyond measure. Much cause had the brethren to nurse so bitter a grudge against Vortigern, since by guile and treason he had slain their brother Constant, and Constantine, their father, before him, as all men held to be the truth. Eldof, Earl of Gloucester, had done homage to Aurelius, and was with him in the host. Much he knew of this land of Wales. "Eldof," said Aurelius, "hast thou forgotten my father who cherished thee, and gave his faith to thee; and dost thou remember no more my brother who held thee so dear! These both honoured thee right willingly, with love and with reverence in their day. They were foully slain by the device of this tyrant, this cozener with oaths, this paymaster with a knife. We who are yet alive must bestir ourselves that we perish not by the

[1] In Hereford.

same means. Let us think upon the dead, and take bitter vengeance on Vortigern for these wrongs." Aurelius and Eldof laced them in their mail. They made the wild fire ready and caused men to cast timber in the moat, till the deep fosse was filled. When this was done they flung wild fire from their engines upon the castle. The fire laid hold upon the castle; it spread to the tower, and to all the houses that stood about. The castle flared like a torch; the flames leaped in the sky; the houses tumbled to the ground. In that place the king was burned with fire, and all his household who fled to Generth with him. Neither dame nor damsel got her living from that pyre; and on the same day perished the king's wife, who was so marvellously fair.

When the new king had brought the realm into subjection to himself, he devised to seek the pagans, that he might deliver the country from their hand. Right fearful was Hengist to hear these tidings, and at once set forth for Scotland. He abandoned all his fiefs, and fled straightway beyond the Humber. He purposed to crave such aid and succour from the Scots as would help him in his need, and made haste to get him to Scotland with all the speed he might. The king pursued him swiftly with his host, making forced marches day by day. On the road his power was increased by a great company of Britons; till with him was a multitude which no man could number, being innumerable as the sand of the sea. The king looked upon his realm, and saw it gnawed to the bone. None drave the plough, nor cast seed in the furrow. The castles and the walled cities were breached and ruined. He marked the villages blackened by fire, and the houses of God stripped bare as a peasant's hovel. The heathen pilled and wasted, but gathered neither corn into barns nor cattle within the byre. He testified that this should not endure, so he returned in safety from the battle.

When Hengist knew that the king followed closely after, and that fight he must, he strove to put heart and hardihood into the breasts of his fellows. " Comrades," said he, " be not dismayed by reason of this rabble. We know well enough what these Britons are, since they never stand before us. If but a handful go against them, not one will stay to fight. Many a time, with but a mean company, have I vanquished and destroyed them. If they be in number as the sand, the more honour is yours. A multitude such as this counts nothing. A host like theirs, led by a weak and foolish captain, what is

it worth? These are a trembling folk, without a chief, and of
them we should have little fear. The shepherd of these sheep is
a child, who is yet too young to bear a spear, or carry harness
on his back. For our part we are heroes and champions, proven
in many a stour, fighting for our very lives, since for us there
will be no other ransom. Now be confident and bold. Let our
bodies serve us for castles and for wall. Be brave and strong,
I say, for otherwise we are but dead men." When Hengist
ceased heartening his comrades, the knights arrayed them for
the battle. They moved against the Britons as speedily as their
horses might bear them, for they hoped to find them naked and
unready, and to take them unawares. The Britons so mis-
doubted their adversary that they watched in their armour,
both day and night. As soon as the king knew that the heathen
advanced to give battle, he ordered his host in a plain that
seemed good for his purpose. He supported the spearmen with
three thousand horsemen, clothed in mail, his own trusty
vassals, who had come with him from Armorica. The Welsh
he made into two companies. The one part he set upon the
hills, so that the Paynim might not climb there if they would.
The other part he hid within the wood, to stay them if they
sought shelter in the forest. For the rest he put every man
into the plain, that it should be the more strongly held and
defended. Now when he had arrayed the battle, and given his
commandment to the captains, the king placed himself amidst
the chosen men of his own household, those whom he deemed
the most loyal to his person. He spoke apart with his friends
concerning the battle. Earl Eldof was near the king's side
that day, together with many another baron. "God," said
Eldof, "what joy will be mine that hour when Hengist and I
meet face to face, with none between us. I cannot forget the
kalends of May, and that murder at Ambresbury, when he
slew all the flower of our chivalry. Right narrowly escaped I
from his net."

Whilst Eldof spake these reproachful words, making complaint
of Hengist, the Saxons drew near the field, and sought to take
it. With no long tarrying the battle was joined. What time
the two hosts looked on each other they hastened together.
There you might see the vassals striving, hand to hand. They
fought body to body, those assailing, these defending. Mighty
blows with the sword were given and received among them.
Many a champion lay stark upon the ground, and the living
passed over the bodies of the dead. Shields were hewn asunder;

spears snapped like reeds; the wounded were trampled beneath men's feet, and many a warrior died that day. The Christians called on Christ, and the heathen answered, clamouring on their gods of clay. Like men the pagans bore them; but the Christians like heroes. The companies of the heathen flinched, giving ground on the field. The Britons pressed about them, redoubling their blows, so that the Saxons were discomfited, and turning their backs, strove no more.

When Hengist saw his champions turn their backs, like children, to the stroke, he fled to the town called Caerconan,[1] where he was persuaded of shelter. The king followed fast after him, crying to the hunters, "On, on." Hengist heard the noise of the pursuit, and had no care to be trapped in his castle. Better to fight in the open at the risk of his body, than to starve behind walls, with none to bring succour. Hengist checked the rout, and rallying the host, set it again in order of battle. The combat was passing sharp and grievous, for the pagans advanced once more in rank and by companies. Each heartened his fellow, so that great damage and loss were sustained by the Christians. The host fell in disarray, and began to give back before the onset of the foe. All would have been lost were it not for those three thousand horsemen, who rode upon the Saxon in one mighty troop, bringing succour and help to the footmen when they were overborne. The pagans fought starkly and grimly. Well they knew not one would escape with his life, if they did not keep them in this peril. In the press, Eldof the Earl lighted on Hengist. Hatred gave him eyes, and he knew him again because of the malice he owed him. He deemed that the time and the means were come to satisfy his lust. Eldof ran in upon his foe, striking him mightily with his sword. Hengist was a stout champion, or he had fallen at the stroke. The two closed together, with naked brands and lifted shields, smiting and guarding. Men forgot to fight, and stared upon them, watching the great blows fall and the gleaming swords.

Whilst the heroes strove, Gorlois, Earl of Cornwall, came hastening like a paladin to the battle. Eldof saw him come, and being assured of the end, arrayed himself against his adversary yet more proudly. He sprang upon Hengist, and seizing him by the nasal of his helmet, dragged him, with fallen head, amongst the Britons. "Knights," he cried, "thanks be to God Who has given me my desire. He is vanquished and

[1] Conisburg in Yorkshire.

taken who has caused such trouble to the land." Eldof showed
the captive to his company, who demanded that he should be
slain with the sword. " A short shrift for the mad dog," they
clamoured, " who knows neither mercy nor pity. This is the
source of the war. This is the shedder of blood. Smite the head
from his body, and the victory is in your hands." Eldof made
answer that Hengist should have the law, good law and just.
He bound him fast in fetters, and delivered him to King Aurelius.
The king chained him, hands and feet, and set him in a strong
prison to await judgment.

Now Octa, Hengist's son, and Ebissa, his cousin, who were in
the field, hardly escaped from the battle, and fleeing, entered
into York. They strengthened the city, and made all ready,
till men might come to their aid. As for the others they hid in
divers places, in the woods and valleys, in caves and in the
hills. But the power of the paynim was broken, for many were
dead, and of the living most were taken, and in bonds, or held
as thralls. The king made merry over his victory, and gave the
glory to God. He abode three full days at Caerconan to heal
the wounded of their hurt, and to give a little leisure to the
weary. At that place he called a council of his captains, to
know what it were good to do with the traitor Hengist; whether
he should be held in prison or slain outright. Eldad got him
to his feet. A right learned clerk was he, a bishop of his orders,
and brother by blood to that Earl Eldof, of whom you have
heard. " My counsel to the king," said the bishop, " is to do
to the traitor Hengist—our earthly adversary—that which holy
Samuel did in old days to King Agag, when he was made captive.
Agag was a prince, passing proud, the right glorious king of the
people of Amalek. He set a quarrel upon the Jews, that he
might work them a mischief, since he sought to do them evil.
He seized their lands; he burned their goods with fire, and very
often he slew them for his pleasure. Then on a day this King
Agag was taken at a battle, the more to his sorrow. He was
led before Saul, whom these Jews so greatly desired for their
king. Whilst Saul was considering what it were well should
be done with Agag, who was delivered into his hand, Samuel
stood upon his feet. This Samuel was a holy prophet of Israel;
a saint of God of the utmost sanctity; never has there lived his
like amongst the sons of men. This holy Samuel seized on Agag,
the proud king. He hewed him in many pieces, dividing him
limb from limb, and his members he sent throughout the realm.
Hearken and learn what Samuel said whilst he was hewing Agag

small. 'Agag, many a man hast thou tormented for thy pleasure; many a fair youth hast thou spoiled and slain. Thou hast drawn out many a soul from its body, and made many a mother troubled for her son. Many a babe hast thou rendered fatherless; but, O Agag, things evil and good come to the like end. Now your mother presently will I make barren, and from thy body shall the soul of thee be wrung.' Mete therefore to your captive, O king, the measure which Samuel counted out to his." Eldof, Earl of Gloucester, was moved by the example furnished by the bishop. He rose in the council, and laying hands on Hengist led him without the city. There Eldof struck the head from Hengist with his own sword. The king caused the head to be set again on the shoulders, and gave Hengist's body seemly burial, according to the rite and fashion of those who observe the law of the paynim.

The king made no long stay at Caerconan, but followed eagerly after his enemies. He came to York with a great host, and sat himself down before the city. Octa, the son of Hengist, was within, and some of his kindred with him. When Octa was persuaded that none might win to his aid, he considered within himself whether he should render him to the king's mercy. If he took his fate in his hand, and humbly besought pity of the king, so mercy were given him all would be well, but if his prayer was scorned, then he would defend himself to the death. Octa did as he devised, and as his kinsfolk approved. He came forth from the gate of the city with a company of all his barons. Octa wore a chain of iron upon his wrists, and walking at the head of his companions, came first to the king. "Sire," said he, "I beseech you for mercy and pity. The gods in whom we put our trust have failed us at need. Your gods are mightier than they. They have wrought wonders, and set strength upon you, since we are stricken to the dust. I am vanquished, and own myself thy servant. Behold the chain of thy bondman! Do with me now according to thy will, to me, and these my men. Life and limb, yea, all that we have, are at thy pleasure. But if it seem good to the king to keep us about his person, we will toil early and late in his service. We will serve him loyally in his quarrels, and become his liege men."

The king was a devout man, very piteous of heart. He looked around him to learn what his barons thought of this matter, and what would be their counsel. Eldad, the fair bishop, spake first as a wise elder. "Good it is, and was, and ever shall be, to show mercy on him who requires mercy to be shown. He who forgives not another his trespass, how may he hope that God will pardon him his sin? These cry loudly upon thee for mercy; mercy they implore, and mercy they must have. Britain is a great realm, long and wide, and in many a place is inhabited of none, save the beast. Grant them enough thereof that they may dig and plant, and live of the increase. But take first of them such hostages, that they will serve thee loyally, and loyally content them in their lot. We learn from Holy Writ that the children of Gibeon sought life and league from the Jew when the Israelites held them in their power. Peace they prayed, peace they received; and life and covenant were g ven in answer to their cry. A Christian man should not be harder than the Jew proved himself to be in his hour. Mercy they crave; mercy they should have; so let not death deceive them in their hope."

The king granted land to the Saxons, according to the counsel of Eldad. The lot was appointed them in Scotland, and they set out speedily to the place where they must dwell. But first they gave to the king hostages of the children of their proudest blood and race. After the king was fifteen days in the city, he sent messages commanding his people to attend him in council. Baron and clerk, abbot and bishop, he summoned to his court. At this council the rights of the heir and the privileges of the orders were re-affirmed. He bade and assured that the houses of religion, destroyed by the Romans, should be rebuilt. He dismissed his soldiers to their homes, making viscounts and provosts to keep his fiefs in peace, and to ensure his revenues and rent. He sought masons and carpenters and built anew the churches. Such chapels in his realm as were hurt or damaged in the wars, the king restored to their former estate, for the fairer service and honour of God. After the council was done the king set forth towards London, where his presence was greatly desired of the citizens. He found the city but the shadow of its former splendour, for the streets were emptied of people, and houses and churches were alike fallen or decayed. Right grievously the king lamented the damage done to his fair city. He founded anew the churches, and bade clerks and burgesses to attend the service of God, as was of wont and right. From thence the king went to Ambresbury, that he might kneel beside the graves of those who were foully slain at Hengist's love-day, near the abbey. He called together a great company of masons, carpenters, and cunning artificers; for it was in his

mind to raise to their worship a monument of stone that would
endure to the world's end.

Thereat spake to the king a certain wise man, Tremonius,
Archbishop of Caerleon, praying him to send for Merlin, and
build according to his bidding, since there was none so skilled
in counsel or labour, more truthful of word or apter in divina-
tion. The king desired greatly to behold Merlin, and to judge
by hearing of his worth. At that time Merlin abode near the
Well of Labenes. This fountain springs in a hidden place, very
deep in Wales, but I know not where, since I have never been.
Merlin came straightway to the king, even as he was bidden.
The king welcomed him with marvellous joy, honouring him
right gladly. He cherished him richly, and was ever about him
with prayers and entreaties that he would show him somewhat
of things that were yet to come, for these he was on itch to
hear. "Sire," replied Merlin, "this I may not do. I dare not
open my lips to speak of such awful matters, which are too
high for me, save only when needs speak I must. Should my
tongue be unloosed by greed or lightness, should I be puffed
up by vanity, then my familiar spirit—that being by whom I
know that which I know—would withdraw his inspiration from
my breath. My knowledge would depart from me, and the
words I speak would be no weightier than the idle words on
every gossip's lips. Let the future take care of itself. Consider
rather the concerns of to-day. If thou art desirous to make a
fair work and a lasting, of which men will brag till the end of
time, cause to be brought hither the carol that a giant wrought
in Ireland. This giant laboured greatly in the building of a
mighty circle of stones. He shaped his carol, setting the stones
one upon another. The stones are so many, and of such a kind;
they are so huge and so weighty; that the strength of man—
as men are in these times—might not endure to lift the least of
his pebbles." The king laughed loudly. "Merlin," said he,
"since these stones are of such heaviness that it passes the
strength of the strong to move them, who shall carry them to
my masons? Have we not in this realm stones mighty enough,
and to spare?" "King," answered Merlin, "knowest thou
not that wit is more than strength! Muscle is good, but craft
is better. Skill devises means when strength fails. Cunning
and engines bring many matters to a good end, that strength
would not venture even to begin. Engines can move these
stones, and by the use of engines we may make them our own.
King, these stones were carried from Africa: there they were

first shapen. The giant who ravished them to Ireland, set up
his carol to his own content. Very serviceable were these stones,
and right profitable to the sick. It was the custom of the
surgeons of that land to wash these stones with fair water.
This water they would make hot in baths, and set therein those
who had suffered hurt, or were grieved by any infirmity. They
washed in this water, and were healed of their sickness. However sore their wound, however grievous their trouble, other
medicine needed they none." When the king and his Britons
heard of the virtue residing in the stones, they all desired them
very greatly. Not one but would gladly have ventured on the
quest for these stones, of which Merlin told such marvels.
They devised therefore to pass the sea with fifteen thousand
men to make war upon the Irish, and to ease them of the stones.
Uther, at his own desire, was chosen as their captain. Merlin
also went with them to furnish engines for their toil. So Uther
and his company crossed to Ireland on such quest. When the
King of Ireland, that men called Guillomer, heard tell that
strangers were arrayed in his land, he assembled his household
and the Irish, and menaced them proudly, seeking to chase
them from the realm. After they had learned the reason of
this quarrel, and that for stones the Britons were come, they
mocked them loudly, making them their mirth and their song.
For mad it seemed in the eyes of these Irish that men should
pain themselves so grievously by land and sea to gain a treasure
of naked stones. " Never a stone," said these, " shall they
have; not one shall they carry with them to their homes."
Very lightly you may scorn your enemy in your heart, but at
your peril you seek to do him mischief with your hands. The
Irish mocked and menaced the stranger, and sought him until
they found. The combat was joined directly the hosts met
together, but the Irish were men of peace, unclad in mail, and
not accustomed to battle. The Britons were their jest, but
they were also their victors. The King of Ireland fled from the
battle discomfited. He went from town to town, with no long
tarrying in any place, so that the Britons might not make him
their captive.

After the Britons had laid aside their armour, and taken rest
from the battle, they were brought by Merlin, their companion,
into a mountain where the carol was builded. This high place
was called Hilomar,[1] by the folk whom they had vanquished,
and the carol was upon the summit of the mount. The Britons

---

[1] Kildare.

stared upon the stones. They went about them, saying each
to his fellow that none had seen so mighty a building. They
marvelled how these stones were set one upon another, and
how they should be got across the sea. "Comrades," said
Merlin," you are strong champions. Strive now if of your
strength you may move these stones, and carry them from their
seat." The young men therefore encompassed the stones before,
behind, and on every side, but heave and tug as mightily as
they could, the stones for all their travail would not budge one
single inch. "Bestir yourselves," cried Merlin, "on, friends,
on. But if by strength you can do no more, then you shall
see that skill and knowledge are of richer worth than thews and
fleshly force." Having spoken these words Merlin kept silence,
and entered within the carol. He walked warily around the
stones. His lips moved without stay, as those of a man about
his orisons, though I cannot tell whether or no he prayed. At
length Merlin beckoned to the Britons. "Enter boldly," cried
he; "there is nought to harm. Now you may lift these pebbles
from their seat, and bear and charge them on your ships." So
at his word and bidding they wrought as Merlin showed them.
They took the stones and carrying them to the ships, bestowed
them thereon. Afterwards the mariners hoisted their sails,
and set out for Britain. When they were safely come to their
own land, they bore the stones to Ambresbury, and placed them
on the mountain near by the burying ground. The king rode
to Ambresbury to keep the Feast of Pentecost. Bishops,
abbots, and barons, he had bidden them all to observe the
Feast. A great company of folk, both rich and poor, gathered
themselves together, and at this fair festival the king set the
crown upon his head. Three days they observed the rite, and
made merry. On the fourth—because of his exceeding reverence—he gave pastoral crosses to two prelates. Holy Dubricius
became Bishop of Caerleon, and York he bestowed upon holy
Sampson. Both these fair prelates were great churchmen, and
priests of devout and spotless life. At the same time Merlin
ranged the stones in due order, building them side by side. This
circle of stones was called by the Britons in their own tongue
The Giant's Carol, but in English it bears the name of Stonehenge.

When the rich feast was come to its appointed end, the court
departed, each man unto his own place. Now Passent, that
was a son of Vortigern, had fled from Wales and Britain, for
fear of Aurelius and his brother Uther. He sought refuge in

Germany, and there purchased to himself ships, and men who
would serve him for guerdon; but of these he had no great
company. This Passent arrived in the north country and
ravaged it, burning the towns and spoiling the land. He dared
make no long stay, for the king hastened to the north to give
him battle, and this he might not endure. Passent took again
to his ships, and fearing to return whence he came, fared so far
with sail and oar that in the end he cast anchor off the coast
of Ireland. Passent sought speech of the king of that realm.
He told over his birth and state, and showed him his bitter
need. Passent prayed the king so urgently; the twain took
such deep counsel together; that it was devised between them
to pass the sea, and offer battle to the Britons. This covenant
was made of Passent that he might avenge his father's death,
and dispute his heritage with Aurelius; but of the King of
Ireland to avenge him upon the Britons, who had vanquished
him in battle, robbed his folk, and taken to themselves the carol
with a strong hand. Thus they plighted faith to satisfy each
the other for these wrongs. Guillomer and Passent made ready
as many soldiers as they might. They ordained their ships,
and with a fair wind crossed the sea, and came safely to Wales.
The host entered in Menevia, that city so praised of the Welsh,
and now called of men, Saint David. It befell that King Aurelius lay sick at Winchester. His infirmity was sore upon him,
for the trouble was long and grievous, and the surgeons knew
not whether he would mend or die. When Aurelius learned
that Passent and the King of Ireland were come together in
Wales to make sorrow in the land, he sent for Uther his brother.
He grieved beyond measure that he could not get him from his
bed. He charged Uther to hasten into Wales, and drive them
from the realm. Uther sent messages to the barons, and summoned the knights to the war. He set out from Winchester;
but partly by reason of the long journey, and partly to increase
the number of his power, he tarried for a great while upon the
road. Very long it was before he arrived in Wales. Whilst he
dallied in this fashion a certain pagan named Appas, a man
born in Saxony, craved speech of Passent. This Appas was
meetly schooled, and apt in parts. He spoke to many people
in their own tongues; he was wise in all that concerned medicine
and surgery; but he was felon and kept bad faith. "Passent,"
said Appas privily, "thou hast hated this King Aurelius for
long. What should be mine if I were to slay him?" "Ease
and riches I will give thee," answered Passent. "Never a day

but I will stand thy friend, so only thy word be fulfilled, and
the king taste death at thy hand." " May your word," said
Appas, " be true as mine." So the covenant was ordained
between them that Passent should count out one thousand
livres, what time Appas had done to death the king. Appas
was very cunning, and right greedy and covetous of wealth.
He put upon him a habit of religion; he shaved his crown, and
caused his hair to be polled close to his head. Like a monk he
was shaven; like a monk he seemed; in gown and hood he
went vested as a monk. In this guise and semblance Appas
took his way to the royal court. Being a liar he gave out that
he was a good physician, and thus won to the king's bed. Him
he promised to make whole very speedily, if he would trust
himself to his hand. He counted the pulse, and sought for the
trouble. " Well I know," said he, " the cause of this evil. I
have such a medicine as will soon give you ease." Who could
misdoubt so sweet a physician? The gentle king desired greatly
to be healed of his hurt, as would any of you in a like case.
Having no thought of treason, he put himself in this traitor's
care. Appas made ready a potion, laced with venom, and gave
the king to drink. He then wrapped the king warmly in a rich
coverlet, and bade him lie in peace and sleep. After the king
was heated, and the poison had lain hold upon his body, ah,
God, the anguish, there was nothing for him but death. When
Aurelius knew that he must die, he took oath of his household,
that so truly as they loved him they would carry his body to
Stonehenge, and bury him within the stones that he had builded.
Thus died the king and was buried; but the traitor, Appas,
escaped and fled with his life.

Uther entered in Wales with his host, and found the folk of
Ireland abiding yet at Menevia. At that time appeared a star,
which was seen of many. This star was hight Comet, and
according to the clerks it signified death and the passing of
kings. This star shone marvellously clear, and cast a beam
that was brighter than the sun. At the end of this beam was
a dragon's head, and from the dragon's mighty jaws issued two
rays. One of these rays stretched over France, and went from
France even to the Mount of St. Bernard. The other ray went
towards Ireland, and divided into seven beams. Each of these
seven beams shone bright and clear, alike on water and on land.
By reason of this star which was seen of all, the peoples were
sorely moved. Uther marvelled greatly what it might mean,
and marvellously was he troubled. He prayed Merlin that he

would read him the sign, and the interpretation thereof. Merlin answered not a word. Sorrow had him by the heart, and he wept bitterly. When speech returned to his mouth he lamented with many words and sighed often. "Ah, God," said he, "sorrow and trouble and grief have fallen on Britain this day. The realm has lost its great captain. The king is dead—that stout champion who has delivered the land from such evil and shame, and plucked his spoil from the pagan."

When Uther was certified that his brother and good lord had finished his course, he was right heavy, and much was he dismayed. But Merlin comforted him as he might. "Uther," said he, "be not altogether cast down, since from Death there is no return. Bring to an end this business of the war. Give battle to thine enemies, for to-morrow shall see Passent and the King of Ireland vanquished. Fight boldly on the morrow; so shalt thou conquer, and be crowned King of Britain. Hearken to the interpretation of the sign. The dragon at the end of the beam betokens thee thyself, who art a stout and hardy knight. One of the two rays signifies a son born of thy body, who shall become a puissant prince, conquering France, and beyond the borders of France. The other ray which parted from its fellow, betokens a daughter who shall be Queen of Scotland. Many a fair heir shall she give to her lord, and mighty champions shall they prove both on land and sea." Uther lent his ear to the counsel of Merlin. He caused his folk to rest the night, and in the morning arm them for the battle. He thought to take the city by assault, but when the Irish saw him approach their walls, they put on their harness, and setting them in companies, issued forth to fight without the gates. The Irish fought valiantly, but right soon were discomfited, for on that day the Britons slew Passent, and the King of Ireland, his friend. Those who escaped from the field fled towards the sea, but Uther following swiftly after, harried them to the death. Such as reached the water climbed wildly upon their ships, and with sail and oar set out to sea, that Uther should work them no more mischief.

When Uther had brought his business to a good end, he took his way towards Winchester, and the flower of his chivalry with him. On his road a messenger met him who told him of a surety the king was dead, and as to the manner of his death. He related how the bishops had laid Aurelius to rest with great pomp in the Giant's Carol, even as he had required of his sergeants and barons whilst he was yet alive. At these tidings

Uther pressed on to Winchester, sparing not the spur. The people came before him on his passage clamouring shrilly. "Uther, sire," cried the common folk, "since he is dead who maintained the poor, and did nought but good to his people, we have none to defend us, save thee. Take then the crown, as thine by heritage and right. Fair sire, we thy poor commons pray this thing, who desire nothing but thy worship and thy gain." Uther rejoiced greatly at their words. He saw clearly where his profit lay, and that no advancement is possible to a king. He hastened, therefore, to do as the folk entreated. He took the crown, and becoming king, loved well his people, and guarded the honour of the realm. In remembrance of the dragon, and of the hardy knight who should be king and a father of kings, which it betokened, Uther wrought two golden dragons, by the counsel of his barons. One of these dragons he caused to be borne before him when he went into battle. The other he sent to Winchester to be set up in the church of the bishop. For this reason he was ever after called Uther Pendragon. Pendragon was his name in the Britons' tongue, but Dragon's head in that of Rome.

Uther was a mighty lord, who had confidence in his power. His sacring at Winchester he held for proof and token that he was a king who would beget puissant princes, by whom great deeds should be done. This faith in his destiny gave him increase of strength. He determined in his heart that he would accomplish all that was foretold of him, and that through good report and ill, never would he turn back. He knew and was persuaded that whatever the task he took in hand, he must in fulness of time bring it to a good end. Merlin was a true prophet; and since no lying spirit was in his mouth, it was impossible to doubt that very swiftly all these things would come to pass.

Now Octa, the son of Hengist, had received from Aurelius broad lands and fair manors for him and his companions. When Octa knew that the mighty captain was dead, he kept neither loyalty nor faith with a king whom he despised in his heart. He called together a great company of his friends and kinsmen, and amongst them Ossa, his cousin. Octa and Ossa were hardy champions, and they were the lords of the host. With them moreover were such folk as had escaped from Uther at the slaying of Passent. These Octa had taken to himself, so that his fellowship was passing strong. This host overran the realm from Humber to Scotland, and subdued it in every part. Octa then came before York, and would have seized it by violence, but the burgesses of the city held it stoutly against him, so that the pagans might not enter within the walls. He sat down, therefore, before the gates, and invested the city straitly, by reason of the numbers of his host. Uther had no thought but to succour his city, and to rescue his friends who were shut within. He marched hot foot to York, calling his men together from every part. Being resolved at all cost to force the heathen to give over the siege, Uther offered them battle without delay. The melley was right sharp and grievous. Many a soul was parted from the body. The heathen played their parts as men, and contended boldly with the sword. The Britons could do them no mischief. They might not force their way into the city, neither could those within prevail to issue forth. The Britons might endure the battle no longer. They gave back in the press, and as they fled, the pursuing Saxons did them marvellous damage. The pursuit lasted until the Britons took refuge in a fastness of those parts, and the night parted the adversaries one from the other. This mountain was named Damen. The peak was very sharp. About its flanks were rocks and precipices, whilst close at hand stood a thicket of hazel trees. Upon this mountain the Britons climbed. By this way and that, they ascended the height, until they sought safety on the summit. There the heathen shut them fast, for they sat beneath them in the plain, whilst all about them stretched the mountain.

The king was very fearful, and not for himself alone. He was in sore straits and perplexity as to what he should do to get his spearmen from the trap. Now Gorlois, Earl of Cornwall, was with the king. This lord was very valiant and courteous, though stricken in years, and was esteemed of all as a right prudent councillor. To him the king went, and unravelled all the coil. Uther prayed Gorlois to counsel him as became his honour, for he knew well that the earl regarded honour beyond the loss of life or limb. "You ask me my counsel," said Gorlois. "My counsel—so it be according to your will—is that we should arm ourselves forthwith, and get down from this hill amongst our foes. They are assuredly sleeping at this hour, for they despise us overmuch to deem that we shall challenge them again to battle. In the morning they will come to seek us—so we await them in the trap. Let us take our fate in our hands like men, and fall upon them suddenly. The foe will then be confused and bewildered, for we must come upon them silently, without battle cry or blowing of trumpets. Before they are awakened from sleep, we shall have slain so many in our onset, that those who escape from our swords will not dare to rally against us in their flight. Only this thing first. Let every man have penitence for that he has done amiss. Let us ask God's pardon for the sins that we have wrought, and promise faithfully to amend our lives. Let us turn from the wickedness wherein we have walked all these days; praying the Saviour to hold us in His hand, and grant us strength against those who fear not His name, and make war upon His Christians. If we do these things God will sustain our quarrel; and if God be with us who then can do us wrong? "

This counsel seemed good to the king and his captains. They did as Gorlois said, and humbled themselves before God with a contrite heart, promising to put away the evil from their lives. After they had made an end of prayer, they took their arms, and stole down the hillside to the valley. The Britons came amongst the pagans lying naked upon the ground, and fast in sleep. The swordplay was right merry, for the slaughter was very great. The Britons thrust their glaives deep in the breasts of the foe. They lopped heads and feet and wrists from their bodies. The Britons ranged like lions amongst their enemies. They were as lions anhungered for their prey, killing ewes and lambs, and all the sheep of the flock, whether small or great. Thus the Britons did, for they spared neither spearman nor captain. The heathen were altogether dismayed. They were yet heavy with sleep, and could neither get to their harness, nor flee from the field. No mercy was shown them for all their nakedness. Armed or naked the sword was thrust through their breast or heart or bowels. In that place the heathen perished from the land, since the Christians destroyed them utterly. Octa and Ossa, the lords of their host—these troublers of Britain—were taken alive. They were led to London, and set fast in a strong prison, bound in iron. If any of their fellows escaped from the battle, it was only by reason of the blackness of the night. He who was able to flee, ran from the field. He tarried not to succour his own familiar friend. But many more were slain in that surprise than got safely away.

When Uther parted from York he passed throughout Northumberland. From Northumberland he entered into Scotland, having many ships and a great host with him. He went about the length and breadth of the land, and purged it throughly in every part. Such folk as were oppressed of their neighbours he confirmed in their rights. Never before had the realm such

rest and peace as in the days of Uther the king. After Uther
had brought his business in the north to an end, he set forth
to London, where he purposed to take the crown on Easter Day.
Uther desired the feast to be very rich and great. He summoned therefore dukes, earls, and wardens, yea, all his baronage
from near and far, by brief and message, to come with their
wedded dames and privy households to London for his feast.
So all the lords came at the king's commandment, bringing
their wives as they were bidden. Very richly the feast was
holden. After the Mass was sung, that fair company went in
hall to meat. The king sat at the head of his hall, upon a daïs.
The lords of his realm were ranged about him, each in his order
and degree. The Earl of Cornwall was near the king's person,
so that one looked upon the other's face. By the earl's side
was seated Igerne, his wife. There was no lady so fair in all
the land. Right courteous was the dame, noble of peerage, and
good as she was fair.

The king had heard much talk of this lady, and never aught
but praise. His eyes were ravished with her beauty. He
loved her dearly, and coveted her hotly in his heart, for certainly
she was marvellously praised. He might not refrain from
looking upon her at table, and his hope and desire turned to her
more and more. Whether he ate or drank, spoke or was silent,
she was ever in his thought. He glanced aside at the lady, and
smiled if she met his eye. All that he dared of love he showed.
He saluted her by his privy page, and bestowed upon her a gift.
He jested gaily with the dame, looking nicely upon her, and
made a great semblance of friendship. Igerne was modest and
discreet. She neither granted Uther's hope, nor denied. The
earl marked well these lookings and laughings, these salutations
and gifts. He needed no other assurance that the king had set
his love upon his wife. Gorlois deemed that he owed no faith
to a lord who would supplant him in her heart. The earl rose
from his seat at table; he took his dame by the hand, and went
straight from the hall. He called the folk of his household about
him, and going to the stables, got him to horse. Uther sent
after Gorlois by his chamberlain, telling him that he did
shame and wrong in departing from the court without taking
leave of his king. He bade him to do the right, and not to
treat his lord so despitefully, lest a worse thing should befall
him. He could have but little trust in his king, if he would not
return for a space. Gorlois rode proudly from the court without
leave or farewell. The king menaced him very grievously, but

the earl gave small heed to his threats, for he recked nothing of what might chance. He went into Cornwall, and arrayed his two castles, making them ready against the war. His wife he put in his castle of Tintagel, for this was the home of his father and of his race. It was a strong keep, easily holden of a few sergeants, since none could climb or throw down the walls. The castle stood on a tall cliff, near by the sea. Men might not win to enter by the gate, and saving the gate, there was no door to enter in the tower.

The earl shut his lady fast in the tower. He dared hide his treasure in no other place, lest thieves broke through, and stole her from him. Therefore he sealed her close in Tintagel. For himself he took the rest of his men-at-arms, and the larger part of his knights, and rode swiftly to the other strong fortress that was his. The king heard that Gorlois had garnished and made ready his castle, purposing to defend himself even against his lord. Partly to avenge himself upon the earl, and partly to be near his vassal's wife, the king arrayed a great host. He crossed the Severn, and coming before the castle where the earl lay, he sought to take it by storm. Finding that he might not speed, he sat down before the tower, and laid siege to those within. The host invested the castle closely for full seven days, but could not breach the walls. The earl stubbornly refused to yield, for he awaited succour from the King of Ireland, whom he had entreated to his aid. King Uther's heart was in another place. He was wearied beyond measure of Gorlois and his castle. His love for Igerne urged and called him thence, for the lady was sweeter to his mind than any other in the world. At the end he bade to him a baron of his household, named Ulfin, who was privy to his mind. Him he asked secretly of that which he should do. " Ulfin," said the king, " my own familiar friend, counsel me wisely, for my hope is in thee. My love for Igerne hath utterly cast me down. I am altogether broken and undone. I cannot go or come about my business; I cannot wake nor sleep; I cannot rise from my bed nor lay my head on the pillow; neither can I eat or drink, except that this lady is ever in my mind. How to gain her to my wish I cannot tell. But this I know, that I am a dead man if you may not counsel me to my hope." " Oh my king," answered Ulfin, " I marvel at your words. You have tormented the earl grievously with your war, and have burned his lands. Do you think to win a wife's heart by shutting her husband close in his tower? You show your love for the dame by harassing the lord! No, the

matter is too high for me, and I have one only counsel to give
you. Merlin is with us in the host. Send after him, for he is
a wise clerk, and the best counsellor of any man living. If
Merlin may not tell you what to do, there is none by whom you
may win to your desire."

King Uther, by the counsel of Ulfin, commanded Merlin to be
brought before him. The king opened out his bitter need.
He prayed that for pity's sake Merlin would find him a way to
his hope, so he were able; since die he must if of Igerne he got
no comfort. But let the clerk seek and buy so that the king
had his will. Money and wealth would be granted plenteously,
if gold were needed; for great as was the king's evil, so large
would be his delight. " Sire," answered Merlin, " have her you
shall. Never let it be said that you died for a woman's love.
Right swiftly will I bring you to your wish, or evil be the
bounty that I receive of the king's hand. Hearken to me.
Igerne is guarded very closely in Tintagel. The castle is shut
fast, and plenteously supplied with all manner of store. The
walls are strong and high, so that it may not be taken by might;
and it is victualled so well, that none may win there by siege.
The castle also is held of loyal castellans; but for all their vigils,
I know well how to enter therein at my pleasure, by reason of
my potions. By craft I can change a man's countenance to the
fashion of his neighbour, and of two men each shall take on his
fellow's semblance. In body and visage, in speech and seeming,
without doubt I can shape you to the likeness of the Earl of
Cornwall. Why waste the time with many words! You, sire,
shall be fashioned as the earl. I, who purpose to go with you
on this adventure, will wear the semblance of Bertel. Ulfin,
here, shall come in the guise of Jordan. These two knights
are the earl's chosen friends, and are very close to his mind and
heart. In this manner we may enter boldly in his castle of
Tintagel, and you shall have your will of the lady. We shall
be known of none, for not a man will doubt us other than we
seem." The king had faith in Merlin's word, and held his counsel
good. He gave over the governance of the host, privily, to a
lord whom he much loved. Merlin put forth his arts, and
transfigured their faces and vesture into the likeness of the
earl and his people. That very night the king and his companions entered in Tintagel. The porter in his lodge, and the
steward within his office, deemed him their lord. They welcomed him gladly, and served him with joy. When meat was
done the king had his delight of a lady who was much deceived.

Of that embrace Igerne conceived the good, the valiant, and the trusty king whom you have known as Arthur. Thus was Arthur begotten, who was so renowned and chivalrous a lord.

Now the king's men learned very speedily that Uther had departed from the host. The captains were wearied of sitting before the castle. To return the more quickly to their homes, they got into their harness and seized their arms. They did not tarry to order the battle, or make ready ladders for the wall, but they approached the tower in their disarray. The king's men assaulted the castle from every side, and the earl defended himself manfully; but at the last he himself was slain, and the castle was swiftly taken. Those who were fortunate enough to escape from the tower fled lightfoot to Tintagel. There they published the news of this misadventure, and the death of their lord. The sorrow and lamentation of those who bewailed the earl's death reached the ears of the king. He came forth from his chamber, and rebuked the messengers of evil tidings. " Why all this noise and coil? " cried he. " I am safe and sound, thank God, as you may see by looking on my face. These tidings are not true; and you must neither believe all that the messengers proclaim, nor deem that they tell naught but lies. The cause is plain why my household think me lost. I came out from the castle taking leave and speaking to no man. None knew that I went secretly through the postern, nor that I rode to you at Tintagel, for I feared treachery upon the way. Now men cry and clamour of my death, because I was not seen when the king won within the tower. Doubtless it is a grievous thing to have lost my keep, and to know that so many goodly spearmen lie dead behind the walls. But whilst I live, my goods at least are my own. I will go forth to the king, requiring a peace, which he will gladly accord me. I will go at once, before he may come to Tintagel, seeking to do us mischief; for if he falls upon us in this trap we shall pipe to deaf ears."

Igerne praised the counsel of him she deemed her lord. The king embraced her by reason of her tenderness, and kissed her as he bade farewell. He departed straightway from the castle, and his familiars with him. When they had ridden for a while upon the road, Merlin again put forth his enchantments, so that he, the king, and Ulfin took their own shapes, and became as they had been before. They hastened to the host without drawing rein; for the king was with child to know how the castle was so swiftly taken, and in what manner the earl was

slain. He commanded before him his captains, and from this
man and that sought to arrive at the truth. Uther considered
the adventure, and took his lords to witness that whoever had
done the earl to death, had done not according to his will. He
called to mind Earl Gorlois' noble deeds, and made complaint
of his servants, looking upon the barons very evilly. He wore
the semblance of a man in sore trouble, but there were few who
were so simple as to believe him. Uther returned with his host
before Tintagel. He cried to those who stood upon the wall
asking why they purposed to defend the tower, since their lord
was dead and his castle taken, neither could they look for
succour in the realm, or from across the sea. The castellans
knew that the king spake sooth, and that for them there was
no hope of aid. They therefore set open the gates of the castle,
and gave the fortress and its keys into the king's hand. Uther,
whose love was passing hot, spoused Igerne forthwith, and
made her his queen. She was with child, and when her time
was come to be delivered, she brought forth a son. This son
was named Arthur, with the rumour of whose praise the whole
world has been filled. After the birth of Arthur, Uther got
upon Igerne a daughter cleped Anna. When this maiden came
of age she was bestowed upon a right courteous lord, called
Lot of Lyones. Of this marriage was born Gawain, the stout
knight and noble champion.

Uther reigned for a long time in health and peace. Then he
fell into a great sickness, failing alike in mind and strength.
His infirmity lay so sore upon him, that he might not get him
from his bed. The warders, who watched over his prison in
London, were passing weary of their long guard, and were
corrupted also by fair promises that were made. They took
rich gifts from Octa, that was Hengist's son, and from Ossa,
his cousin, and delivering them out of their bonds, let them go
free from their dungeon. Octa and Ossa returned swiftly to
their own place. They purchased war galleys to themselves,
and gathering their men about them menaced Uther very
grievously. With a great company of knights, and spearmen,
and archers they passed the marches of Scotland, burning and
spoiling all the realm. Since Uther was sick, and could do
little to defend his life and land, he called Lot, the husband
of his daughter, to his aid. To this lord he committed the
guidance of his host, and appointed him constable of his knights.
He commanded these that they should hearken Lot as himself,
and observe all his biddings. This Uther did because he knew

Lot for a courteous and liberal lord, cunning in counsel, and mighty with the spear.

Now Octa vexed the Britons very sorely. He boasted himself greatly, by reason of the number of his folk, and of the king's weakness. To avenge his father's death and his own wrongs, he made Britain fearful of his name; for he neither granted truce nor kept faith. Lot met Octa once and again in battle. Many a time he vanquished his foe; but often enough the victory remained with Octa. The game of war is like a game of tables. Each must lose in his turn, and the player who wins to-day will fail to-morrow. At the end Octa was discomfited, and was driven from the country. But it afterwards befell that the Britons despised Lot. They would pay no heed to his summons, this man for reason of jealousy, this other because of the sharing of the spoil. The war, therefore, came never to an end, till the king himself perceived that something was amiss, whilst the folk of the country said openly that the captains were but carpet knights, who made pretence of war. At this certain men of repute came before the king, praying him to remain no longer hidden from his people. " Come what may," said these counsellors, " you must get to the host, and show yourself to the barons." The king took them at their word. He caused himself to be set within a horse litter, and carried, as though in a bier, amongst his people. " Now we shall see," said these, " which of these recreant lords will follow him to the host." The king sent urgent messages to the knights who were so disdainful of Lot, summoning them on their allegiance to hasten to his aid. For himself he was carried straight to Verulam.[1] This once was a fair city where St. Alban fell upon his death, but was now altogether ravaged and destroyed of the heathen. Octa had led his people to the city, and seized thereon, making fast the gates. The king sat down without the town. He caused great engines to be arrayed to break through the wall, but it was very strong, and he might make no breach. Octa and his friends made merry over the catapults set over against them. On a morning they opened wide their gates, and came forth to do battle with the king. A vile matter it seemed to them that the door should be locked and barred because of a king lying sick within a litter. They could not endure to be so despised that he should fight against them from his coffin. As I deem their pride went before a fall. That captain won who was deserving of the victory. The

[1] St. Albans.

heathen were defeated, and in that battle Octa and his fair
cousin Ossa were slain. Many who escaped from the field fled
into Scotland. There they made Colgrin their chieftain, who
was a friend of Octa and his cousin. Uther rejoiced so greatly
by reason of his victory, and of the honour God had shown
him, that for sheer joy he was as a man healed and altogether
whole. He set himself to hearten his barons, and inspire them
with his own courage. He said to his men, with mirth, " I like
rather to lie on my bier, languishing in long infirmity, than to
use health and strength in fleeing from my foe. The Saxons
disdained me, holding me in despite because I cannot rise from
my bed; but it has befallen that he who hath one foot in the
grave hath overthrown the quick. Forward then, and press
hardly on their heels who seek to destroy our religion from the
land."

When the king had rested him for a space, and had encouraged
the lords with his words, he would have followed after the
heathen. Seeing that his sickness was yet heavy upon him,
the barons prayed that he would sojourn awhile in the city,
until it pleased God to give him solace from his hurt. This
they said fearing lest his courage should bring him to his death.
It chanced, therefore, that the host departed, leaving Uther at
Verulam, because of his infirmity, none being with him, save
the folk of his private household. Now the Saxons who were
driven from the land, when they had drawn together, considered
within themselves that if the king were but dead, he had no
heir who might do them a mischief, and despoil them of their
goods. Since they had no trust in their weapons, doubting
that they could slay him with the sword, they devised to murder
the king by craft and poison. They suborned certain evil-
doers, whose names I do not know, by promises of pennies and
of land. These men they conveyed to the king's court, arrayed
in ragged raiment, the better to spy in what fashion they might
draw near his person and carry out their purpose. The male-
factors came to Verulam, but for all their cunning and craft
of tongues, in no way could they win anigh the king. They
went to and fro so often; they listened to the servitors' talk so
readily; that in the end they knew that the king drank nothing
but cold water, that other liquor never passed his lips. This
water was grateful to his sickness. It sprang from a well very
near his hall, and of this water he drank freely, for none other
was to his mind. When these privy murderers were persuaded
that they might never come so close to the king's body as to

slay him with a knife, they sowed their poison in the well.
They lurked secretly about the country, until it came to their
ears when and how he died, and then fled incontinent whence
they came. Presently the king was athirst, and called for drink.
His cupbearer gave him water, laced with venom, from the
spring. Uther drank of the cup, and was infected by the
plague, so that there was no comfort for him save in death.
His body swelled, becoming foul and black, and very soon he
died. Right quickly all those who drank of the water from
that fountain died of the death from which their lord lay dead.
After this thing became known, and the malice of these evil-
doers was made clear, the burgesses of the city met together,
and choked the well for evermore. They cast therein so much
earth, that a pyre stood above the source, as a witness to this
deed. Uther the king having fallen asleep, his body was borne
to Stonehenge, and laid to rest close by Aurelius, his brother;
the brethren lying side by side. The bishops and barons of
the realm gathered themselves together, and sent messages to
Arthur, Uther's son, bidding him to Cirencester to be made their
king. Arthur at the time of his coronation was a damoiseau of
some fifteen years, but tall and strong for his age. His faults
and virtues I will show you alike, for I have no desire to lead
you astray with words. He was a very virtuous knight, right
worthy of praise, whose fame was much in the mouths of men.
To the haughty he was proud; but tender and pitiful to the
simple. He was a stout knight and a bold: a passing crafty
captain, as indeed was but just, for skill and courage were his
servants at need: and large of his giving. He was one of
Love's lovers; a lover also of glory; and his famous deeds are
right fit to be kept in remembrance. He ordained the courtesies
of courts, and observed high state in a very splendid fashion.
So long as he lived and reigned he stood head and shoulders
above all princes of the earth, both for courtesy and prowess,
as for valour and liberality. When this Arthur was freshly
crowned king, of his own free will he swore an oath that never
should the Saxons have peace or rest so long as they tarried in
his realm. This he did by reason that for a great while they
had troubled the land, and had done his father and his uncle
to their deaths. Arthur called his meinie to his aid. He
brought together a fair company of warriors, bestowing on them
largely of his bounty, and promising to grant largely of the
spoil. With this host he hastened into the land that lay about
York. Colgrin—who was the chief and captain of these Saxons

since the slaying of Octa—had many Picts and Scots in his
fellowship, besides a goodly company of his own people. He
desired nothing more hotly than to meet Arthur in battle, and
to abate his pride. The armies drew together upon the banks
of the Douglas. The two hosts fell one upon the other furiously,
and many a sergeant perished that day, by reason of lance
thrust, or quarrel, or dart. At the end Colgrin was discomfited,
and fled from the field. Arthur followed swiftly after, striving
to come upon his adversary, before he might hide him in York.
But Colgrin, for all his pains, took refuge in the city; so Arthur
sat him down without the walls.

Now Baldulph, the brother of Colgrin, tarried by the shore,
awaiting the coming of Cheldric, the king, and his Saxons from
Germany. When he heard the tidings of what had befallen
Colgrin at the Ford of Douglas, and of how he was holden
straitly by Arthur in York, he was passing heavy and sorrowful,
for with this Colgrin was all his hope. Baldulph made no
further tarrying for Cheldric. He broke up his camp, and
marching towards York, set his comrades in ambush, within a
deep wood, some five miles from the host. Together with the
folk of his household, and the strangers of his fellowship, Baldulph had in his company six thousand men in mail. He
trusted to fall upon Arthur by night, when he was unready, and
force him to give over the siege. But certain of the country
who had spied Baldulph spread this snare, ran to the king, and
showed him of the matter. Arthur, knowing of the malice of
Baldulph, took counsel with Cador, Earl of Cornwall, a brave
captain, who had no fear of death. He delivered to the earl's
care seven hundred horsemen, and of spearmen three thousand,
and sent him secretly to fall upon Baldulph in his lurking place.
Cador did the king's bidding. The Saxons heard no rumour of
his coming; for the host drew to the wood privily without
trumpet or battle cry. Then when Cador was near the foe, he
cried his name, and burst fiercely upon the heathen with the
sword. In this combat there perished of the Saxons more than
three thousand men. Had it not been for the darkness of the
night, and the hindrance of the wood, not one might have fled
on his feet. Baldulph, the cunning captain, got him safely
from the field, by hiding beneath every bush and brake. He
had lost the fairer and the stronger half of his meinie, and was
at his wits' end to know how to take counsel with his brother,
or to come to his aid. But speak with him he would, so that
craft and courage might find a way. Baldulph devised to seek

the besiegers' camp in the guise of a jongleur. He arrayed himself in all points as a harper, for he knew well how to chant songs and lays, and to touch the strings tunably. For his brother's sake he made himself as a fool. He shaved off one half of his beard and moustache, and caused the half of his head to be polled likewise. He hung a harp about his neck, and showed in every respect as a lewd fellow and a jester. Baldulph presently went forth from his abode, being known again of none. He went to and fro harping on his harp, till he stood beneath the walls of the city. The warders on the towers hearkened to his speech, so that they drew him up by cords upon the wall. At Baldulph's tale the folk within the city despaired of succour, and knew not how to flee, nor where to escape. In their extremity the news was bruited amongst them that Cheldric had come to a haven in Scotland, with a fleet of five hundred galleys, and was speeding to York. Cheldric knew and was persuaded that Arthur dared not abide his onset. This was a right judgment, for Arthur made haste to begone. The king called a council of his captains, and by their rede decided not to await Cheldric at York, neither to give him battle, because of the proud and marvellous host that was with him. " Let the king fall back upon London," said the lords, " and summon his meinie about him. The king's power will increase daily, and if Cheldric have the hardihood to follow, with the more confidence we shall fight." Arthur took his captains at their word. He let well the siege, and came to London, that he might strengthen his castle, choose his own battle ground, and trouble his adversary the more surely. Arthur, by the rede of his counsellors, sent letters to his nephew, the son of his sister, Hoel, King of Little Britain. For in that country dwelt many strong barons, sib to his flesh, and the stoutest knights of his race. In these letters, and by the mouth of his ambassadors, Arthur prayed the king to hasten to his rescue. If Hoel came not swiftly over sea—wrote the king—certainly his realm would be taken from him, and shame would always be on those who watched tamely their cousin stripped of his heritage.

When this bitter cry came to Hoel he sought neither hindrance nor excuse. His vassals and kinsmen got in their harness forthwith. They arrayed their ships, and set thereon the stores. Within these ships there entered twelve thousand knights alone, without taking count of the sergeants and archers. So in a good hour they crossed the sea, coming with a fair wind to the port of Southampton. Arthur welcomed them with

great joy, showing them the honour which it became him
to offer. They made no long tarrying at Southampton, nor
wasted the day in fair words and idle courtesies. The king had
summoned his vassals, and had brought together his household.
Without speeches and blowings of trumpets the two hosts set
forth together towards Lincoln, which Cheldric had besieged
but had not yet taken. Arthur came swiftly and secretly upon
Cheldric. He fell silently upon the Saxons, making no stir with
horns and clarions. King Arthur and his men slew so many in
so grim and stark a fashion, that never was seen such slaughter,
such sorrow and destruction, as they made of the Saxons in one
single day. The Saxons thought only of flight. They stripped
off their armour to run the more lightly, and abandoned their
horses on the field. Some fled to the mountains; others by the
valleys; and many flung themselves into the river, and were
drowned miserably, striving to get them from their foe. The
Britons followed hotly at their heels, giving the quarry neither
rest nor peace. They struck many a mighty blow with the
sword, on the heads, the necks, and bodies of their adversaries.
The chase endured from Lincoln town to the wood of Celidon.
The Saxons took refuge within the thick forest, and drew
together the remnants of their power. For their part, the
Britons watched the wood, and held it very strictly. Now
Arthur feared lest the Saxons should steal from their coverts by
night, and escape from his hand. He commanded, therefore,
his meinie to cut down the trees on the skirts of the forest.
These trunks he placed one upon another, lacing the branches
fast together, and enclosing his foe. Then he sat down on the
further side of his barrier, so that none might issue forth, nor
enter in. Those within the wood were altogether dismayed,
since they might neither eat nor drink. There was no man so
cunning or strong, so rich or valiant, who could devise to carry
bread and wine, flesh and flour, for their sustenance. Three
days they endured without food, till their bodies were weak
with hunger. Since they would not die of famine, and might
not win forth from the wood by arms, they took counsel as to
what it were well to do. They approached Arthur, praying
him to keep raiment and harness and all that they had, saving
only their ships, and let them depart to their own land. They
promised to put hostages in his power, and render a yearly
tribute of their wealth, so only the king allowed them to go on
foot to the shore, and enter naked in the ships. Arthur set
faith in their word. He gave them leave to depart, receiving

hostages for assurance of their covenant. He rendered them the ships, but kept their armour as a spoil; so that they left the realm without a mantle to their bodies, or a sword for their defence. The Saxons set out across the water, until their sails were lost to sight. I know not what was their hope, nor the name of him who put it in their mind, but they turned their boats, and passed through the channel between England and Normandy. With sail and oar they came to the land of Devon, casting anchor in the haven of Totnes. The heathen breathed out threatenings and slaughter against the folk of the country. They poured forth from their ships, and scattered themselves abroad amongst the people, searching out arms and raiment, firing homesteads and slaying Christian men. They passed to and fro about the country, carrying off all they found beneath their hands. Not only did they rob the hind of his weapon, but they slew him on his hearth with his own knife. Thus throughout Somerset and a great part of Dorset, these pirates spoiled and ravaged at their pleasure, finding none to hinder them at their task. For the barons who might have made head against them were in Scotland with the king. So by road and country, laden with raiment and all manner of spoil, the Saxons came from their ships to Bath. But the citizens of the town shut fast their gates, and defended the walls against them.

Arthur was in Scotland, punishing the folk of that realm, because of the war they had made upon him, and of the aid they had afforded Cheldric. When the king learned what mischief the pagans had done to his land, and of the siege they laid to Bath, he hanged his hostages straightway. He dared tarry no longer in Scotland, but hastened south, leaving Hoel of Brittany lying sick at Dumbarton, I know not of what infirmity. With what men he might, Arthur came to Bath as swiftly as he was able, since he was resolved to chase the Saxons from before the gates, and succour the burgesses of his city. Now, near this town a wood stands within a wide country, and there Arthur arranged his men and ordered the battle. He saw to the arming of his meinie, and for himself got him into his harness. Arthur donned thigh pieces of steel, wrought strong and fairly by some cunning smith. His hauberk was stout and richly chased, even such a vesture as became so puissant a king. He girt him with his sword, Excalibur. Mighty was the glaive, and long in the blade. It was forged in the Isle of Avalon, and he who brandished it naked in his hand deemed himself a happy man. His helmet gleamed upon his head. The nasal was of gold; circlets of gold adorned the headpiece, with many a clear stone; and a dragon was fashioned for its crest. This helm had once been worn by Uther, his sire. The king was mounted on a destrier, passing fair, strong, and speedy, loving well the battle. He had set his shield about his neck, and, certes, showed a stout champion, and a right crafty captain. On the buckler was painted in sweet colours the image of Our Lady St. Mary. In her honour and for remembrance, Arthur bore her semblance on his shield. In his hand the king carried his lance, named Ron. Sharp it was at the head, tough and great, and very welcome at need in the press of battle. Arthur gave his commands to his captains, and ordained the order of the combat. He caused his host to march in rank and company at a slow pace towards the foe, so that when the battle was joined none might flinch but that he was sustained of his comrades. The host drew near to a certain mountain of those parts, and began to climb the hill. The Saxons held this mountain strongly, and defended the height, as though they were shut fast and safely behind walls. Small cause had the heathen for such assurance of safety, for a mighty captain was upon them, who would not endure their presence in his realm. Arthur led his spearmen upon the slope, and there admonished his men. " Behold," said he, " and see before you those false and scornful heathen, who have destroyed and ravished your kith and kin, your near ones and neighbours, and on your own goods and bodies have done so much mischief. Avenge now your friends and your kinsfolk: avenge the great ruin and burnings: avenge all the loss and the travail that for so long a space we have suffered at their hands. For myself this day I will avenge me for all these bitter wrongs. I will avenge the oaths these perjurers have broken. I will silence the crying of my fathers' blood. This day I will exact the price for all they have cost me in loss and in sorrows, and avenge the bad faith which led them to return to Totnes. If but this day we bear us in the battle like men, and smite the heathen in their fastness, never again will they array themselves proudly against us, but will be for ever before us as naked men without a shield." With these words Arthur set his buckler before him, and hastened to the playing of the swords. I know not the name of the Saxon who ran upon him in the stour, but the king smote him so fiercely that he died. Before Arthur passed across the body he cried aloud, " God aid, Saint Mary succour. He gives twice," said he, gaily, " who gives quickly. Here lies one whose lodging for the night I have paid." When the Britons saw this deed they aided the king mightily, beating down and slaying the Saxons very grievously. They pressed upon them from every side, thrusting shrewdly with the spear, and striking lustily with the sword. Arthur was of marvellous hardihood. Strong beyond the common strength and of great prowess, with lifted shield and terrible sword he hewed a path towards the summit of the mount. He struck to right and to left, slaying many, so that the press gave back before so stout a champion. To himself alone he slew four hundred heathen that day, working them more mischief than was done by all his men. To an evil end came the captains of these Saxons. Baldulph lay dead upon the mount, and dead also was Colgrin. Cheldric and some others fled from the field, and would have got them to their ships that they might enter therein and garnish for their needs.

When Arthur heard tidings of Cheldric's flight, and that he sought again his ships, he bade Cador of Cornwall to follow swiftly after the fugitives, giving ten thousand horsemen to his keeping, chosen from his best and closest friends. For his part, Arthur himself turned his face to Scotland; for a messenger came who told that the wild Scots held Hoel close within his city, and for a little would take him where he lay. Cheldric made in all haste to his ships, but Cador was a crafty captain, and by a way that he knew well he rode swiftly to Totnes, before Cheldric might come to the town. He seized the galleys, manning them with archers and country folk, and then hastened hotly on the track of the fugitives. Two by two, and three by three, these drew near the shore, as best they might hide them from the pursuers. To go the more lightly, to run the more nimbly, they had thrown away their harness, and carried nothing save their swords. They pained themselves to get to the ships, deeming that if they might enter therein their troubles would be at an end. As they strove to ford the river Teign, Cador, the huntsman, came winding upon their slot. The Saxons were dismayed beyond measure, and without stay or delay fled from their foe. Cador lighted upon Cheldric in the steep mountain, called Tenedic, and slew him in that place. As Cador came on Cheldric's companions he killed them with the sword, in sore sorrow. For those who escaped from Cador they made their way from every part to the ships. There they were slain by the archers, or perished miserably in the sea. The Britons took no captives; he who cried for mercy perished alike with him who strove with his sword. The rest of the Saxons fled to the

coverts of the woods and the mountains, by large companies.
In such desolate and waste places they lurked and hid from their
enemies until hunger and thirst put a term to their miseries.

When Cador had made an end of his slaying, and given quiet
to the land, he followed after Arthur, and took the road towards
Scotland. He came upon the king at Dumbarton, where he had
brought succour to his nephew, Hoel of Brittany. Arthur found
Hoel safe in body and in wealth, and altogether whole of his
infirmity. The Scots had departed from before the city when
they heard that Arthur drew near, and hastening to Murray,
made strong the towers, and set barriers at the gates. This
they did because they were resolved to await Arthur in the
city, thinking to hold themselves against him behind the walls.
Arthur knew well that the Scots were gathered together to make
head against him in that place. He came therefore to Murray
with all his power, but they dared not abide his coming, and for
dread fled to Lake Lomond, scattering themselves abroad
amongst the isles thereof. Passing wide and deep is this fair
mere. From the hills and valleys round about sixty rivers fall
therein, and making together one sweet water, pass swiftly by
a single river to the sea. Sixty islands lie upon this water, the
haunt and home of innumerable birds. Each island holds an
eyrie, where none but eagles repair to build their nests, to cry
and fight together, and take their solace from the world. When
evil folk arrive to raven and devour the realm, then all these
eagles gather themselves together, making great coil and
clamour, and arraying themselves proudly one against another.
One day, or two days, three or four, the mighty birds will strive
together; and the interpretation thereof portends horror and
grim destruction amongst men.

On this fair lake the Scots sought hiding, going and coming
upon its waters. Arthur followed swiftly after. He caused to
be made shallops, barges, and light, speedy boats, and harassed
them grievously in their refuge. By reason of famine and the
sword, they died by twenties, by hundreds, and by thousands
in those secret ways.

Now Guillomer, a certain king from Ireland, wishful to aid
the Scots in this quarrel, drew towards Arthur with his host.
Arthur went his way to give him battle. When the battle was
joined the Irish king was discomfited anon. He and his men
fled to their ships, getting them back to Ireland, and Arthur
came again to the mere, where he had left his harrying of the
Scots.

Then the bishops and abbots of the realm, with divers monks and other orders, carrying in their hands bodies of the saints and many holy relics, came before the king beseeching him to show mercy on the Scots. With these went a pitiful company of ladies of that country, naked of foot, spoiled of visage, with streaming hair and rent raiment, bearing their babes in their bosoms. These with tears and shrill lamentations fell at Arthur's knees right humbly, weeping, clamouring, and imploring his grace. "Sire, gentle king, have mercy and pity," cried these lamentable women, "on this wasted land, and on those wretched men who are dying of hunger and misery. If thou hast no bowels of pity for the fathers, look, sire, and behold these babes and these mothers; regard their sons and their daughters, and all the distressful folk thou art bringing down to death. Give again the fathers to the little children, restore to the ladies their husbands, and to this sad company of damsels return their brothers and their lords. Have we not paid enough by reason of the Saxon passing this way? It was not for our pleasure they sojourned awhile in the land. We went the more heavily for their presence, for much pain and sorrow we suffered because of the heathen, and passing weary were we of their speech. If we sheltered them in our houses, the greater sorrow is ours, since we have endured the more at their hands. Our beasts they have slain and eaten; and for our goods, these they have taken, and sent the gear into their own realm. There was none to help us, nor was any man so strong as to deliver us from their power. Sire, if we prepared them a feast, it was because we feared to drink their wine cup to the dregs. Might was theirs, and we were as the captive who sees no succour on the road. These Saxons were pagan men. Thy servants are Christians. Therefore the heathen oppressed us the more mightily, and laid the heavier burdens upon us. But great as was the mischief these Saxons wrought us, thou hast done us the sorer harm. Theirs were the whips, but thine are the stinging scorpions. It should prove little honour to the Christian king that he slay by hunger amongst these rocks those folk who cry his pardon for their trespass. We die, sire, of famine and of all misease. Nothing is left us save cold and wretchedness. Thou hast overcome us, every one; destroy us not from the land, but suffer us to live of thy bounty. Grant that we and all our race—so it be thy pleasure—may find peace in the king's service. Have mercy on thy poor Christians. We hold the faith that you, too, count dear. How foully then should

Christianity be wronged, if you destroy the whole realm. Alas, has not mischief enough been wrought already!" Arthur was tender of heart and marvellously pitiful. He took compassion on this doleful company of ladies, and by reason of those holy bodies of the saints and those fair prelates, he granted life and member to his captives, and forgave them their debts.

The Scots, having done homage to the king and owned themselves his men, departed, and went their way. Hoel gazed long upon the mere, calling to him the folk of his house. He wondered exceedingly because of the grandeur of the lake, and because of the greatness of the water. He marvelled altogether to behold so many islands therein, and at the rocks thereof. He was astonied beyond measure at the number of the eagles and their eyries, at the clamour and the shrilling of their cries. He deemed in his heart that never had he gazed upon so beautiful a sight. " Hoel, fair nephew," said Arthur, " very marvellous this water seems in your eyes. Your astonishment will be the more when you look upon yet another mere that I know. Near this lake, in this very country, lies a water held in a cup, not round but square. This pond is twenty feet in length, twenty in breadth, and the water thereof is five feet deep. In the four corners of this pond are many fish of divers fashions. These fish pass never from their corner to another. Yet none can certify by touch or sight whether craft keeps these fish each in his place, or what is that hindrance they may not overcome. Yea, I cannot tell whether the pond was digged by the wit of man, or if Nature shaped it to her will. Moreover I know of another mere, whereof you would be more amazed than of both these marvels. This lake is close by the Severn in the land of Wales. The sea pours its tide into this lake; yet empty itself as it may, the waters of the lake remain ever at the same height, never more and never less. The ocean itself may not suffice to heap its waters above the lake, neither to cover its shores. Yet at the ebbing of the tide, when the sea turns to flee, then the lake spues forth the water it has taken to its belly, so that the banks are swallowed up, the great waves rise tall in their wrath, and the wide fields round about are hid, and all is sodden with the foam. The folk of that country tell that should a man stare upon the wave in its anger, so that his vesture and body be wetted of the spray, then, whatever be his strength, the water will draw him to itself, for it is mightier than he. Many a man has struggled and fallen on the brink, and been drowned in its clutch. But if a man turn his back upon the water, then he may stand safely upon the bank, taking his pleasure as long as he will. The wave will pass by him, doing him no mischief; he will not be wetted even of the flying foam." So Hoel marvelled greatly at these wonders told him by the king. Then Arthur bade sound his horns, his clarions and trumpets to call his meinie to himself. He granted leave to all but the folk of his privy household to return to their homes. The host went therefore each to his own place, loudly praising the king. Even in Brittany men told that there was no more valiant captain than he.

Arthur turned south to York, abiding there till Christmas was past. He kept the Feast of the Nativity within its walls. He marked clearly the weakness and impoverishment of the city, and how deeply it was fallen from its former state. The churches were empty and silent; whilst for the houses they were either breached or fallen to the ground. The king appointed Pyramus, a learned clerk who had been diligent in his service, to the vacant see, so that the chapels might be maintained, and those convents built anew which the heathen had destroyed. Arthur commanded that the criers should proclaim that all honest folk must return to their toil. He sent messages to every place, bidding those who were dispossessed of their lands to repair to his court. There he gave them again their heritage, and confirmed them in their fiefs and rents. Now there were three brethren of right good birth and high peerage, kin to many a fair family, having to name Lot, Aguisel, and Urian. The forefather of these lords was the earl of that great country beyond the Humber; and these in their turn held justly their father's lands, doing wrong to none. Arthur rendered these brothers their own, and restored them their heritage. On Urian, as head of his house, Arthur bestowed the province of Murray, and without fee or recompense proclaimed him king of that realm. Scotland was given to Aguisel, who claimed it as his fief. As for Lot, who had the king's sister to wife, Arthur confirmed him in that kingdom of Lyones, which he had held for a great while, and gave him many another earldom besides. This Lot was the father of Gawain, who as yet was a damoiseau, young and debonair.

When Arthur had settled his realm in peace, righted all wrongs, and restored the kingdom to its ancient borders, he took to wife a certain fresh and noble maiden, named Guenevere, making her his queen. This damsel was passing fair of face and courteous, very gracious of manner, and come of a noble

Roman house. Cador had nourished this lady long and richly
in his earldom of Cornwall. The maiden was the earl's near
cousin, for by his mother he, too, was of Roman blood. Marvellously dainty was the maiden in person and vesture; right
queenly of bearing; passing sweet and ready of tongue. Arthur
cherished her dearly, for his love was wonderfully set upon the
damsel, yet never had they a child together, nor betwixt them
might get an heir.

As soon as winter was gone, and the warm days were come
when it was good to wend upon the sea, Arthur made ready his
ships to cross the straits to Ireland and conquer the land.
Arthur made no long tarrying. He brought together the most
lusty warriors of his realm, both poor and rich, all of the people
who were most vigorous and apt in war. With these he passed
into Ireland, and sent about the country seeking provand for
his host. So the sergeants took seisin of cows and oxen, and
brought to the camp in droves all that was desirable for meat.
Guillomer, the king of that realm, heard that Arthur had
fastened this quarrel upon him. He hearkened to the cries and
the tidings, the plaints and the burdens, raised by those villeins
whose granges and bields were pillaged for the sustenance of his
foes. Guillomer went forth to give battle to Arthur, but in an
ill hour he drew to the field. His men were naked to their
adversaries, having neither helmets nor coats of leather nor
shields. They knew nothing of archery, and were ignorant of
catapults and slings. The Britons were mighty bowmen.
They shot their shafts thickly amongst their enemies, so that
the Irish dared not show their bodies, and might find no shelter.
The Irish could endure the arrows no longer. They fled from
the fight, taking refuge where they were able. They hid in
woods and thickets, in towns and in houses, seeking refuge from
the stour. Right grievous was their discomfiture. Guillomer,
their king, sought shelter within a forest, but his fate was upon
him, and he might not conceal him from his foes. Arthur
searched him out so diligently, following so hotly on his track,
that at the last he was taken captive. Guillomer did very
wisely. He paid fealty and homage to Arthur, and owned that
of him he held his heritage. Moreover he put hostages within
Arthur's power, for surety that he would render a yearly tribute
to the king. When Arthur had subdued Ireland, he went
further and came even so far as Iceland. He brought the land
in subjection to himself, so that the folk thereof owned themselves his men, and granted him the lordship. Now three

princes, by name Gonfal, King of the Orkneys, Doldamer, King
of Gothland, and Romarec, King of Finland, heard the rumour
of these deeds. They sent spies to Iceland, and learned from
their messengers that Arthur was making ready his host to pass
the sea, and despoil them of their realms. In all the world—
said these messengers—there was no such champion, nor so
crafty a captain in the ordering of war. These three kings
feared mightily in case Arthur should descend upon them, and
waste their land. Lest a worse thing should befall them, with
no compulsion and of their own free wills, they set forth for
Iceland and came humbly before the king. They gave of their
substance rich gifts and offerings, and kneeling before Arthur
did him fealty, putting their countries between his hands, and
proclaiming themselves his men. They owned that of grace
they held their inheritance; they swore to render tribute to his
treasury, and gave hostages for assurance of their covenant.
So they departed in peace to their own place. For his part
Arthur came again to his ships. He returned to England, where
he was welcomed of his people with marvellous joy. Twelve
years he abode in his realm in peace and content, since none
was so bold as to do him a mischief, and he did mischief to none.
Arthur held high state in a very splendid fashion. He ordained
the courtesies of courts, and bore himself with so rich and noble
a bearing, that neither the emperor's court at Rome, nor any
other bragged of by man, was accounted as aught besides that
of the king. Arthur never heard speak of a knight in praise,
but he caused him to be numbered of his household. So that
he might he took him to himself, for help in time of need. Because of these noble lords about his hall, of whom each knight
pained himself to be the hardiest champion, and none would
count him the least praiseworthy, Arthur made the Round
Table, so reputed of the Britons. This Round Table was
ordained of Arthur that when his fair fellowship sat to meat
their chairs should be high alike, their service equal, and none
before or after his comrade. Thus no man could boast that he
was exalted above his fellow, for all alike were gathered round
the board, and none was alien at the breaking of Arthur's bread.
At this table sat Britons, Frenchmen, Normans, Angevins,
Flemings, Burgundians, and Loherins. Knights had their place
who held land of the king, from the furthest marches of the
west even unto the Hill of St. Bernard. A most discourteous
lord would he be deemed who sojourned not awhile in the king's
hall; who came not with the countenance, the harness, and the

vesture that were the garb and usage of those who served Arthur
about his court. From all the lands there voyaged to this court
such knights as were in quest either of gain or worship. Of
these lords some drew near to hear tell of Arthur's courtesies;
others to marvel at the pride of his state; these to have speech
with the knights of his chivalry; and some to receive of his
largeness costly gifts. For this Arthur in his day was loved
right well of the poor, and honoured meetly by the rich. Only
the kings of the world bore him malice and envy, since they
doubted and feared exceedingly lest he should set his foot upon
them every one, and spoil them of their heritage.

I know not if you have heard tell the marvellous gestes and
errant deeds related so often of King Arthur. They have been
noised about this mighty realm for so great a space that the
truth has turned to fable and an idle song. Such rhymes are
neither sheer bare lies, nor gospel truths. They should not be
considered either an idiot's tale, or given by inspiration. The
minstrel has sung his ballad, the storyteller told over his story
so frequently, little by little he has decked and painted, till by
reason of his embellishment the truth stands hid in the trappings of a tale. Thus to make a delectable tune to your ear,
history goes masking as fable. Hear then how, because of his
valour, the counsel of his barons, and in the strength of that
mighty chivalry he had cherished and made splendid, Arthur
purposed to cross the sea and conquer the land of France.
But first he deemed to sail to Norway, since he would make
Lot, his sister's lord, its king. Sichelin, the King of Norway,
was newly dead, leaving neither son nor daughter of his body.
In the days of his health, as alike when he fell on death, Sichelin
had appointed Lot to succeed him in his realm and fief. The
crown was Lot's by right, even as Sichelin proclaimed, since
Lot was the king's nephew, and there was no other heir. When
the folk of Norway learned that Sichelin had bequeathed his
realm to Lot, they held his command and ordinance in derision.
They would have no alien for their lord, nor suffer a stranger to
meddle in their business, lest he should deem them an ancient
and feeble people, and give to outland folk what was due to the
dwellers in the realm. The Norwegians resolved to make king
one of their own house, that he might cherish them and their
children; and for this reason they chose from amongst them a
certain lord named Ridulph to be their king.

When Lot perceived that his right was despised, save that he
took his heritage by force, he sought help of Arthur, his lord.

Arthur agreed to aid him in his quarrel, promising to render
him his own, and to avenge him bitterly on Ridulph. Arthur
gathered together many ships and a mighty host. He entered
into Norway with this great company, wasting the land, seizing
on the manors, and spoiling the towns. Ridulph was no
trembler, and had no thought to leave the country to its fate.
He assembled his people, and prepared to give battle to the
king. Since however his carles were not many, and his friends
but few, Ridulph was defeated in the fight and slain. The
greater part of his fellowship perished with him, so that no
large number remained. In this manner Lot the King of Lyones
destroyed the Norwegians from the land. Having delivered
Norway from itself Arthur granted the kingdom to Lot, so only
that he did Arthur homage as his lord. Amongst the barons
who rode in this adventure was Gawain, the hardy and famous
knight, who had freshly come from St. Sulpicius the Apostle,
whose soul may God give rest and glory. The knight wore
harness bestowed on him by the Apostle, and wondrously was
he praised. This Gawain was a courteous champion, circumspect in word and deed, having no pride nor blemish in him.
He did more than his boast, and gave more largely than he
promised. His father had sent him to Rome, that he might be
schooled the more meetly. Gawain was dubbed knight in the
same day as Wavain, and counted himself of Arthur's household. Mightily he strove to do his devoir in the field, for the
fairer service and honour of his lord.

After Arthur had conquered Norway, and firmly established
his justice in the land, he chose of his host those men who were
the most valiant and ready in battle, and assembled them by
the sea. He brought to the same haven many ships and barges,
together with such mariners as were needful for his purpose.
When a quiet time was come, with a fortunate wind, Arthur
crossed the sea into Denmark; for the realm was very greatly
to his desire. Acil, the Danish king, considered the Britons and
the folk from Norway. He considered Arthur, who had prevailed against so many kings. Acil knew and was persuaded
that Arthur was mightier than he. He had no mind to suffer
hurt himself, or to see his goodly heritage spoiled in a useless
quarrel. What did it profit to waste wealth and honour alike,
to behold slain friends and ruined towers? Acil wrought well
and speedily. He sought peace, and ensued it. He gave costly
gifts, and made promises which were larger still; till by reason
of his words, his prayers, and supplications, concord was estab-

lished between Arthur and the king. Acil paid fealty and
homage; he became Arthur's man, and owned that of Arthur's
grace he held his fief. King Arthur rejoiced greatly at this
adventure, and of the conquest he had made. He desired
honour the more greedily because of the worship he had gained.
From out of Denmark he chose, by hundreds and by thousands,
the stoutest knights and archers he could find. These he joined
to his host, purposing to lead this fair company into France.
Without any long tarrying the king acted on his purpose.
Towns, cities, and castles fell before him, so that Flanders and
the country about Boulogne were speedily in his power. Arthur
was a prudent captain. He perceived no profit in wasting his
own realm, burning his towns, and stealing from his very purse.
His eyes were in every place, and much was forbidden by his
commandment. No soldier might rob nor pill. If there was
need of raiment, meat, or provand, then must he buy with good
minted coin in the market. Nothing he dared to destroy or
steal.

Now in Arthur's day the land of France was known as Gaul.
The realm had neither king nor master, for the Romans held
it strongly as a province. This province was committed to the
charge of Frollo, and the tribune had governed the country
for a great space. He took rent and tribute of the people, and
in due season caused the treasure to be delivered to the emperor
at Rome. Thus had it been since the time of Cæsar, that mighty
emperor, who brought into subjection France and Germany,
and all the land of Britain. Frollo was a very worthy lord,
come of a noble Roman race, fearful of none, however hardy.
He knew well, by divers letters, the loss and the mischief done
by Arthur and his host. Frollo had no mind tamely to watch
the Romans lose their heritage. The tribune summoned to his
aid all the men abiding in the province who carried arms and
owned fealty to Rome. He assembled these together, ordaining
a great company, clad in harness and plenteously supplied with
stores. With these he went out to battle against Arthur, but
he prospered less than his merit deserved. The Roman tribune
was discomfited so grievously that he sought safety in flight.
Of his fellowship he had lost a great number. Many were slain
outright in battle, others were sorely wounded, or made captive,
or returned sorrowing to their own homes. Out of the meinie
Frollo had gathered from so many cities, more than two thousand
were destroyed. This was no great marvel, since the count of
Arthur's host was more than Frollo might endure. From every

land he had subdued to himself, from every city that was taken, Arthur saw to it that not a spearman nor knight of fitting years and strength of body, but was numbered in the host, and commanded to serve Arthur as his lord. Of these outland folk, Arthur chose a fair company of the hardiest knights and most proven champions to be of his private household. The very French began to regard him as their king, so only that they had the courage of their minds. This man loved him for his wise and comely speech: this by reason of his liberal hand: this because of his noble and upright spirit. Whether men were driven to his presence by fear, or considered him a refuge in the storm, all found cause enough to seek his court, to make their peace, and to acknowledge him as their suzerain. Now Frollo, after his discomfiture by the king, fled to Paris with all the speed he might, making no stop upon the road. The tribune feared Arthur and his power very sorely, and since he sought a fortress to defend his person, he would not trust his fortune to any other city. He resolved, therefore, to await Arthur within Paris, and to fight the king beneath the walls. Frollo called to himself such legions as were yet in towns near by. Because of the number of the fugitives who were come to that place, together with the burgesses abiding therein, a great concourse of people filled the city. All these folk toiled diligently to furnish the city with corn and meat, and to make sure the walls and gates against their foes.

Arthur learned that Frollo was making strong his towers, and filling the barns with victuals. He drew to Paris, and sat down without the city. He lodged his men in the suburbs beyond the walls, holding the town so close that food might not enter whether by the river or the gates. Arthur shut the city fast for more than a month, since the French defended them well and manfully. A mighty multitude was crowded within the walls, and there was a plentiful lack of meat. All the provand bought and gathered together in so short a space was quickly eaten and consumed, and the folk were afterwards anhungered. There was little flesh, but many bellies; so that the women and children made much sorrow. Had the counsel of the poor been taken, right soon would the keys of the city have been rendered. " Diva," clamoured the famished citizens, " what doest thou, Frollo? Why requirest thou not peace at Arthur's hand? " Frollo regarded the common people who failed for famine. He looked upon the folk dying by reason of their hunger, and knew that they would have him yield the city. Frollo perceived

that of a surety the end of all was come. The tribune chose
to put his own body in peril—yea, rather to taste of death, than
to abandon Paris to her leaguers. Frollo had full assurance
of Arthur's rectitude. In the simplicity of his heart he sent
urgent messages to the king, praying him to enter in the Island,
that body to body they might bring their quarrel to an end. He
who prevailed over his fellow, and came living from the battle,
should take the whole realm as his own and receive all France
for his guerdon. Thus the land would not perish, nor the folk
be utterly destroyed. Arthur hearkened willingly to the
heralds, for very greatly was their message to his mind. He
accorded that the battle should be between the two captains,
even as Frollo desired. Gauntlets were taken from one and
the other, and hostages given on behalf of Paris and on the part
of the besiegers for better assurance of the covenant that was
made.

On the morrow the two champions arrayed them in harness,
and coming to the Island, entered boldly in the lists. The
banks were filled with a mighty concourse of people, making
great tumult. Not a man or woman remained that day in his
chamber. They climbed upon the walls, and thronged the
roofs of the houses, crying upon God, and adjuring Him by
His holy Name to give victory to him who would guard the
realm in peace, and preserve the poor from war. Arthur's
meinie, for their part, awaited the judgment of God, in praying
the King of Glory to bestow the prize and honour on their lord.
The two champions were set over against the other, laced each
in his mail, and seated on his warhorse. The strong destriers
were held with bit and bridle, so eager were they for the battle.
The riders bestrode the steeds with lifted shields, brandishing
great lances in their hands. It was no easy matter to perceive
—however curiously men looked—which was the stouter
knight, or to judge who would be victor in the joust. Certainly
each was a very worthy lord and a right courageous champion.
When all was made ready the knights struck spurs to their
steeds, and loosing the rein upon the horses' necks, hurtled
together with raised buckler and lance in rest. They smote
together with marvellous fierceness. Whether by reason of the
swerving of his destrier, I cannot tell, but Frollo failed of his
stroke. Arthur, on his side, smote the boss of his adversary's
shield so fairly, that he bore him over his horse's buttock, as
long as the ash staff held. Arthur drew forth his sword, and
hastened to Frollo to bring the battle to an end. Frollo climbed

stoutly on his feet. He held his lance before him like a rod, and the king's steed ran upon the spear, so that it pierced deeply in his body. Of this thrust the destrier and his rider alike came tumbling to the ground. When the Britons saw this thing, they might not contain themselves for grief. They cried aloud, and seizing their weapons, for a little would have violated the love-day. They made ready to cross the river to the Island, and to avenge their lord upon the Gauls. Arthur cried loudly to his Britons to observe their covenant, commanding that not a man should move to his help that day. He gripped Excalibur sternly in his hand, resolving that Frollo should pay dearly for his triumph. Arthur dressed his shield above his head, and handselling his sword, rushed upon Frollo. Frollo was a passing good knight, hardy and strong, in no whit dismayed by the anger of his adversary. He raised his own glaive on high, striking fiercely at Arthur's brow. Frollo was strong beyond the strength of man. His brand was great and sharp, and the buffet was struck with all his power. The blade sheared through helm and coif alike, so that King Arthur was wounded in his forehead, and the blood ran down his face.

When Arthur felt the dolour of his hurt, and looked upon his blood, he desired nothing, save to wreak evil on the man who had wrought this mischief. He pressed the more closely upon Frollo. Lifting Excalibur, his good sword, in both hands, he smote so lustily that Frollo's head was cloven down to his very shoulders. No helmet nor hauberk, whatever the armourer's craft, could have given surety from so mighty a blow. Blood and brains gushed from the wound. Frollo fell upon the ground, and beating the earth a little with his chausses of steel, presently died, and was still.

When men saw this bitter stroke the burgesses and sergeants raised a loud cry. Arthur's household rejoiced beyond measure; but those of the city wept, making great sorrow for Frollo, their champion. Nevertheless, the citizens of Paris ran to their gates. They set the doors wide, and welcomed Arthur, his meinie, and company within their walls. When Arthur perceived the French were desirous to offer him their fealty, he suffered them so to do, taking hostages that they would abide in peace. He lodged within the city certain days, and appointed governors, for the assurance of his power. After quiet was established, Arthur divided the host into two parts. The one of these companies he delivered into the charge of Hoel, the king's nephew. With the other half he devised to conquer Anjou,

Auvergne, Gascony, and Poitou; yea, to overrun Lorraine and
Burgundy, if the task did not prove beyond his power. Hoel did
his lord's commandment, even as Arthur purposed. He conquered Berri, and afterwards Touraine, Auvergne, Poitou, and
Gascony. Guitard, the King of Poitiers, was a valiant captain,
having good knights in his service. To uphold his realm and
his rights Guitard fought many a hard battle. The luck went
this way and that. Sometimes he was the hunter, sometimes
the quarry: often he prevailed, and often, again, he lost. At
the end Guitard was persuaded Arthur was the stronger lord,
and that only by submission could he keep his own. The land
was utterly wasted and ravaged. Beyond the walls of town
and castle there was nothing left to destroy; and of all the fair
vineyards not a vine but was rooted from the ground. Guitard
made overtures of peace, and accorded himself with Hoel. He
swore Arthur fealty and homage, so that the king came to love
him very dearly. The other parcels of France Arthur conquered them every one by his own power. When there was
peace over all the country, so that none dared lift a spear
against the king, Arthur sought such men as were grown old
in his quarrels, and desired greatly to return to their homes.
To these feeble sergeants Arthur rendered their wages and
gifts, and sent them rejoicing from whence they had come.
The knights of his household, and such lusty youths as were
desirous of honour, having neither dame nor children to their
hearths, Arthur held in his service for yet nine years. During
these nine years that Arthur abode in France, he wrought
divers great wonders, reproving many haughty men and their
tyrannies, and chastising many sinners after their deservings.
Now it befell that when Easter was come, Arthur held high
feast at Paris with his friends. On that day the king recompensed his servants for their losses, and gave to each after his
deserts. He bestowed guerdon meetly on all, according to his
zeal and the labour he had done. To Kay, the master seneschal
of his house, a loyal and chivalrous knight, the king granted all
Anjou and Angers. Bedevere, the king's cup-bearer and very
privy counsellor, received that fief of Normandy, which aforetime was called Neustria. These lords, Kay and Bedevere, were
Arthur's faithful friends, knowing the inmost counsel of his
mind. Boulogne was given to Holden: Le Mans to Borel, his
cousin. On each and all, according to his gentleness of heart
and diligence in his lord's service, Arthur bestowed honours
and fees, and granted largely of his lands.

After Arthur thus had feoffed his lords, and given riches to his friends, in April, when winter was gone, he passed the sea to England, his own realm. Marvellous joy was shown of all good folk at the return of the king. Dames held those husbands close from whom they had been parted so long. Mothers kissed their sons, with happy tears upon their cheeks. Sons and daughters embraced their fathers. Cousin clipped cousin, and neighbour that friend who once was his companion. The aunt made much of her sister's son. Ladies kissed long that lover who returned from France; yea, when the place was meet, clasped him yet more sweetly in their arms. Wondrous was the joy shown of all. In the lanes and crossways, in the highways and by-ways, you might see friends a many staying friend, to know how it fared with him, how the land was settled when it was won, what adventures chanced to the seeker, what profit clave to him thereof, and why he remained so great a while beyond the sea. Then the soldier fought his battles once again. He told over his adventures, he spoke of his hard and weary combats, of the toils he had endured, and the perils from which he was delivered.

Arthur cherished tenderly his servants, granting largely, and promising richly, to the worthy. He took counsel with his barons, and devised that for the louder proclamation of his fame and wealth, he would hold a solemn feast at Pentecost, when summer was come, and that then in the presence of his earls and baronage he would be crowned king. Arthur commanded all his lords on their allegiance to meet him at Caerleon in Glamorgan. He desired to be crowned king in Caerleon, because it was rich beyond other cities, and marvellously pleasant and fair. Pilgrims told in those days that the mansions of Caerleon were more desirable than the palaces of Rome. This rich city, Caerleon, was builded on the Usk, a river which falls within the Severn. He who came to the city from a strange land, might seek his haven by this fair water. On one side of the town flowed this clear river; whilst on the other spread a thick forest. Fish were very plentiful in the river, and of venison the burgesses had no lack. Passing fair and deep were the meadows about the city, so that the barns and granges were very rich. Within the walls rose two mighty churches, greatly praised. One of these famed churches was called in remembrance of Saint Julius the Martyr, and held a convent of holy nuns for the fairer service of God. The second church was dedicate to Saint Aaron, his companion. The bishop had his seat therein. Moreover, this church was furnished with many wealthy clergy and canons of seemly life. These clerks were students of astronomy, concerning themselves diligently with the courses of the stars. Often enough they prophesied to Arthur what the future would bring forth, and of the deeds that he would do. So goodly was the city, there was none more delectable in all the earth. Now by reason of the lofty palaces, the fair woods and pastures, the ease and content, and all the delights of which you have heard, Arthur desired to hold his court at Caerleon, and to bid his barons to attend him every one. He commanded, therefore, to the feast, kings and earls, dukes and viscounts, knights and barons, bishops and abbots. Nor did Arthur bid Englishmen alone, but Frenchman and Burgundian, Auvergnat and Gascon, Norman and Poitivin, Angevin and Fleming, together with him of Brabant, Hainault, and Lorraine, the king bade to his dinner. Frisian and Teuton, Dane and Norwegian, Scot, Irish, and Icelander, him of Cathness and of Gothland, the lords of Galway and of the furthest islands of the Hebrides, Arthur summoned them all. When these received the king's messages commanding them to his crowning, they hastened to observe the feast as they were bidden, every one. From Scotland came Aguisel the king, richly vested in his royal robes; there, too, was Urian, King of Murief, together with his son Yvain the courteous; Lot of Lyones also, to take a brave part in the revels, and with him that very frank and gentle knight Gawain, his son. There besides were Stater and Cadual, kings of South Wales and of North; Cador of Cornwall, right near to Arthur's heart; Morud, Earl of Gloucester; and Guerdon, Earl of Winchester. Anavalt came from Salisbury, and Rimarec from Canterbury. Earl Baldulph drew from Silchester, and Vigenin from Leicester. There, too, was Algal of Guivic, a baron much held in honour by the court. Other lords were there a many, in no wise of less reputation than their fellows. The son of Po that was hight Donander; Regian, son of Abauder; Ceilus the son of Coil; that son of Chater named Chatellus; Griffin, the heir of Nagroil; Ron, the son of Neco; Margoil, Clefaut, Ringar, Angan, Rimar and Gorbonian, Kinlint, Neco and that Peredur, whom men deemed to be gotten by Eladur. Besides these princes there drew to Caerleon such knights as were of the king's house, and served him about his court. These were his chosen friends, who had their seats at the King's Round Table, but more of them I cannot tell. Many other lords were there of only less wealth and worship than those

I have named. So numerous was this fair company that I
have lost count of their numbers. A noble array of prelates
came also to Arthur's solemn feast. Abbots and mitred bishops
walked in their order and degree. The three archbishops of the
realm came in his honour, namely, the Archbishop of London,
his brother of York, and holy Dubricius, whose chair was in that
self same city. Very holy of life was this fair prelate. Very
abundantly he laboured, being Archbishop of Caerleon and
Legate of Rome. Many wonderful works were wrought by his
hands. The sick were brought to him gladly, and by reason
of his love and his prayers, oftentimes they were healed of their
hurt. In olden days this Dubricius abode in London, but now
was Bishop in Wales, by reason of the evil times when kings
regarded not God, and the people forsook the churches of their
fathers. These clergy assembled at Arthur's court, for the
king's feast, together with so great a fellowship of barons that
I know not even to rehearse you their names.

Yet these must be remembered, whomsoever I forget. Vil-
lamus, King of Ireland, and Malinus, King of Iceland, and
Doldamer, lord of that lean and meagre country, known as the
land of Goths. Acil, the King of the Danes; Lot, who was
King of Norway, and Gonfal, jarl of the lawless Orkneys, from
whence sail the pirates in their ships. From the parts beyond
the seas came Ligier, holding the dukedom and honour of
Burgundy; Holden, Earl of Flanders; and Guerin, Earl of
Chartres, having the twelve peers of France in his company, for
the richer dignity and splendour of his state. Guitard was
there, the Earl of Poitiers; Kay, whom the king had created
Earl of Angers; and Bedevere of Neustria, that province which
men now call Normandy. From Le Mans drew Earl Borel, and
from Brittany Earl Hoel. Passing noble of visage was Hoel, and
all those lords who came forth from France. They voyaged
to Arthur's court in chased harness and silken raiment, riding
on lusty horses with rich trappings, and wearing jewels, with
many golden ornaments. There was not a prince from here
even unto Spain, yea, to the very Rhine in the land of Germany,
but hastened to Arthur's solemn feast, so only that he was bidden
to that crowning. Of these some came to look on the face of the
king; some to receive of his largeness costly gifts; some to have
speech with the lords of his council. Some desired to marvel
over the abundance of Arthur's wealth, and others to hear tell
of the great king's courtesies. This lord was drawn by the cords
of love; this by compulsion of his suzerain's ban; this to learn

by the witness of his eyes whether Arthur's power and prosperity exceeded that fame of which the whole world bragged.

When this proud company of kings, bishops, and princes was gathered together to observe Arthur's feast, the whole city was moved. The king's servants toiled diligently making ready for so great a concourse of guests. Soldiers ran to and fro, busily seeking hostels for this fair assemblage. Houses were swept and garnished, spread with reeds, and furnished with hangings of rich arras. Halls and chambers were granted to their needs, together with stables for the horses and their provand. Those for whom hostelries might not be found abode in seemly lodgings, decently appointed to their degree. The city was full of stir and tumult. In every place you beheld squires leading horses and destriers by the bridle, setting saddles on hackneys and taking them off, buckling the harness and making the metal work shining and bright. Grooms went about their business. Never was such a cleansing of stables, such taking of horses to the meadows, such a currying and combing, shoeing and loosing of girths, washing and watering, such a bearing of straw and of grass for the litter, and oats for the manger. Nor these alone, but in the courtyards and chambers of the hostels you might see the pages and chamberlains go swiftly about their tasks, in divers fashions. The varlets brushed and folded the habiliments and mantles of their lords. They looked to the stuff and the fastenings of their garments. You saw them hurry through the halls carrying furs and furred raiment, both vair and the grey. Caerleon seemed rather a fair than a city, at Arthur's feast.

Now telleth the chronicle of this geste, that when the morning was come of the day of the high feast, a fair procession of archbishops, bishops, and abbots wended to the king's palace, to place the crown upon Arthur's head, and lead him within the church. Two of these archbishops brought him through the streets of the city, one walking on either side of his person. Each bishop sustained the king by his arm, and thus he was carried to his throne. Four kings went before Arthur and the clerks, bearing swords in their hands. Pommel, scabbard, and hilt of these four swords were of wrought gold. This was the office of these kings when Arthur held state at his court. The first of the princes was from Scotland, the second from South Wales, the third was of North Wales, and as to the last it was Cador of Cornwall who carried the fourth sword. All these fair princes were at one in their purpose, being altogether at unity, when Arthur was crowned king. To holy Dubricius it fell, as prelate of Caerleon and Roman legate, to celebrate the office and perform such rites as were seemly to be rendered in the church.

That the queen might not be overshadowed by her husband's state, the crown was set on her head in another fashion. For her part she had bidden to her court the great ladies of the country, and such dames as were the wives of her friends. Together with these had assembled the ladies of her kindred, such ladies as were most to her mind, and many fair and gentle maidens whom she desired to be about her person at the feast. The presence of this gay company of ladies made the feast yet more rich, when the queen was crowned in her chamber, and brought to that convent of holy nuns for the conclusion of the rite. The press was so great that the queen might hardly make her way through the streets of the city. Four dames preceded their lady, bearing four white doves in their hands. These dames were the wives of those lords who carried the golden swords before the king. A fair company of damsels followed after the queen, making marvellous joy and delight. This fair fellowship of ladies came from the noblest of the realm. Passing dainty were they to see, wearing rich mantles above their silken raiment. All men gazed gladly upon them, for their beauty was such that none was sweeter than her fellows. These dames and maidens went clothed in their softest garments. Their heads were tired in their fairest hennins, and they walked in their most holiday vesture. Never were seen so many rich kirtles of divers colours, such costly mantles, such precious jewels and rings. Never were seen such furs and such ornaments, both the vair and the grey. Never was known so gay and noble a procession of ladies, as this which hastened to the church, lest it should be hindered from the rite.

Now within the church Mass was commenced with due pomp and observance. The noise of the organ filled the church, and the clerks sang tunably in the choir. Their voices swelled or failed, according as the chant mounted to the roof, or died away in supplication. The knights passed from one church to the other. Now they would be at the convent of St. Julius, and again at the cathedral church of St. Aaron. This they did to compare the singing of the clerks, and to delight their eyes with the loveliness of the damsels. Although the knights passed frequently between the churches, yet no man could answer for certain at which they remained the longer. They could not surfeit the heart by reason of the sweetness of the melody. Yea, had the song endured the whole day through, I doubt those knights would ever have grown weary or content.

When the office drew to its appointed end, and the last words were chanted, the king put off his crown that he had carried to the church. He took another crown which sat more lightly on his head; and in such fashion did the queen. They laid aside their heavy robes and ornaments of state, and vested them in less tiring raiment. The king parted from St. Aaron's church, and returned to his palace for meat. The queen, for her part, came again to her own house, carrying with her that fair fellowship of ladies, yet making marvellous joy. For the Britons held still to the custom brought by their sires from Troy, that when the feast was spread, man ate with man alone, bringing no lady with him to the board. The ladies and damsels ate apart. No men were in their hall, save only the servitors, who served them with every observance, for the feast was passing rich, as became a monarch's court. When Arthur was seated in his chair upon the daïs, the lords and princes sat around the board, according to the usage of the country, each in his order and degree. The king's seneschal, hight Sir Kay, served Arthur's table, clad in a fair dalmatic of vermeil silk. With Sir Kay were a thousand damoiseaux, clothed in ermine, who bore the dishes from the buttery. These pages moved briskly about the tables, carrying the meats in platters to the guests. Together with these were yet another thousand damoiseaux, gentle and goodly to see, clothed likewise in coats of ermine. These fair varlets poured the wine from golden beakers into cups and hanaps of fine gold. Not one of these pages but served in a vesture of ermine. Bedevere, the king's cupbearer, himself set Arthur's cup upon the board; and those called him master who saw that Arthur's servants lacked not drink.

The queen had so many servitors at her bidding, that I may not tell you the count. She and all her company of ladies were waited on, richly and reverently. Right worshipfully were they tended. These ladies had to their table many rich meats, and wines and spiced drink of divers curious fashions. The dishes and vessels from which they ate were very precious, and passing fair. I know not how to put before you the wealth and the splendour of Arthur's feast. Whether for goodly men or for chivalrous deeds, for wealth as for plenty, for courtesy as for honour, in Arthur's day England bore the flower from all the lands near by, yea, from every other realm whereof we know.

The poorest peasant in his smock was a more courteous and valiant gentleman than was a belted knight beyond the sea. And as with the men, so, and no otherwise, was it with the women. There was never a knight whose praise was bruited abroad, but went in harness and raiment and plume of one and the self-same hue. The colour of surcoat and armour in the field was the colour of the gown he wore in hall. The dames and damsels would apparel them likewise in cloth of their own colour. No matter what the birth and riches of a knight might be, never, in all his days, could he gain fair lady to his friend, till he had proved his chivalry and worth. That knight was accounted the most nobly born who bore himself the foremost in the press. Such a knight was indeed cherished of the ladies; for his friend was the more chaste as he was brave.

After the king had risen from the feast, he and his fellowship went without the city to take their delight amongst the fields. The lords sought their pleasure in divers places. Some amongst them jousted together, that their horses might be proven. Others fenced with the sword, or cast the stone, or flung pebbles from a sling. There were those who shot with the bow, like cunning archers, or threw darts at a mark. Every man strove with his fellow, according to the game he loved. That knight who proved the victor in his sport, and bore the prize from his companions, was carried before the king in the sight of all the princes. Arthur gave him of his wealth so goodly a gift, that he departed from the king's presence in great mirth and content. The ladies of the court climbed upon the walls, looking down on the games very gladly. She, whose friend was beneath her in the field, gave him the glance of her eye and her face; so that he strove the more earnestly for her favour. Now to the court had gathered many tumblers, harpers, and makers of music, for Arthur's feast. He who would hear songs sung to the music of the rote, or would solace himself with the newest refrain of the minstrel, might win to his wish. Here stood the viol player, chanting ballads and lays to their appointed tunes. Everywhere might be heard the voice of viols and harp and flutes. In every place rose the sound of lyre and drum and shepherd's pipe, bagpipe, psaltery, cymbals, monochord, and all manner of music. Here the tumbler tumbled on his carpet. There the mime and the dancing girl put forth their feats. Of Arthur's guests some hearkened to the teller of tales and fables. Others called for dice and tables, and played games of chance for a wager. Evil befalls to winner and loser alike from such sport as this. For the most part men played at chess or draughts. You might see them, two by two, bending over the board. When one player was beaten by his fellow, he borrowed moneys to pay his wager, giving pledges for the repayment of his debt. Dearly enough he paid for his loan, getting but eleven to the dozen. But the pledge was offered and taken, the money rendered, and the game continued with much swearing and cheating, much drinking and quarrelling, with strife and with anger. Often enough the loser was discontented, and rose murmuring against his fellow. Two by two the dicers sat at table, casting the dice. They threw in turn, each throwing higher than his fellow. You might hear them count, six, five, three, four, two, and one. They staked their raiment on the cast, so there were those who threw half naked. Fair hope had he who held the dice, after his fellow had cried his number. Then the quarrel rose suddenly from the silence. One called across the table to his companion, " You cheat, and throw not fairly. Grasp not the dice so tightly in your hand, but shake them forth upon the board. My count is yet before yours. If you still have pennies in your pouch bring them out, for I will meet you to your wish." Thus the dicers wrangled, and to many of Arthur's guests it chanced that he who sat to the board in furs, departed from the tables clothed in his skin.

When the fourth day of the week was come, on a certain Wednesday, the king made knights of his bachelors, granting them rents to support their stations. He recompensed those lords of his household who held of him their lands at suit and service. Such clerks as were diligent in their Master's business he made abbots and bishops; and bestowed castles and towns on his counsellors and friends. To those stranger knights who for his love had crossed the sea in his quarrel, the king gave armour and destrier and golden ornaments, to their desire. Arthur divided amongst them freely of his wealth. He granted lordship and delights, greyhound and brachet, furred gown and raiment, beaker and hanap, sendal and signet, bliaut and mantle, lance and sword and quivers of sharp barbed arrows. He bestowed harness and buckler and weapons featly fashioned by the smith. He gave largesse of bears and of leopards, of palfreys and hackneys, of chargers with saddles thereon. He gave the helm as the hauberk, the gold as the silver, yea, he bestowed on his servants the very richest and most precious of his treasure. Never a man of these outland knights, so only he was worthy of Arthur's bounty, but the king granted him such gifts as he might

brag of in his own realm.   And as with the foreign lords, so to
the kings and the princes, the knights and all his barons, Arthur
gave largely many precious gifts.

Now as King Arthur was seated on a daïs with these princes
and earls before him, there entered in his hall twelve ancient
men, white and greyheaded, full richly arrayed in seemly raiment.
These came within the palace two by two.   With the one hand
each clasped his companion, and in the other carried a fair
branch of olive.   The twelve elders passed at a slow pace down
the hall, bearing themselves right worshipfully.   They drew
near to Arthur's throne, and saluted the king very courteously.
They were citizens of Rome, said the spokesman of these aged
men, and were ambassadors from the emperor, bringing with
them letters to the king.   Having spoken such words, one
amongst them made ready his parchment, and delivered it in
Arthur's hands.   This was the sum of the writing sent by the
Emperor of Rome.

"Lucius, the Emperor and lord of Rome, to King Arthur,
his enemy, these, according to his deservings.   I marvel very
greatly, and disdain whilst yet I marvel, the pride and ill-will
which have puffed you up to seek to do me evil.   I have nothing
but contempt and wonder for those who counsel you to resist
the word of Rome, whilst yet one Roman draws his breath.
You have acted lightly, and by reason of vanity have wrought
mischief to us who are the front and avengers of the world.
You resemble a blind man, whose eyes the leech prepares to
open.   You know not yet, but very soon you will have learned,
the presumption of him who teaches law to the justice of Rome.
It is not enough to say that you have acted after your kind, and
sinned according to your nature.   Know you not whom you
are, and from what dust you have come, that you dare to dispute the tribute to Rome!   Why do you steal our land and our
truage?   Why do you refuse to render Cæsar that which is his
own?   Are you indeed so strong that we may not take our
riches from your hand?   Perchance you would show us a
marvellous matter.   Behold—you say—the lion fleeing from
the lamb, the wolf trembling before the kid, and the leopard
fearful of the hare.   Be not deceived.   Nature will not suffer
such miracles to happen.   Julius Cæsar, our mighty ancestor—
whom, maybe, you despise in your heart—conquered the land
of Britain, taking tribute thereof, and this you have paid until
now.   From other islands also, neighbours of this, it was our
custom to receive truage.   These in your presumption you have

taken by force, to your own most grievous hurt. Moreover, you have been so bold as to put yet greater shame and damage upon us, since Frollo, our tribune, is slain, and France and Britain, by fraud, you keep wrongfully in your power. Since, then, you have not feared Rome, neither regarded her honour, the senate summon you by these letters, and command you under pain of their displeasure, to appear before them at mid August, without fail or excuse. Come prepared to make restitution of that you have taken, whatever the cost; and to give satisfaction for all those things whereof you are accused. If so be you think to keep silence, and do naught of that you are bidden, I will cross the Mont St. Bernard with a mighty host, and pluck Britain and France from your hand. Do not deem that you can make head against me, neither hold France in my despite. Never will you dare to pass that sea, for my dearer pleasure; yea, were your courage indeed so great, yet never might you abide my coming. Be persuaded that in what place soever you await me, from thence I will make you skip. For this is my purpose, to bind you with bonds, and bring you to Rome, and deliver you, bound, to the judgment of the senate."

When this letter was read in the hearing of those who were come to Arthur's solemnity, a great tumult arose, for they were angered beyond measure. Many of the Britons took God to witness that they would do such things and more also to those ambassadors who had dared deliver the message. They pressed about those twelve ancient men, with many wild and mocking words. Arthur rose hastily to his feet, bidding the brawlers to keep silence. He cried that none should do the Romans a mischief, for they were an embassy, and carried the letters of their lord. Since they were but another's mouthpiece, he commanded that none should work them harm. After the noise was at an end, and Arthur was assured that the elders were no longer in peril, he called his privy council and the lords of his household together, in a certain stone keep, that was named the Giant's Tower. The king would be advised by his barons—so ran the summons—what answer he should give to the messengers of Rome. Now as they mounted the stairs, earl and prince, pell-mell, together, Cador, who was a merry man, saw the king before him. "Fair king," said the earl gaily, "for a great while the thought has disturbed me, that peace and soft living are rotting away the British bone. Idleness is the stepdame of virtue, as our preachers have often told us. Soft living makes a sluggard of the hardiest knight, and steals away his strength.

She cradles him with dreams of woman, and is the mother of chambering and wantonness. Folded hands and idleness cause our young damoiseaux to waste their days over merry tales, and dice, raiment to catch a lady's fancy and things that are worse. Rest and assurance of safety will in the end do Britain more harm than force or guile. May the Lord God be praised Who has jogged our elbow. To my mind He has persuaded these Romans to challenge our country that we may get us from sleep. If the Romans trust so greatly in their might that they do according to their letters, be assured the Briton has not yet lost his birthright of courage and hardness. I am a soldier, and have never loved a peace that lasts over long, since there are uglier things than war." Gawain overheard these words. "Lord earl," said he, " by my faith be not fearful because of the young men. Peace is very grateful after war. The grass grows greener, and the harvest is more plenteous. Merry tales, and songs, and ladies' love are delectable to youth. By reason of the bright eyes and the worship of his friend, the bachelor becomes knight and learns chivalry."

Whilst the lords jested amongst themselves in this fashion, they climbed the tower, and were seated in the chamber. When Arthur marked that each was in his place, silent and attentive to the business, he considered for a little that he had to speak. Presently he lifted his head, and spoke such words as these. "Lords," said the king, "who are here with me, nay, rather my companions and my friends, companions alike, whether the day be good or evil, by whose sustenance alone I have endured such divers quarrels, hearken well to me. In the days that are told, have we not shared victory and defeat together; partners, you with me, as I with you, in gain and in loss? Through you, and by reason of your help in time of trouble, have I won many battles. You have I carried over land and sea, far and near, to many strange realms. Ever have I found you loyal and true, in business and counsel. Because of your prowess I hold the heritage of divers neighbouring princes in subjection. Lords, you have hearkened to the letters carried by the ambassadors of Rome, and to the malice they threaten if we do not after their commandment. Very despiteful are they against us, and purpose to work us bitter mischief. But if God be gracious to His people, we shall yet be delivered from their hand. Now these Romans are a strong nation, passing rich and of great power. It becomes us therefore to consider prudently what we shall say and do in answer to their message, looking always to the end.

He who is assured of his mark gets there by the shortest road. When the arrows start to fly, the sergeant takes shelter behind his shield. Let us be cautious and careful like these. This Lucius seeks to do us a mischief. He is in his right; and it is ours to take such counsel, that his mischief falls on his own head. To-day he demands tribute from Britain and other islands of the sea. To-morrow he purposes in his thought to receive truage of France. Consider first the case of Britain, and how to answer wisely therein. Britain was conquered by Cæsar of force. The Britons knew not how to keep them against his host, and perforce paid him their tribute. But force is no right. It is but pride puffed up and swollen beyond measure. They cannot hold of law what they have seized by violence and wrong. The land is ours by right, even if the Roman took it to himself by force. The Romans really reproach us for the shame and the damage, the loss and the sorrow Cæsar visited upon our fathers. They boast that they will avenge such losses as these, by taking the land with the rent, and making their little finger thicker than their father's loins. Let them beware. Hatred breeds hatred again, and things despiteful are done to those who despitefully use you. They come with threats, demanding truage, and reproving us for the evil we have done them. Tribute they claim by the right of the strong; leaving sorrow and shame as our portion. But if the Romans claim to receive tribute of Britain because tribute was aforetime paid them from Britain, by the same reasoning we may establish that Rome should rather pay tribute to us. In olden days there lived two brothers, British born, namely, Belinus, King of the Britons, and Brennus, Duke of Burgundy, both wise and doughty lords, These stout champions arrived with their men before Rome, and shutting the city close, at the end gained it by storm. They took hostages of the citizens to pay them tribute; but since the burgesses did not observe their covenant, the brethren hanged the hostages, to the number of four-and-twenty, in the eyes of all their kinsfolk. When Belinus went to his own place, he commended Rome to the charge of Brennus, his brother. Now Constantine, the son of Helena, drew from Brennus and Belinus, and in his turn held Rome in his care. Maximian, King of Britain, after he had conquered France and Germany, passed the Mont St. Bernard into Lombardy, and took Rome to his keeping. These mighty kings were my near kinsmen, and each was master of Rome. Thus you have heard, and see clearly, that not only am I King of Britain, but by law Emperor of Rome also, so we maintain the rights of our fathers. The Romans have had truage of us, and my ancestors have taken seisin of them. They claim Britain, and I demand Rome. This is the sum and end of my counsel as regards Britain and Rome. Let him have the fief and the rent who is mightier in the field. As to France and those other countries which have been removed from their hands, the Romans should not wish to possess that which they may not maintain. Either the land was not to their mind, or they had not the strength to hold it. Perchance the Romans have no rights in the matter, and it is by reason of covetousness rather than by love of law, that they seek this quarrel. Let him keep the land who can, by the right of the most strong. For all these things the emperor menaces us very grievously. I pray God that he may do us no harm. Our fiefs and goods he promises to take from us, and lead us captive in bonds to Rome. We care not overmuch for this, and are not greatly frighted at his words. If he seek us after his boast, please God, he will have no mind to threaten when he turns again to his own home. We accept his challenge, and appeal to God's judgment, that all may be rendered to his keeping, who is able to maintain it in his hand."

When Arthur the king had made an end of speaking in the ears of his barons, the word was with those who had hearkened to his counsel. Hoel followed after the king. " Sire," said he, " you have spoken much, and right prudently; nor is there any who can add wisdom to your speech. Summon now your vassals and meinie, together with us who are of your household. Cross the sea straightway into France, and make the realm sure with no further tarrying. From thence we can pass Mont St. Bernard, and overrun Lombardy. By moving swiftly we shall carry the war into the emperor's own land. We shall fright him so greatly that he will have the less leisure to trouble Britain. Your movements, moreover, will be so unlooked for that the Romans will be altogether amazed, and quickly confounded. Sire, it is the Lord's purpose to exalt you over all the kings of the earth. Hinder not the will of God by doubtfulness. He is able to put even Rome in your power, so only it be according to His thought. Remember the books of the Sibyl, and of the prophecies therein. The Sibyl wrote that three kings should come forth from Britain, who of their might should conquer Rome. Of these three princes, two are dead. Belinus is dead, and Constantine is dead; but each in his day was the master of Rome. You are that third king destined to be stronger than

the great city. In you the prophecy shall be fulfilled, and the
Sibyl's words accomplished. Why then scruple to take what
God gives of His bounty? Rise up then, exalt yourself, exalt
your servants, who would see the end of God's purpose. I tell
you truly that nothing of blows or hurt, neither weariness nor
prison nor death, counts aught with us in comparison with what
is due to the king's honour. For my part, I will ride in your
company, so long as this business endures, with ten thousand
armed horsemen at my back. Moreover, if your treasury
has need of moneys for the quarrel, I will put my realm in
pledge, and deliver the gold and the gain to your hand. Never
a penny will I touch of my own, so long as the king has
need."

After Hoel had ended his counsel, Aguisel, King of Scotland,
who was brother to Lot and to Urian, stood on his feet. "Sire,"
said he, "the words you have spoken in this hall, where are
gathered the flower of your chivalry, are dear to their ears, for
we have listened to the disdainful messages of Rome. Be
assured that each of your peers will aid you to the utmost of
his power. Now is the time and occasion to show forth the
counsel and help we can afford to our king. Not one of us here
who is a subject of your realm, and holds his manors of the
crown, but will do his duty to his liege, as is but just and right.
No tidings I have heard for a great while past sounded so good
and fair as the news that presently we shall have strife with
Rome. These Romans are a people whom I neither love with
my heart, nor esteem in my mind; but hate because they are
very orgulous and proud. Upright folk should avoid their
fellowship, for they are an evil and a covetous race, caring for
no other matter but to heap treasure together, and add to their
store. The emperor of this people, by fraud and deceit, has
fastened this quarrel upon us, sending you letters with an
embassy. He deems that Britain is no other than it was, or he
would not demand his measure of tribute, pressed down and
running over. The Roman has raised such a smoke that his
fingers will quickly be scorched in the flame. Moreover, had
the Roman kept quiet, even had he refrained from threats, it
becomes our honour, of our own choice, to enter on this war, to
avenge the wrongs of our fathers, and to abase his pride. The
Romans' logic is that they are entitled to receive tribute at our
hands, by reason that their fathers, in their day, took truage
of our ancestors. If this be so, it was no free-will offering of our
fathers, but was wrenched from them by force. So be it. By

force we take again our own, and revenge ourselves for all the pilling of the past. We are a perilous people, who have proved victors in divers great battles, and brought many a bitter war to a good end. But what profit is ours of all these triumphs, so long as we cry not ' check ' to Rome! I desire not drink to my lips when athirst, nor meat to my mouth when an hungered, as I desire the hour when we hurtle together in the field. Then hey for the helm laced fast, the lifted shield, for the brandished sword, and the mighty horse. God! what spoil and rich ransom will he gain whose body God keeps with His buckler that day. Never again will he be poor till his life's end. Cities and castles will be his for the sacking; and mules, sumpters, and destriers to the heart's desire. On then, comrades, to the conquest of Rome, and to the parcelling of the Romans' lands. When the proud city is destroyed, and its wardens slain, there remains yet a work for us to do. We will pass into Lorraine, and seize the realm. We will make our pleasaunce of all the strongholds of Germany. So we will do, till there endures not a land to the remotest sea but is Arthur's fief, nor one only realm to pluck them from his power. Right or wrong this is our purpose. That my blow may be heavy as my word, and the deed accord with the speech, I am ready to go with the king, and ten thousand riders with me, besides men-at-arms in such plenty that no man may count them."

When the King of Scotland had spoken, there was much stir and tumult, all men crying that he would be shamed for ever who did not his utmost in this quarrel. Arthur and his baronage being of one mind together, the king wrote certain letters to Rome, and sealed them with his ring. These messages he committed to the embassy, honouring right worshipfully those reverend men. " Tell your countrymen," said the king, " that I am lord of Britain: that I hold France, and will continue to hold it, and purpose to defend it against the Roman power. Let them know of a surety that I journey to Rome presently at their bidding; only it will be not to carry them tribute, but rather to seek it at their hand." The ambassadors, therefore, took their leave, and went again to Rome. There they told where and in what fashion they were welcomed of the king, and reported much concerning him. This Arthur—said these ancient men—is a lord amongst kings, generous and brave, lettered and very wise. Not another king could furnish the riches spent on his state, by reason of the attendance of his ministers, and the glory of their apparel. It was useless to seek

tribute from Arthur, since in olden days Britain received tribute
of Rome.

Now when the senate had heard the report of the messengers,
and considered the letters wherewith they were charged, they
were persuaded of ambassador and message alike that Arthur
neither would do homage nor pay them the tribute they demanded. The senate, therefore, took counsel with the emperor,
requiring him to summon all the empire to his aid. They
devised that with his host he should pass through the mountains
into Burgundy, and giving battle to King Arthur deprive him
of kingdom and crown. Lucius Tiberius moved very swiftly.
He sent messages to kings, earls, and dukes, bidding them as
they loved honour to meet him on a near day at Rome, in
harness for the quest. At the emperor's commandment came
many mighty lords, whose names I find written in the chronicles
of those times. To meet Lucius came Epistrophius, King of the
Greeks; Ession, King of Bœotia; and Itarc, King of the Turks,
a passing strong and perilous knight. With these were found
Pandras, King of Egypt, and Hippolytus, King of Crete. These
were lords of very great worship; a hundred cities owning their
tyranny. Evander drew from Syria, and Teucer from Phrygia;
from Babylon came Micipsa, and from Spain, Aliphatma. From
Media came King Bocus, from Libya, Sertorius, from Bithynia,
Polydetes, and from Idumea, King Xerxes. Mustansar, the
King of Africa, came from his distant home, many a long days'
journey. With him were black men and Moors, bearing their
king's rich treasure. The senate gave of their number these
patricians: Marcellus and Lucius Catellus, Cocta, Caius, and
Metellus. Many other lords gladly joined themselves to that
company, whose names for all my seeking I have not found.
When the host was gathered together, the count of the footmen
was four hundred thousand armed men, besides one hundred
and eighty thousand riders on horses. This mighty army,
meetly ordered and furnished with weapons, set forth on a day
to give Arthur battle from Rome.

Arthur and his baronage departed from the court to make
them ready for battle. The king sent his messengers to and fro
about the land, calling and summoning each by his name, to
hasten swiftly with his power, so that he valued Arthur's love.
Not a knight but was bidden to ride on his allegiance, with all
the men and horses that he had. The lords of the isles, Ireland,
Gothland, Iceland, Denmark, Norway and the Orkneys, promised
for their part one hundred and forty thousand men, armed and

clad according to the fashion of their country. Of these not a
horseman but was a cunning rider; not a footman but bore his
accustomed weapon, battle-axe, javelin, or spear. Normandy
and Anjou, Auvergne and Poitou, Flanders and Boulogne
promised, without let, eighty thousand sergeants more, each
with his armour on his back. So much it was their right and
privilege to do, they said. The twelve peers of France, who
were of the fellowship of Guerin of Chartres, promised every one
to ride at Arthur's need, each man with a hundred lances. This
was their bounden service, said these peers. Hoel of Brittany
promised ten thousand men; Aguisel of Scotland two thousand
more. From Britain, his proper realm, that we now call England, Arthur numbered forty thousand horsemen in hauberks of
steel. As for the count of the footmen—arbalestriers, archers,
and spearmen—it was beyond all measure, for the number of
the host was as the grains of the sand. When Arthur was certified of the greatness of his power, and of the harness of his men,
he wrote letters to each of his captains, commanding him that
on an appointed day he should come in ships to Barfleur in
Normandy. The lords of his baronage, who had repaired from
the court to their fiefs, hastened to make ready with those
whom they should bring across the sea. In like manner Arthur
pushed on with his business, that nothing should hinder or delay.

Arthur committed the care of his realm, and of Dame Guenevere, his wife, to his nephew, Mordred, a marvellously hardy
knight, whom Arthur loved passing well. Mordred was a man
of high birth, and of many noble virtues, but he was not true.
He had set his heart on Guenevere, his kinswoman, but such
a love brought little honour to the queen. Mordred had kept
this love close, for easy enough it was to hide, since who would
be so bold as to deem that he loved his uncle's dame? The
lady on her side had given her love to a lord of whom much good
was spoken; but Mordred was of her husband's kin! This
made the shame more shameworthy. Ah, God, the deep wrong
done in this season by Mordred and the queen.

Arthur, having put all the governance in Mordred's power,
save only the crown, went his way to Southampton. His
meinie was lodged about the city, whilst his vessels lay within
the haven. The harbour was filled with the ships. They
passed to and fro; they remained at anchorage; they were
bound together by cables. The carpenter yet was busy upon
them with his hammer. Here the shipmen raised the mast,
and bent the sail. There they thrust forth bridges to the land,

and charged the stores upon the ship. The knights and the
sergeants entered therein in their order, bearing pikes, and
leading the fearful horses by the rein. You could watch them
crying farewell, and waving their hands, to those remaining on
the shore. When the last man had entered in the last ship
the sailors raised the anchors, and worked the galleys from the
haven. Right diligently the mariners laboured, spreading the
sails, and making fast the stays. They pulled stoutly upon the
hoists and ropes, so that the ships ran swiftly out to sea. Then
they made the ropes secure, each in its wonted place. The
captain who was charged with the safety of the ship set his
course carefully, whilst pilot and steersman heedfully observed
his word. At his bidding they put the helm to port, to lee, as
they might better fill their sails with the wind. As need arose
the shipmen drew upon the cords and bowlines, or let the canvas
fall upon the deck, that the vessel might be the less beaten of
the waves. Thus, loosing and making fast, letting go and
bringing quickly to the deck, hauling and tugging at the ropes—
so they proceeded on their way. When night was come, they
steered their courses by the stars, furling the sails that the wind
should not carry them from their path. Very fearful were the
mariners of the dark, and went as slowly as they were able.
Passing bold was he, that first courteous captain, who builded
the first ship, and committing his body to the wind and waves,
set forth to seek a land he might not see, and to find such haven
as men had never known.

Now it came to pass that whilst the host voyaged in great
content with a fair wind towards Barfleur, that Arthur slept,
for he was passing heavy, and it was night. As the king slum-
bered he beheld a vision, and, lo, a bear flying high in air towards
the east. Right huge and hideous of body was the bear, and
marvellously horrible to see. Also the king saw a dragon flying
over against him towards the west. The brightness of his eyes
was such, that the whole land and sea were filled with the radi-
ance of his glory. When these two beasts came together, the
dragon fell upon the bear, and the bear defended himself valiantly against his adversary. But the dragon put his enemy
beneath him, and tumbling him to the earth, crushed him
utterly in the dust. When Arthur had slept for awhile, his spirit
came to him again, and he awoke and remembered his dream.
The king called therefore for his wise clerks, and related to them
and his household the vision that he had seen of the bear and
of the dragon. Then certain of these clerks expounded to the

king his dream, and the interpretation thereof. The dragon
that was beholden of the king signified himself. By the bear
was shown forth a certain horrible giant, come from a far land,
whom he should slay. The giant desired greatly that the
adventure should end in another fashion; nevertheless all would
be to the king's profit. But Arthur replied, " My interpretation
of the dream is other than yours. To me it typifies rather the
issue of the war between myself and the emperor. But let the
Creator's will be done."

After these words no more was spoken until the rising of the
sun. Very early in the morning they came to haven at Barfleur
in Normandy. Presently the host issued from the ships, and
spread themselves abroad, to await the coming of those who
tarried on the way. Now they had but dwelled for a little while
in the land when tidings were brought to the king that a marvellously strong giant, newly come from Spain, had ravished
Helen, the niece of his kinsman, Hoel. This doleful lady the
giant had carried to a high place known as St. Michael's Mount,
though in that day there was neither church nor monastery on
the cliff, but all was shut close by the waves of the sea. There
was none in the country so hardy and strong, whether gentle
or simple of birth, that dared to do battle with the giant, or
even to come where he lay. Often enough the folk of the land
had gathered themselves together, and compassed about the
rock both by land and sea, but little had they gained from their
labour. For the giant had beaten their boats amongst the rocks,
so that they were slain or drowned. Therefore they left him to
himself, since there was none to hinder his pleasure. The
peasants of the realm were exceeding sorrowful. Their enemy
spoiled their houses, harried their cattle, bore away their wives
and children, and returned to his fastness on the mount. The
villeins lurked in the woods from his wrath. They perished of
misery in secret places, so that the whole land was barren,
because there was none to labour in the fields. This marvellous
giant had to name Dinabuc. Not a soul but prayed that he
might come to an evil end. When Arthur heard these lamentable tidings he called to him Kay the seneschal and Bedevere
his cupbearer, for he would open his counsel to no other man.
He told them his purpose to depart from the camp that same
night privily, taking none with him, save themselves alone.
None but they would know of his errand, for he rode to the
mount to be assured as to whether he or the giant was the
stouter champion. All through the night the three rode to-

gether, sparing not the spur. At daybreak they came upon the
ford that leads across the water to the mount. Looking towards
the mount they beheld a burning fire upon the hill, that might
be seen from very far. Over against the mount was set another
hill, near by, and of lesser height, and upon this hill also a fire
of coals. Arthur gazed from hill to mountain. He doubted
where the giant lodged, and in which of these two high places
he should come upon him. There was no man to ask of his
dwelling, nor to tell of his outgoings. Arthur bade Bedevere
to go first to the one and then to the other hill, seeking news of
the giant. When he had found that which he sought, he must
return swiftly, bringing good tidings. Bedevere set forth upon
his quest. He entered into a little boat, and rowed over to that
mount which was nearer. He could cross in no other manner,
for the tide was very full, and all the sand was covered of the
sea. Bedevere got him from the boat, and began to climb the
hill. As he climbed he stood still for a space, and hearkened.
From above Bedevere might hear a noise of sore weeping, and
loud lamentation, and doleful sighs. The knight grew cold at
the heart root by reason of his exceeding fear, since he deemed
to have come upon the giant at his play. Presently the courage
returned to his breast, and drawing the sword from its sheath,
he advanced stoutly up the hill. Bedevere considered within
himself that it were better for a knight to die, rather than know
himself a coward. He reproached himself for his fearfulness,
and in heart and hope desired only to bring the adventure to a
good end. His wish proved but vain. When Bedevere won
the summit of the mountain, there was no giant, but only a
flaming fire, and close by the fire a new-digged grave. The
knight drew near this fire, with the sword yet naked in his
hand. Lying beside the grave he found an old woman, with rent
raiment and streaming hair, lamenting her wretched case. She
bewailed also the fate of Helen, making great dole and sorrow,
with many shrill cries. When this piteous woman beheld
Bedevere upon the mount, " Oh, wretched man," she exclaimed,
" what is thy name, and what misadventure leads you here!
Should the giant find thee in his haunt, this very day thy life
will end in shame and grief and hurt. Flee, poor wretch, upon
thy road, before he spies thee. Be pitiful to thyself, nor seek
to die, for who art thou to deliver thyself from his wrath! "
" Good dame," made reply Sir Bedevere, " give over weeping
and answer my words. Tell me who you are, and why you shed
these tears. For what reason do you abide in this isle, and

crouch beside this tomb? Answer me plainly concerning your adventure." "Fair lord," replied the ancient lady, "I am a forsaken and a most unhappy woman. I make my lamentation for a damsel, named Helen, whom I nourished at my breast, the niece of Duke Hoel of this realm. Here lies her body in this tomb, that was given to me to cherish. Alas, for her who was set upon my knees! Alas, for her I cherished in my bosom! A certain devil ravished her away, and me also, bearing us both to this his lair. The giant would have had to do with the maiden, but she was so tender of her years that she might not endure him. Passing young was the maid; whilst he, for his part, was so gross and weighty of bone and flesh, that her burden was more than she could bear. For this the soul departed from her body. Alas, wretch that I am, I remain alive, and she, my joy and my love, my sweetness and my delight, was foully done to death by this giant. Nothing was left for me to do, but to put her body in the earth." "For what reason do you abide in this hill," asked Sir Bedevere, "since Helen is gone before?" "Will thou learn of the reason," said the ancient damsel, "then it shall not be hidden; for easy it is to see that thou art a gentle and a courteous man. When Helen had gone her way in shame and sorrow, the giant constrained me to abide that I might suffer his pleasure. This he did, although my heart was hot because I had seen my lady die in sore anguish. Force keeps me in this haunt; force makes me his sport. You cannot think that I stay of my own free will on the mount. I but submit to the will of the Lord. Would to God that I were dead, as for a little more I should be slain of the giant. But if I am older of years, I am also stronger, and harder, and more firm in my purpose, than ever was my frail Lady Helen. Nevertheless I am well-nigh gone, and have little longer to endure. Perchance even this very day will be my last. Friend, tarry here no further whomsoever thou mayst be. Flee while you can, for behold the fire smokes upon the mountain, and the devil makes him ready to ascend, according to his custom. Be not snared within his net. Depart, and leave an old woman to her tears and sorrow; for I have no care to live, since Helen and her love are spoiled with dust."

When Bedevere heard this adventure he was filled with pity. With his whole heart he comforted the damsel as gently as he might. He left her for a season, and hastening down the hill came straightway to the king. Bedevere showed his lord of all that he had heard and seen. He told over the tale of that ancient nurse lamenting by a grave; of Helen who was dead, and of the giant's haunt upon the higher of the hills which smoked. Arthur was passing heavy at Helen's fate. He wasted no time in tears, nor suffered himself to be fearful. Arthur bade his companions get into their harness, and ride with him to the ford. The tide was now at the ebb, so that they crossed on their horses, and came speedily to the foot of the hill. There they dismounted, giving their mantles and destriers to the charge of the squires. Arthur, Bedevere, and Kay, the three together, began briskly to climb the mount. After they had climbed for a while Arthur spake to his fellows: " Comrades, I go before to do battle with the giant. For your part you must follow a little after. But let neither of you be so bold as to aid me in my quarrel, so long as I have strength to strive. Be the buffets what they may, stand you still, unless he beats me to the ground. It is not seemly that any, save one, should have lot in this business. Nevertheless so you see me in utmost peril and fear, come swiftly to my succour, nor let me find death at his hands." Sir Kay and Sir Bedevere made this covenant with their lord, and the three knights together set forth again up the hill. Now when Arthur drew near to the summit of the mount, he beheld the giant crouched above his fire. He broiled a hog within the flame upon a spit. Part of the flesh he had eaten already, and part of the meat was charred and burning in the fire. He was the more hideous to see because his beard and hair were foul with blood and coal. Arthur trusted to take him thus unready, before he could get to his mace. But the giant spied his adversary, and all amarvelled leapt lightly on his feet. He raised the club above his shoulder, albeit so heavy that no two peasants of the country could lift it from the ground. Arthur saw the giant afoot, and the blow about to fall. He gripped his sword, dressing the buckler high to guard his head. The giant struck with all his strength upon the shield, so that the mountain rang like an anvil. The stroke was stark, and Arthur stood mazed at the blow, but he was hardy and strong, and did not reel. When the king came to himself, and marked the shield shattered on his arm, he was marvellously wroth. He raised his sword and struck full at the giant's brow. The blow was shrewd, and would have brought the combat to an end had not the giant parried with his mace. Even so, his head was sorely hurt, and the blood ran down his face, that he might not see. When the giant knew that he was wounded to his hurt, he became in his rage as a beast possessed. He turned grimly on his adversary, even as the boar, torn of the hounds and mangled by the hunting knife, turns on the hunter. Filled with ire and malice the giant rushed blindly on the king. Heedless of the sword, he flung his arms about him, and putting forth the full measure of his might, bore Arthur to his knees. Arthur was ardent and swift and ready of wit. He remembered his manhood, and struggled upright on his feet. He was altogether angered, and fearful of what might hap. Since strength could not help, he called subtlety to his aid. Arthur made his body stiff like a rod, and held himself close, for he was passing strong. He feigned to spring on his foe, but turning aside, slipped quickly from under the giant's arms. When Arthur knew his person free of these bands, he passed swiftly to and fro, eluding his enemy's clasp. Now he was here, now there, ofttimes striking with the sword. The giant ran blindly about, groping with his hands, for his eyes were full of blood, and he knew not white from black. Sometimes Arthur was before him, sometimes behind, but never in his grip; till at the end the king smote him so fiercely with Excalibur that the blade clove to his brain, and he fell. He cried out in his pain, and the noise of his fall and of this exceeding bitter cry was as fetters of iron tormented by the storm.

Arthur stood a little apart, and gazed upon his adversary. He laughed aloud in his mirth; for his anger was well-nigh gone. He commanded Bedevere, his cupbearer, to strike off the giant's head, and deliver it to the squires, that they might bear it to the host, for the greater marvel. Bedevere did after his lord's behest. He drew his sword, and divided the head from the shoulders. Wonderfully huge and hideous to sight was the head of this giant. Never, said Arthur, had he known such fear; neither had met so perilous a giant, save only that Riton, who had grieved so many fair kings. This Riton in his day made war upon divers kings. Of these some were slain in battle, and others remained captive in his hand. Alive or dead, Riton used them despitefully; for it was his wont to shave the beards of these kings, and purfle therewith a cloak of furs that he wore, very rich. Vainglorious beyond measure was Riton of his broidered cloak. Now by reason of folly and lightness, Riton sent messages to Arthur, bidding him shave his beard, and commend it forthwith to the giant, in all good will. Since Arthur was a mightier lord and a more virtuous prince than his fellows, Riton made covenant to prefer his beard before theirs, and hold it in honour as the most silken fringe of his mantle. Should

Arthur refuse to grant Riton the trophy, then nought was there
to do, but that body to body they must fight out their quarrel,
in single combat, alone. He who might slay his adversary, or
force him to own himself vanquished, should have the beard
for his guerdon, together with the mantle of furs, fringes and
garniture and all. Arthur accorded with the giant that this
should be so. They met in battle on a high place, called Mount
Aravius, in the far east, and there the king slew Riton with the
sword, spoiling him of that rich garment of furs, with its border
of dead kings' beards. Therefore, said Arthur, that never since
that day had he striven with so perilous a giant, nor with one
of whom he was so sorely frighted. Nevertheless Dinabuc
was bigger and mightier than was Riton, even in the prime of
his youth and strength. For a monster more loathly and
horrible, a giant so hideous and misshapen, was never slain by
man, than the devil Arthur killed to himself that day, in Mont
St. Michel, over against the sea.

After Arthur had slain the monster, and Bedevere had taken
his head, they went their way to the host in great mirth and
content. They reached the camp, and showed the spoil to all
who would, for their hearts were high with that which they had
done. Hoel was passing sorrowful for that fair lady, his niece,
making great lamentation for a while over her who was lost in
so fearsome a fashion. In token of his dolour he builded on the
mount a chapel to Our Lady St. Mary, that men call Helen's
Tomb to this very day. Although this fair chapel was raised
above the grave of this piteous lady, and is yet hight Tomb-
elaine, none gives a thought to the damsel after whom it is
named. Nothing more have I to relate concerning this adventure, and would tell you now of that which happened to the host.

When the men of Ireland, and those others for whom Arthur
tarried, had joined themselves to the host, the king set forth,
a day's march every day, through Normandy. Without pause
or rest he and his fellowship passed across France, tarrying
neither at town nor castle, and came speedily into Burgundy.
The king would get to Autun as swiftly as he might, for the
Romans were spoiling the land, and Lucius their emperor,
together with a great company, purposed to enter in the city.
Now when Arthur drew to the ford, leading across the waters of
the Aube, his spies and certain peasants of those parts came
near and warned him privily concerning the emperor, who lay
but a little way thence, so that the king could seek him, if he
would. The Romans had sheltered them in tents, and in lodges

of branches. They were as the sand of the shore for multitude, so that the peasants marvelled that the earth could bring forth for the footmen and horses. Never might the king store and garner in that day; for where he reaped with one, Lucius the emperor would reap with four. Arthur was in no wise dismayed at their words. He had gone through many and divers perils, and was a valiant knight, having faith and affiance in God. On a little hill near this river Aube, Arthur builded earthworks for his host, making the place exceeding strong. He closed the doors fast, and put therein a great company of knights and men-at-arms to hold it close. In this fortress he set his harness and stores, so that he could repair thither to his camp in time of need. When all was done Arthur summoned to his counsel two lords whom he esteemed for fair and ready speech. These two lords were of high peerage. Guerin of Chartres was one, and the other was that Boso, Earl of Oxford, right learned in the law. To these two barons Arthur added Gawain, who had dwelt in Rome for so long a space. This Arthur did by reason that Gawain was a good clerk, meetly schooled, and held in much praise and honour by his friends in Rome. These three lords the king purposed to send as an embassy to the emperor. They were to bear his message, bidding the Romans to turn again to their own land, nor seek to enter France, for it pertained to the king. Should Lucius persist in his purpose, refusing to return whence he came, then let him give battle on the earliest day, to determine whether Arthur or he had the better right. This thing was certain. So long as Arthur had breath he would maintain his claim to France, despite the Roman power. He had gained it by the sword, and it was his by right of conquest. In ancient days Rome, in her turn, held it by the same law. Then let the God of battles decide whether Britain or Rome had the fairer right to France.

The messengers of the king apparelled themselves richly for their master's honour. They mounted on their fairest destriers, vested in hauberks of steel, with laced helmets, and shields hung round their necks. They took their weapons in their hands, and rode forth from the camp. Now when certain knights and divers bold and reckless varlets saw the embassy make ready to seek the emperor, they came to Gawain and gave him freely of their counsel. These exhorted him that when he reached the court, to which he fared, he should act in such fashion, right or wrong, that a war would begin which had threatened overlong. Yea, to use such speech that if no matter of dispute should be found at the meeting, there might yet be quarrel enough when they parted. The embassy accorded, therefore, that they would so do as to constrain the Romans to give battle. Gawain and his comrades crossed a mountain, and came through a wood upon a wide plain. At no great distance they beheld the tents and lodges of the host. When the Romans saw the three knights issue from the wood, they drew near to look upon their faces and to inquire of their business. They asked of them concerning whom they sought, and if for peace they had come within the camp. But the three knights refused to answer, for good or evil, until they were led before the lord of Rome. The embassy got from their horses before the emperor's pavilion. They gave their bridles to the hands of the pages, but as to their swords concealed them beneath their mantles. The three knights showed neither salutation nor courtesy when they stood in the emperor's presence. They rehearsed over Arthur's message, whilst Lucius hearkened attentively to their words. Each of the ambassadors said that which pleased him to be said, and told over what he held proper to be told. The emperor listened to each and all without interruption. After he had considered at his leisure he purposed to reply. " We come from Arthur, our lord," said Gawain, " and bear to thee his message. He is our king, and we are his liegemen, so it becomes us to speak only the words he has put in our mouth. By us, his ambassadors, he bids you refrain from setting a foot in France. He forbids you to intermeddle with the realm, for it is his, and he will defend his right with such power, that very certainly you may not snatch it from his hand. Arthur requires you to seek nothing that is his. If, however, you challenge his claim to France, then battle shall prove his title good, and by battle you shall be thrown back to your own land. Once upon a time the Romans conquered this realm by force, and by force they maintained their right. Let battle decide again whether Rome or Britain has the power to keep. Come forth to-morrow with thy host, so that it may be proven whether you or we shall hold France. If you fear this thing, then go your way in peace, as indeed is best, for what else is there to do! The game is played, and Rome and you have lost." Lucius the emperor made answer that he did not purpose to return to his realm. France was his fief, and he would visit his own. If he might not pursue his road to-day, why, then to-morrow. But in heart and hope he deemed himself mighty enough to conquer France, and to take all in his seisin.

Now Quintilian, the nephew of the emperor, was seated by his side. He took the word suddenly from his uncle's mouth, for he was a passing proud youth, quick to quarrel, and very bitter in speech. " The Britons," cried he, " are known to all as a vainglorious people. They threaten readily, and they boast and brag more readily still. We have listened to their menaces, but we remember they are of those who boast the more because they act the less." Quintilian, as I deem, would have continued with yet other grievous words, but Gawain, who was hot with anger, drew forth his sword, and springing forward, made the head fly from his shoulders. He cried to his comrades that they should get to their horses, and the earls won their way from the pavilion, Gawain with them, and they with him. Each seized his steed by the bridle, and climbed nimbly in the saddle. Then they rode forth from the camp, shield on shoulder, and lance in hand, asking no leave of any.

The patricians within the pavilion sat silent for a space after that bitter stroke. The emperor was the first to come from his amazement. " Why sit you here? " cried Lucius; " Follow after those men who have set this shame upon us. Ill fall the day, if they come not to my hand!" The bravest of his household ran from the tent crying for harness and horses. From every side arose the shouting, " Swiftly, swiftly; bridle and spur; gallop, gallop." The whole host was mightily moved together. They set saddles on destriers, and led the steeds from the stable. They girt their baldrics about them, and taking their lances, spurred after the fugitives. The three barons pricked swiftly across the plain. They looked this way and that; often glancing behind them to mark how nearly they were followed. The Romans pursued them pell-mell; some on the beaten road, and others upon the heavy fields. They came by two, or three, or five, or six, in little clumps of spears. Now a certain Roman rode in advance of his fellows, by reason of his good horse, which was right speedy. He followed closely after the Britons, calling loudly, " Lords, stay awhile. He knows himself guilty who flees the pursuer." At his word Guerin of Chartres turned him about. He set his buckler before him, and lowering the lance, hurtled upon his adversary. Guerin rode but the one course. He smote the Roman so fiercely, midmost the body, that he fell from his destrier, and died. Guerin looked on the fallen man. He said, " A good horse is not always great riches. Better for you had you lain coy in your chamber, than to have come to so shameful an end." When Boso beheld this adventure of Guerin, and heard his words, he was filled with desire of such honour. He turned his horse's head, and seeing before him a knight seeking advancement, ran upon him with the spear. Boso smote his adversary in the throat, where the flesh is soft and tender. The Roman fell straightway to the ground, for his hurt was very grievous. Boso cried gaily to his stricken foe, "Master Roman, you must needs be fed with gobbets and dainties. Take now your rest, till your comrades may tend you. Then give them the message that I leave you in their care." Among the pursuers spurred a certain patrician named Marcellus, who was come of a very noble house. This Marcellus was amongst the last to get in his saddle, but by reason of the strength and swiftness of his destrier he rode now with the foremost. He had forgotten his lance, in his haste to follow his fellows. Marcellus strove hotly to overtake Gawain. He rode furiously with bloody spur and loosened rein. His horse approached nearly to Gawain's crupper, and the knight was persuaded that in no wise might he shake off his pursuer. Already Marcellus had stretched forth his hand, promising Gawain his life if he would yield as his prisoner. Gawain watched his hunter warily. When Marcellus was upon him, Gawain drew his rein sharply, so that the Roman overran the chace. As he passed, Gawain plucked forth his sword, and smote Marcellus terribly on the helmet. No coif could have hindered the stroke, for it divided the head down to the very shoulders. Marcellus tumbled from his horse and went to his place. Then said Gawain, of his courtesy, "Marcellus, when you greet Quintilian deep in hell, tell him, I pray, that you have found the Britons as bold as their boast. Tell him that they plead the law with blows, and bite more fiercely than they bark." Gawain called upon his companions, Guerin and Boso, by their names, to turn them about, and enter the lists with their pursuers. The two knights did cheerfully after his counsel, so that three Romans were shocked from their saddles. Then the messengers rode swiftly on their way, whilst the Romans followed after, seeking in all things to do them a mischief. They thrust at the Britons with lances, they struck mightily with the sword, yet never might wound nor hurt, neither bring them to the earth, nor make them their captives. There was a certain Roman, a kinsman of Marcellus, who bestrode a horse that was right speedy. This Roman was very dolent, because of his cousin's death, for he had seen his body lying in the dust. He spurred his steed across the plain, and gaining upon the three knights, made ready to avenge his kinsman's blood. Gawain watched him ride, with lifted sword, as one who deemed to smite the shield. When Gawain perceived his purpose, he dropped the lance, for he had no need of a spear. He drew his sword, and as the Roman, with brand raised high above his head, prepared to strike, Gawain smote swiftly at the lifted limb. Arm and sword alike flew far off in the field, the fist yet clasped about the hilt. Gawain dressed his glaive again. He would have bestowed yet another buffet, but the Romans hastened to the succour of their fellow, and he dared not stay. In this fashion the huntsmen followed after the quarry, till the chase drew near a wood, close by the entrance to that fortress Arthur had newly built.

Now Arthur had appointed six thousand horsemen of his host to follow after his messengers. He commanded these horsemen to go by hill and valley to guard against surprise. They were to watch diligently for the ambassadors, affording them succour, so they were beset. This great company of spears was hidden in the wood. They sat upon their horses, helmet on head, and lance in hand, scanning the road for the return of Arthur's embassy. Presently they were aware of many armed men riding swiftly across the plain, and in their midst three knights, in harness, fleeing for their lives. When the Britons marked the quarry, and were assured of the hunters, they cried out with one voice, and burst from their ambush. The Romans dared not abide their coming, but scattered on the plain. The Britons rode hardly upon them, doing them all the mischief they might, for they were passing wroth to see their comrades handselled so despitefully. Many a Roman had reason to rue his hunting, for some were seized and made captive, others were sorely wounded, and divers slain. There was a certain rich baron named Peredur. Amongst the captains of Rome not one was counted his peer. This captain had ten thousand armed men in his bailly, who marched at his bidding. Tidings were carried to Peredur of the snare the Britons had limed. Peredur moved promptly. He hastened with ten thousand shields to the plain, and by sheer force and numbers bore the Britons back to the wood, for they were not mighty enough to contend against him in the field. The Britons held the wood strongly, and defended it right manfully. Peredur might not take it for all his cunning, and lost there largely of his company. The Britons lured the Romans within the covert, and slew them in the glooms. So hot and so perilous was the melley, fought between the valley and the wood.

Arthur took thought to the tarrying of his messengers, and
remembered that those came not again whom he sent to their
aid. The king summoned Yder, the son of Nut, to his counsel.
He committed to his charge seven thousand horses and riders,
and despatched them after the others, bidding him seek until he
found. Yder drew to the plain. Gawain and Boso yet strove
like champions, and for the rest there was not one but did what
he could. From afar Yder heard the cry and the tumult as the
hosts contended together. When the Britons beheld Yder's
company, they were refreshed mightily in heart and hope. They
assailed their adversaries so fiercely that they won back the
ground which was lost. Yder led his horsemen like a brave
knight and a cunning captain. He charged so vigorously with
his company, that many a saddle was emptied, many a good
horse taken, and many a rider shocked. Peredur sustained
the battle stoutly, and wheeling about, returned to the field.
He was a crafty captain, knowing well the hour to charge and
to wheel, to press hard on the fugitive, or to wait. Many a fair
charge did he lead that day. He who was valiant, found
Peredur yet more bold. Whoso was minded to tourney, found
Peredur yet more willing to break a spear. His bailly smote
more terribly with the sword than ever they were stricken, so
that three hundred horsemen and over lay dead upon the field.
When the Britons marked the deeds of Peredur they could not
be contained. They broke from their ranks and companies, and
ran upon the foe. They were desirous beyond measure to joust
with their adversaries, and to show forth their prowess. Above
all things they were covetous of honour, so that for chivalry
they brought the battle to confusion. So only they strove hand
to hand with the Romans, they gave no thought to the end.
Peredur wished nothing better. He held his bailly closely
together, pushing home and drawing off according to need.
Many a time he charged amongst the Britons, and many a time
he returned, bringing his wounded from their midst. Boso of
Oxford regarded the battle. He saw his dead upon the ground.
He marked the craft with which Peredur—that great captain—
sustained the Romans, and knew well that all was lost, save
that Peredur were slain. How might the courage of a rash and
foolish company prevail against the discipline of the Roman
host! Boso called about him the best and bravest of his captains. "Lords," he said, "give me your counsel. You, in
whom Arthur put his trust, have entered on this battle without
any commandment of our lord. If well befalls, all will be well;

if ill, he will require his sergeants at our hands. Should we be
vile and niddering enough to gain no honour on the field, very
surely we shall receive yet more shame as our portion when we
come into his presence. Our one hope is to fight against none,
great or small, save only with Peredur. Alive or dead he must
be made captive, and delivered into Arthur's power. Until
Peredur be taken we shall never draw off in honour from the
stour, but must suffer yet greater loss than before. If then you
would make him prisoner, follow after where I will lead, and do
that thing which you shall see me do." The captains, therefore, plighted faith to follow his ensample, and in no wise to
depart from his command.

Boso brought together as many horsemen as he might, and
ranged them in order of battle. He sent out spies to bring him
tidings where that Peredur should be met, who led the Romans
so craftily. The spies departed on their perilous errand, and
returning presently, proclaimed that Peredur rode with the host
in that place where the press was thickest, and the battle drew
never to an end. Boso rode with his company straight to the
heart of the stour. He hurtled upon the Romans, and looking on
Peredur, fought his way to his side. When their horses stood
together, Boso flung his arms about his adversary, and dragged
him amongst the Britons. Then of his will he hurled himself to
the ground, and with him tumbled Sir Peredur. A very marvellous adventure was it to behold Boso fall from his destrier
in the hottest of the battle, clasping Peredur closely in his arms.
The two champions strove mightily, but Boso was above, and
for nothing would unloose his hold. The bailly of Peredur
hastened fiercely to the rescue of their captain. Those whose
lances were still unbroken charged till the staves were splintered;
when their lances failed them at need, they laid on with their
swords, working havoc amongst the Britons. At any price the
Romans would rescue their captain, and the Britons were in the
same mind to succour Boso in his jeopardy. Never might
heart desire to see battle arrayed more proudly. Never was
there a fairer strife of swords; never a more courteous contention of valiant men. Plume and helmet were abased to the
dust, shields were cloven, the hauberk rent asunder, ash staves
knapped like reeds, girths were broken, saddles voided, and
strong men thrown, and brave men wounded to the death. The
thunder of the shouting filled the field. The Britons cried as
Arthur had taught them, and the Romans answered with the
name of Rome. The one party did all that valiant men were

able to guard their captive in their midst, and the other to
pluck their captain from amongst them. So confused was the
contention, so disordered the combat, that men as they strove
together hardly knew Roman from Briton, friend from foe, save
only by the cry they shouted, and by the tongue they spoke in
the stour. Gawain flung himself in the press, hewing a path
towards Boso, with mighty strokes of the sword. With point
and edge, thrust and cut, he beat down many, and put divers
to flight. Not a Roman of them all could prevail against him,
nor, so he might, would strive to hinder him in his road. From
another side of the field Yder set his face to the same end. A
woodman was he, clearing a bloody path amongst the trees.
Guerin of Chartres aided him like a loyal comrade, each covering
his fellow with the shield. The three champions drew before
Peredur and Boso, and dragged them to their feet. They
brought a steed to Boso, and gave a sword to his hand. As for
Peredur, the crafty captain who had done them so many and
such great mischiefs, they held him strongly. They carried him
from the press to their own lines for the greater surety. There
they left him, bound, under the charge of trusty warders, and
straightway returned to the battle. Now the Romans had lost
their captain. They were as a ship upon the waters, without
a rudder, that drifts here and there, having neither aim nor
direction, at the bidding of the winds and waves. Such was
the plight of the bailly which was spoiled of its captain; for an
army without a constable is less an army than a flock of sheep.
The Britons dealt mercilessly with their beaten foe. They
pressed hardly upon the Romans, smiting down and slaying
many. They made captives of the fallen, stripping them of
wealth and armour, and pursued hotly after the fugitives.
These they bound with cords, and came again in triumph to
their companions in the wood, together with their prisoners.
The Britons carried Peredur, the wise captain, to the camp,
and bestowed him upon Arthur, their lord. They rendered also
to his hand divers other prisoners of less value than he. Arthur
thanked them for their gift. He promised to recompense each
for his goodwill, when he returned a victor to his realm. Arthur
set his captives fast in prison, whence they could in nowise
break out. Afterwards he took counsel with his barons to convey
the prisoners to Paris, and guard them close in his castle, until
the king's pleasure concerning them was known. He feared to
keep them with the host, lest—watch as he would—they should
escape from his ward. Arthur made ready a strong company

to bring them to Paris, and set governors over them. He gave
Peredur and his fellows into the charge of four earls of high
lineage, namely, Cador, Borel, Richier, and Bedevere his butler.
These barons rose very early in the morning, and brought the
Romans from their prison. Like careful warders they put the
captives in their midst, and set out on their journey, riding
right warily.

Now Lucius, the emperor, had learned from his spies that
the earls purposed to start at daybreak on their road to Paris.
Lucius prepared ten thousand riders on horses. He bade them
travel the whole night through, outstripping the Britons, and
devise such ambush as would rescue their comrades from these
barons. He committed this company to Sertorius, lord of
Libya, and Evander, the King of Syria. With these princes
were Caritius and Catellus Vulteius, patricians of Rome. Each
of these lords was a wealthy man of his lands, and a skilful
captain in war. Lucius had chosen them from all their fellows,
and laid his charge straitly upon them, to succour their comrades in their need. These were the lords of the host. The
ten thousand horsemen in mail set out at nightfall on their
errand. Certain peasants of the land went with them, to guide
them by the surest way. They travelled throughout the night,
sparing not the spur, till they came forth on the Paris road.
There they searched out a likely place where they might hide
them in ambush, and held themselves close and coy until it was
day. Very early in the morning the prickers of the host sent
tidings that the Britons were near at hand. Arthur's men rode
in all surety, deeming they had nought to fear. They were
ordered in two companies. Cador and Borel led the first company, and were the vanguard of the host. A little space after
came Richier, the earl, and Bedevere, the king's cupbearer.
These had Peredur and his fellows in their care. Six hundred
horsemen in harness followed at the earls' backs, having the
captives in their midst. They had tied their wrists behind them,
and fastened their feet with ropes under the bellies of the horses.
So they pricked, all unwitting, into the snare the Romans had
spread. When Cador and Borel were in the net, the Romans
sallied forth from their hiding. The hard ground trembled
beneath the thunder of the destriers' hoofs. They charged home
fiercely amongst their adversaries; but for all their amazement
the Britons sustained the shock like men. Bedevere and
Richier gave ear to the tumult, and the noise of the shouting.
Their first thought was to the prisoners. These they set in a

sure place, giving them to the charge of their squires, and commanding that they should be guarded strictly. Then they hastened amain to the breaking of spears. The adversaries clashed together with all their strength. The Romans drifted here and there, in little clumps of lances, for their mind was less to discomfit the Britons than to release the captives from their bonds. For their part the Britons kept their order, and fared boldly among the enemy. Passing heavy were the Romans because of the prisoners they might not find. Very grievous was the count of their horsemen who perished in the search. Now the captains divided the Britons by companies into four strong columns of battle. Cador of Cornwall commanded the folk of his earldom; Bedevere the Frenchmen of Beauce; Borel had with him the levies of Le Mans, and to Richier was committed a company drawn from the men of his household. King Evander perceived the loss and the peril caused to his host by reason of their divided mind. Since the captives could not be met with, he checked the hastiness of his meinie. He drew back his horsemen, and ranged them in order. Then he returned to the battle. It befell, therefore, that the Romans bore away the prize, and had the better of their adversaries. They wrought much damage to the Britons, making many prisoners. They slew, moreover, four of the mightiest and most valiant lords of their enemies. At that time perished Yder, a faithful knight, courageous and passing strong. Hirelgas of Peritum died, too, this day; there was no hardier knight than he. Aliduc of Tintagel also, for whom his kin made wondrous sorrow. Besides these was slain Sir Amaury of the Islands; but whether he was Welsh or Briton I do not know. Earl Borel of Le Mans, a rich lord, and a right honoured and puissant prince amongst his own, did well and worshipfully. He checked the Romans boldly, slaying of them more than one hundred men. Evander hastened against him. He thrust his lance head through Borel's throat, so that the point came out at his neck. Borel fell from his horse, for he was sped. The Britons were dismayed beyond measure. They fled before their adversaries, since many were killed, and where one Briton stood, ten Romans opposed themselves over against him. Doubtless they had been utterly discomfited, and the captives wrested from their hand, had not Guitard of Poitiers drawn to their succour. Earl Guitard, that day, was warden of the marches. He learned from his prickers tidings that a company of Romans was despatched to rescue the captives. Guitard saddled his destrier. He took with him three thousand horsemen, without counting the spearmen and archers, and rode swiftly in aid. As they drew near to the battle they heard the shouts of the Romans in praise of their victory. Guitard and his company rode into the press with lowered lances and scarlet spurs. A hundred horsemen and more were hurled from their steeds in that shock, never to climb in the saddle again. The Romans were altogether fearful and esmayed, making complaint of their pitiful plight. They deemed that Arthur himself had fallen upon them with all his meinie at his back. Their hearts turned to water, by reason of the number of their dead. The levies of Poitou closed about them, and the Britons failed not at need. Each company strove to outvie its fellow, contending earnestly for the greater glory. The Romans could do no more. They turned about and fled the field, utterly discomfited and abased. Their one thought was to get to shelter, or else they were all dead men. The Britons pressed hardly on the fugitives, slaying many. In the flight King Evander and Catellus were taken, and of their fellowship six hundred and more were destroyed. Of these divers were slain, and others made captive. The Britons took spoil of prisoners according to their desire, and retained of these as they might. Then they returned by the road, to the place where the combat was won. The Britons went about the field searching amongst the dead for Borel, the stout Earl of Le Mans. They found him among the fallen, bebled with blood, and gashed with many a grisly wound. Afterwards they carried the hurt to the surgeons, and the dead they laid in their graves. As for Peredur and his companions they committed them afresh to those whom Arthur had charged with their keeping, and sent them on their way to Paris. The rest of the prisoners they bound straitly, and carrying them before Arthur, delivered them to his hand. They rehearsed to the king the tale of this adventure, and not a man of them all but pledged his word that so the Romans made offer of battle, without doubt they should be utterly destroyed.

The tidings of this heavy discomfiture were brought to the emperor. Lucius learned of the capture of Evander, and of the others who were slain. He saw his men had no more spirit in them, and that the beginning of the war went very ill. Lucius considered the failure of his hopes; that in nothing was he conqueror. He was passing heavy, being altogether cast down and dismayed. He thought and thought and feared. He knew not whether to give Arthur battle without delay, or to

await the coming of the rearward of his host. He doubted
sorely that which he should do, for wondrously affrighted was
he of this battle, by reason of the losses he had known. Lucius
took counsel with his captains, and devised to bring his company
to Autun, passing by way of Langres. He set forth with the
host, and moving towards Langres, entered the city when the
day was far spent. Now Langres is builded on the summit of
a mount, and the plain lies all about the city. So Lucius and
part of his people lodged within the town, and for the rest they
sought shelter in the valley. Arthur knew well where the
emperor would draw, and of his aim and purpose. He was
persuaded that the Roman would not fight till the last man
was with him. He cared neither to tarry in the city, nor to
pacify the realm. Arthur sounded his trumpets, and bade his
men to their harness. As speedily as he might he marched out
from camp. He left Langres on the left hand, and passed
beyond it bearing to the right. He had in mind to outstrip
the emperor, and seize the road to Autun. All the night
through, without halt or stay, Arthur fared by wood and plain,
till he came to the valley of Soissons. There Arthur armed his
host, and made him ready for battle. The highway from Autun
to Langres led through this valley, and Arthur would welcome
the Romans immediately they were come. The king put the
gear and the camp followers from the host. He set them on a
hill near by, arrayed in such fashion as to seem men-at-arms.
He deemed that the Romans would be the more fearful, when
they marked this multitude of spears. Arthur took six thousand
six hundred and sixty-six men, and ranged them by troops in a
strong company. This company he hid within a wood upon a
high place. Mordup, Earl of Gloucester, was the constable of
the meinie. " Your part in the battle," said Arthur, " is to be
still. Let nothing induce you to break from your post. Should
evil befall, and the battle roll back to the wood, charge boldly
on your adversaries, that your comrades may find rest. If it
chance that the Romans turn their backs in the battle, then
hurtle upon them without delay, sparing none in the flight."
So these answered, promising to do after his word. Arthur
straightway ordered another legion. It was formed of mighty
men, chosen from amongst his vassals, with laced helmets,
riding on their destriers. This fair company he arrayed in
open ground, and it owned no other captain save the king.
With this legion rode those of his privy household, whom he
had cherished and nourished at his own table. In their midst

was guarded the royal Dragon, that was the king's own gonfalon. From the rest of his host the king made six companies, each company having ten captains. Half of these companies were horsemen, and the others went on foot. On each and all Arthur laid prayer and commandment, that rider and sergeant alike should bear them as men, and contend earnestly against the Romans. Not one of these legions but was numbered of five thousand five hundred and fifty-five horsemen, chosen soldiers, mighty men of valour, and mightily armed for war. Of the eight legions, four companies were set over against their enemy, supported by four behind. Every man was armed and clad according to the custom of his land. Aguisel of Scotland had the forefront of the first legion in his keeping; Cador of Cornwall being charged with the rear. Boso and Earl Guerin of Chartres were the constables of another company. The third company, formed of outland folk, and armed in divers manners, was delivered to Echil, King of the Danes, and to Lot, the King of Norway. The fourth had Hoel for constable, and with him Gawain, who, certes, was no faintheart. Behind these four legions were arrayed and ordered yet four other companies. Of one, Kay the sewer and Bedevere the cupbearer were the captains. With Kay were the men of Chinon and the Angevins; whilst under Bedevere were the levies of Paris and of Beauce. To Holdin of Flanders and Guitard the Poitivin were committed another company—right glad were they of their trust. Earls Jugein of Leicester and Jonathan of Dorchester were lords and constables of the seventh legion. Earl Curfalain of Chester and Earl Urgain of Bath held the eighth legion as their bailly; for these were lords by whom Arthur set great store. As for the spearmen, the archers, and the stout arbalestriers Arthur separated them from the press. He divided them into two portions—one for either wing of his army. All these were about the king's person, and embattled near his body.

When Arthur had arrayed his legions, and set his battle in order, hearken now that which he spake to his lords, his household, and his vassals. "Lords," said Arthur, "I take wondrous comfort when I remember your manhood and virtues, seeing you always so valiant and praiseworthy. In the past you have accomplished great things; but day by day your prowess grows to the full, abating the pride of all who set themselves against you. When I call to mind and consider that Britain, in our day, is the lady of so many and so far lands by reason of you and your fellows, I rejoice mightily, mightily I boast thereof, and in my God and you right humbly do I put my trust. God grant that you may do more marvellous works than ever you have wrought, and that your orb has not yet reached its round. Lords, your valiance and manhood have conquered these Romans twice already. My heart divines the decree of fate that you will overthrow them once again. Three times then have we discomfited these Romans. You have smitten down the Danes; you have abated Norway, and vanquished the French. France we hold as our fief in the teeth of the Roman power. Right easily should you deal with the varlet, who have overborne so many and such perilous knights. The Romans desire to make Britain their province, to grow fat with our tribute, and to bring France once more to their allegiance. For this cause they have ransacked the east, and carried hither these strange, outland people, who amaze Christendom, to fight in their quarrel. Be not fearful of their numbers. Ten christened men are worth a hundred of such paynims. The battle will be less a battle, than a tournament of dames. Have therefore good trust in God, and be confident of the issue. We shall deal with them lightly, so only we show a little courage. Well I am assured what each of you will do this day, and how he will bear him in the melley. For my part I shall be in the four quarters of the field, and with every one of my legions. Where the press is thickest, where the need most dire, my Dragon shall raise his crest."

When the proud words were ended which Arthur rehearsed in the ears of his people, the host made answer with one loud voice. Not a man of them all, who hearkened to his speech, but replied that he loved better to lie stark upon the field, than to know himself vanquished at the end. The whole host was mightily moved together. They defied the foe; they promised with oaths to bear them like men, and there were those who wept. Such tears were not shed by reason of fearfulness. It was the weeping of men who were utterly purposed never to fail their king.

Now Lucius, the emperor, was born in Spain, of a valiant and noble stock. He was in the most comely flower of his age, having more than thirty years, but less than forty. He was a proven knight, of high courage, who had done great deeds already. For such feats of arms the Roman senate had chosen him to be their emperor. Lucius rose early in the morning, purposing to set forth from Langres to Autun. His host was now a great way upon the road, when tidings were brought of the stratagem Arthur had practised against him. The emperor knew well that either he must fight or retreat. Go back he would not, lest any deemed him fearful. Moreover, should the Britons follow after, their triumph was assured, for how may soldiers bear them with a stout heart, who flee already from the field! Lucius called about him his kings, his princes, and his dukes. He drew together his wisest counsellors, and the most crafty captains of his host. To these he spake, and to the bravest of his legions, numbering one hundred thousand men and more besides. "Hearken, gentle lords," cried Lucius, "give ear, ye liege men, fair conquerors, honest sons of worthy sires, who bequeathed you so goodly an inheritance. By reason of your fathers' glorious deeds, Rome became the empery of the world. That she will remain whilst one only Roman breathes. Great as is the glory of your fathers who subdued this empire, so great will be the shame of their sons in whose day it is destroyed. But a valiant father begets a valiant son. Your ancestors were gentle knights, and you do them no wrong. Not one of you but comes of hardy stock, and the sap rises in your blood like wine. Let every man strive valiantly this day to be what his father was in his. Remember the grief that will be his lot who loses his heritage, and whose cowardice gives to another what he holds of his father's courage. But I know, and am persuaded, that you will maintain your portions. Bold as were the dead, so bold are the living, and I speak to knights who are mighty men of valour. Lords, the road is shut which would lead us to Autun. We cannot wend our way till we have forced the gate. I know not what silent thief, or picker, or sturdy knave, has closed the road by which we fared. He deems that I shall flee, and abandon the realm like a dropped pouch. He is wrong. If I went back it was but to lure him on. Now that he has arrayed his battle against you, brace your harness and loosen your swords. If the Briton awaits us, he shall not be disappointed of his hope. Should he flee he shall find us on his track. The time is come to put bit and bridle in the jaws of this perilous beast, and to hinder him from further mischief."

The Romans hastened to get to their arms, for they were passing eager to fight. They arrayed and embattled the host, setting the sergeants in rank and company, and forming the columns in due order. The Romans were a mingled fellowship. Divers outland kings, and many paynim and Saracens, were mixed with the Christian folk; for all these people owned fealty

to Rome, and were in the service of the emperor. By thirties
and forties, by fifties, by sixties, by hundreds and by legions,
the captains apparelled the battle. In troops and in thousands
the horsemen pricked to their appointed place. Multitudes
of spearmen, multitudes of riders, were ranged in close order,
and by hill and valley were despatched against Arthur's host.
One mighty company, owning fealty to Rome and employed
in the service of the emperor, descended within the valley.
Another great company assaulted the Britons where they lay.
Thereat broke forth a loud shrilling of clarions and sounding of
trumpets, whilst the hosts drew together. As they approached,
the archers shot so deftly, the spearmen launched their darts
so briskly, that not a man dared to blink his eye or to show his
face. The arrows flew like hail, and very quickly the melley
became yet more contentious. There where the battle was
set you might mark the lowered lance, the rent and piercéd
buckler. The ash staves knapped with a shriek, and flew in
splinters about the field. When the spear was broken they
turned to the sword, and plucked the brand from its sheath.
Right marvellous was the melley, and wondrously hideous and
grim. Never did men hew more mightily with the glaive. Not
a man who failed at need; not a man of them all who flinched
in the press; not one who took thought for his life. The sword
smote upon the buckler as on an anvil. The earth shuddered
beneath the weight of the fighting men, and the valley rang
and clanged like a smithy with the tumult. Here a host
rushed furiously against a legion which met it with unbroken
front. There a great company of horsemen crashed with spears
upon a company as valiant as itself. Horse and rider went
down before the adversary; arrows flew and darts were hurled;
lances were splintered and the sword shattered upon the covering
shield. The strong prevailed against the weak, and the living
brought sorrow to the dead. Horses ran madly about the field,
with voided saddles, broken girths, and streaming mane. The
wounded pitied their grievous hurts, choosing death before life;
but the prayer of their anguish was lost in the tumult and the
cries. Thus for a great while the two hosts contended mightily
together, doing marvellous damage, one to the other. Neither
Roman nor Briton could gain ground, so that no man knew
who would triumph in the end. Bedevere and Kay considered
the battle. They saw that the Romans held themselves closely.
They were filled with anger at the malice of the Romans, and
led their company to that place where the press was the most

perilous. Ah, God, but Arthur had men for his seneschal and
cupbearer. Knights of a truth were these who sat at his table.
Kay and Bedevere smote like paladins with their brands of
steel. Many fair deeds had they done, but none so fair as they
did that day. They divided the forefront of the battle, and
cleaving a passage with the sword, opened a road for their
fellows. The Britons followed after, taking and rendering
many strokes, so that divers were wounded and many slain.
Blood ran in that place like water, and the dead they lay in
heaps. Bedevere adventured deeper into the melley, giving
himself neither pause nor rest. Kay came but a stride behind,
beating down and laying low, that it was marvellous to see.
The two companions halted for a breathing space, turning them
about to encourage their men. Great was the praise and
worship they had won, but they were yet desirous of honour.
They were over anxious for fame, and their courage led them
to rashness. In their hope of destroying the Romans, they
took no heed to their own safety. They trusted beyond measure
in their strength, and in the strength of their company. There
was a certain pagan, named Bocus, King of the Medes. He
was a rich lord in his land, and captain of a strong legion.
Bocus hastened his men to the battle, for he was fearful of none,
however perilous the knight. When the two hosts clashed
together the contention was very courteous, and the melley
passing well sustained. Pagan and Saracen were set to prove
their manhood against Angevins and the folk of Beauce. King
Bocus took a sword, and discomfited the two paladins. May
his body rot for his pains. He thrust Bedevere through the
breast, so fiercely that the steel stood out beyond his back.
Bedevere fell, for his heart was cloven. His soul went its way.
May Jesus take it in His keeping! Kay lighted upon Bedevere
lying dead. Since he loved him more than any living man,
he was determined the pagans should not triumph over his body.
He called around him as many men as he might, and did such
deeds that the Medians fled before him, leaving the Britons on
the field. Sertorius, King of Libya, beheld this adventure, and
was passing wroth. He had with him a great company of
pagans whom he had carried from his realm. Sertorius, hot
with anger, drew near, and dealt much mischief to his adversaries. He wounded Kay to the death, and slew the best of his
men. Mauled as he was with many grim strokes, Kay guarded
his comrade's body. He set it amidst his men, and carried the
burthen from the press, fighting as they went. With him, also,

he bore Arthur's banner, the golden Dragon, let the Romans rage as they would. Now Hiresgas, the nephew of Bedevere, loved his uncle passing well. He sought his kinsfolk and friends, and gathered to his fellowship some three hundred men. This company wore helmet and hauberk and brand, and rode fair destriers, fierce and right speedy. Hiresgas ordered his house for the battle. " Come now with me," said he to his friends, " and crave the price of blood." Hiresgas drew near that place where Bocus, King of the Medians, displayed his banner. When Hiresgas beheld his enemy he became as a man possessed. He cried the battle cry of Arthur, and together with his company charged terribly upon Bocus. He had but one only thought, to avenge his uncle's death. Hiresgas and his fellows burst amongst the Medians with lowered lances and covering shields. They slew many, and flung many others from their saddles. They rode over the fallen, trampling them beneath the hoofs of the horses, till they reached the very cohort of that king who had slain Sir Bedevere. Mounted on strong destriers the bold vassals followed after Hiresgas, wheeling to right or left, as he led, till they pierced to the gonfalon, showing the arms of the king. Hiresgas spied his foe. He turned his horse, and pushing through the press, drew near, and smote Bocus full on the helm. The baron was a mighty man; the stroke was fierce, and his blade was keen and strong. He struck well and craftily. The blow sheared through helmet and coif. It divided the head to the shoulders, so that the soul of King Bocus sped away to the Adversary. Hiresgas stretched out his arm, seizing the body ere it might fall to the ground. He set his enemy before him on his horse, and held him fast, the limbs hanging on either side. Then he made his way from the stour, the dead man uttering neither lamentation nor cry. The knight was grim, and his war-horse mighty. His kinsfolk gathered behind him, that the Medians should do him no mischief. By the aid of his fellows he won out of the battle, and carried his burthen to the very place where his uncle lay. There, joint by joint, he hacked King Bocus asunder. When his task was ended, Sir Hiresgas called his comrades about him. " Come," said he, " come, true men's sons, to the slaying of these Romans. Romans! nay, cutpurses, rather, whoresons, paynims who have neither trust in God, nor faith in our true religion. Rome has brought them from the east for the destruction of our lives and our kin. On then, friends, let us wipe out these pagans; the pagans, and such renegade Christians as have joined them to slay Christendom more surely. Forward, to sharpen your manhood upon them." Hiresgas led his household back to the battle. Tumult and shouting filled the plain. Helmet and brand glittered in the sun, but the steel often was dulled with blood, or was shattered on the shield. The fair duke, Guitard of Poitiers, bore him as a valiant man. He held his own stoutly against the King of Afric. The two lords contended together, hand to hand, but it was the King of Afric died that day. Guitard passed across his body, smiting down many Africans and Moors. Holdin, Duke of the Flemings, was a wise prince, circumspect and sober in counsel. He strove with the legion of Aliphatma, a King of Spain. The two princes fought one with the other, in so great anger, that Aliphatma was wounded to the death, and Holdin was in no better case. Ligier, Earl of Boulogne, ran a course with the King of Babylon. I know not who was the fairer knight, for both were shocked from their seats. Dead upon the field lay earl and king alike. With Ligier were slain three other earls, masters of many carles in their own lands. Urgent, Lord of Bath, Balluc, Earl of Guitsire, and Earl Cursa of Chester, warden of the marches of Wales, perished in a little space, so that their men were sorely grieved. The company which followed after their pennons flinched in the press. It gave back before the Romans, and fled for shelter to the legion which had Gawain for its captain, and with him Hoel, his fair friend and companion. Two such champions you would not find, search the whole world through. Never had knighthood seen their peers for courtesy and kindliness, as for wisdom and chivalry.

Now Hoel was captain of the men of Brittany. His fellowship were proud and debonair. They were reckless of danger to such a degree that they neither cared nor feared to whom they were opposed. As one man they charged, and as one man they pierced through the foe. The men of Brittany swept down on the Romans, who were pursuing their comrades, and trampling them under in thousands. They put them speedily to the rightabout, and rode over many in their turn. Ahi, for the griding of their swords, and, ahi, for the captives who were taken. The company hurtled on, till they drew to the golden eagle which was the gonfalon of the emperor. Lucius, himself, was very near his pennon, and with him the flower of his meinie, the gentle men and gallant knights of Rome. Then angels and men witnessed so mortal an encounter, as never I deem was beheld of any, since time began. Chinmark, Earl of Tigel,

rode in Hoel's cohort. He was a great baron, and wrought
much mischief to his adversaries. His day was come; for a
Roman, mean of his station, and fighting on his feet, flung a
javelin at his body, so that he died. With the earl perished
two thousand of the Britons, every man hardier than his
fellows. There, too, were slain three other earls. Jagus, to his
loss, had come from Boloan. The second was hight Cecor-
manus; the third, Earl Boclonius. Few indeed of Arthur's
barons might compare with these lords in valour and worth.
Had they been sons of kings, who were but earls, the story of
their gestes would be sung by the minstrels, as I deem, about
the world; so marvellous were their feats. These three fair
lords raged wondrously amongst the Romans. Not one who
came to their hands but gasped out his life, whether by lance-
thrust or sword. They forced a path to the eagle of the
emperor, but the bearers arrayed themselves against them, and
cutting them off from their companions, slew them amidst their
foes. Hoel and Gawain, his cousin, were distraught with anger
when they regarded the mischief dealt them by the Romans.
To avenge their comrades, to wreak damage upon their adversaries, they entered amongst them as lions in the field. They
smote down and did much havoc to their adversaries, cleaving
a way with many terrible blows of their swords. The Romans
defended their bodies to the death. If strokes they received,
strokes they rendered again. They opposed themselves stoutly
to those who were over against them, and were as heroes contending with champions. Gawain was a passing perilous
knight. His force and manhood never failed, so that his
strength was unabated, and his hand unwearied in battle. He
showed his prowess so grimly that the Romans quailed before
him. Gawain sought the emperor in every place, because of
his desire to prove his valour. He went to and fro, seeking so
tirelessly and diligently, that at the last he found. The captains
looked on the other's face. The emperor knew again the
knight, and Gawain remembered Lucius. The two hurtled
together, but each was so mighty that he fell not from his horse.
Lucius, the emperor, was a good knight, strong and very valiant.
He was skilled in all martial exercises and of much prowess.
He rejoiced greatly to adventure himself against Gawain, whose
praise was so often in the mouths of men. Should he return
living from the battle, sweetly could he boast before the ladies
of Rome. The paladins strove with lifted arm and raised
buckler. Marvellous blows they dealt with the sword. They

pained themselves greatly, doing all that craft might devise to bring the combat to an end. Neither of them flinched, nor gave back before the other. Pieces were hewn from the buckler, and sparks flew from the brands. They joined together, smiting above and thrusting under, two perfect knights, two gentle paladins, so fierce and so terrible, that had they been left to themselves very quickly must one have come to a fair end.

The Roman legions recovered from the panic into which they had fallen. They ranged themselves beneath the golden eagle, and brought succour to the emperor at the moment of his utmost need. The legions swept the Britons before them, and won again the field from which they were driven. Arthur watched the fortunes of the day. He marked the discomfiture of his host, and hearkened to the triumphant shouts of the legionaries. He could not, and dared not, wait longer. Arthur hastened with his chosen company to the battle. He rallied the rout, crying to the fleeing sergeants, " Whom seek you? Turn about, for it were better to be slain of the Romans than by your king. I am Arthur, your captain; and mortal man shall not drive me from the field. Follow me, for I will open a road; and beware lest the maidens of Britain hold you as recreant. Call to mind your ancient courage, by which you have overcome so many proud kings. For my part I will never go from this field alive, till I have avenged me on my adversaries." Arthur did wondrously in the eyes of all the people. He struck many a Roman to the ground. Shield, and hauberk, and helmet he hewed asunder; heads, arms, and gauntlets were divided by his sword. Excalibur waxed red that day, for whom Arthur smote he slew. I cannot number the count of his blows, and every blow a death. For as the ravenous lion deals with his prey, so likewise did the fair king raven amongst his enemies. Not one he spared; he turned aside from none. That man he wounded required no surgeon for his hurt. All the press gave back before so stark a champion, till in his path stood neither great nor small. The King of Libya—Sertorius to name—was a lord exceeding rich. Arthur struck the head from his shoulders. " In an ill hour you drew from the east to bear arms in this quarrel, and to furnish drink for Excalibur." But the dead man answered never a word. Polybetes, King of Bithynia, fought upon his feet. This was a pagan lord, and passing rich. Arthur found the paynim before him. He smote but one marvellous blow, and divided his head to the shoulders. Polybetes crashed to the earth. His soul rushed from his body, and his brains were spattered about the field. "Roman, speed to your doom," cried Arthur loudly, in the hearing of all. When the Britons beheld Arthur's deeds, and hearkened to his high words, they took courage and charged upon the Romans. The Romans met them boldly with sword and spear, doing them many and great mischiefs. When Arthur saw that the battle was stayed, he increased in valour, and did yet more dreadfully with Excalibur. He slew and cast down divers, so that the ground was cumbered with the fallen. Lucius, the emperor, for his part, was not backward in the melley, and avenged himself grievously on the Britons. Emperor and king, for all their seeking, might not come together. This was heavy upon them, for each was a very courteous champion. The battle rolled this way and that, since the contention was passing perilous. The Romans did well, nor might the Britons do better. A thousand men came swiftly to their deaths, for the two hosts arrayed themselves proudly one against the other, and strove right scornfully. Not a judge on earth could declare which host should be vanquished, nor what man of them all would come victor and quick from the tourney.

Now Mordup, Earl of Gloucester, was constable of the bailly Arthur had hidden on a high place within a wood. Mordup remembered Arthur's counsel that should evil befall, and the battle draw back to the wood, he must charge boldly on his adversaries. Mordup rode from his hiding with a company of six thousand six hundred and sixty-six riders, clad in gleaming helmets and coats of mail, and carrying sharp lances and swords. These drew down the hillside, unnoticed of the Romans, and coming out on their rear, charged hotly on the legion. The legion was altogether discomfited. Its ranks were pierced, its order was broken, with the loss of more than one thousand men. The Britons rode amongst the Romans, parting each from his fellow, trampling the fallen beneath the horses' hoofs, and slaying with the sword. The Romans could endure no longer, for the end of all was come. They broke from their companies, and fled fearfully down the broad road, climbing one upon the other in their haste. There Lucius, the emperor, fell on death, being smitten in the body by a spear. I cannot tell who smote him down, nor of whose lance he was stricken. He was overtaken in the press, and amongst the dead he was found slain. Beneath the thickest of the battle he was discovered, dead, and the hurt within his breast was dealt him by a spear.

The Romans and their fellows from the east fled before the

pursuers, but the Britons following after did them sore mischief.
They waxed weary of slaying, so that they trod the Romans
underfoot. Blood ran in runnels, and the slain they lay in
heaps. Fair palfreys and destriers ran masterless about the
field, for the rider was dead, and had neither joy nor delight in
the sun. Arthur rejoiced and made merry over so noble a
triumph, which had brought the pride of Rome to the dust.
He gave thanks to the King of Glory, who alone had granted
him the victory. Arthur commanded search to be made about
the country for the bodies of the slain, whether they were friend
or foe. Many he buried in the self-same place, but for the others
he carried them to certain fair abbeys, and laid them together
to rest. As for the body of Lucius, the emperor, Arthur bade
it to be held in all honour, and tended with every high observance. He sealed it in a bier, and sent it worshipfully to Rome.
At the same time he wrote letters to the senate that no other
truage would he pay them for Britain, which he guarded as his
realm. If truage they yet required, then truage they should
receive coined in the very mint. Kay, who was wounded to
death in the battle, was carried to Chinon, the castle he had
builded, and called after his own name. There he was interred
in a holy hermitage, standing in a little grove, near by the city.
Bedevere was brought to Bayeux in Normandy, a town of his
lordship. He was lain in the ground beyond the gate, looking
over towards the south. Holdin was borne to Flanders, and
buried at Tervanna. Ligier was buried at Boulogne.

Arthur, for his part, sojourned all through the winter in
Burgundy, giving peace and assurance to the land. He purposed when summer was come to pass the mountains, and get
him to Rome. He was hindered in his hope by Mordred, of
whose shame and vileness you shall now hear. This Mordred
was the king's kin, his sister's very son, and had Britain in his
charge. Arthur had given the whole realm to his care, and
committed all to his keeping. Mordred did whatever was good
in his own eyes, and would have seized the land to his use. He
took homage and fealty from Arthur's men, demanding of every
castle a hostage. Not content with this great sin he wrought
yet fouler villainy. Against the Christian law he took to himself
the wife of the king. His uncle's queen, the dame of his lord,
he took as wife, and made of her his spouse.

These tidings were carried to Arthur. He was persuaded that
Mordred observed no faith towards him, but had betrayed the
queen, stolen his wife, and done him no fair service. The king

gave half his host to Hoel, committing Burgundy and France
to his hand. He prayed him to keep the land shut from its
foes till he came again in peace. For himself he would return
to Britain, to bring the kingdom back to its allegiance, and to
avenge himself on Mordred, who had served his wife and honour
so despitefully. Britain, at any cost, must be regained, for if
that were lost all the rest would quickly fall a prey. Better to
defer for a season the conquest of Rome, than to be spoiled of
his own realm. In a little while he would come again, and then
would go to Rome. With these words Arthur set forth towards
Wissant, making complaint of the falseness of Mordred, who
had turned him away from his conquest; for the warships lay
at Wissant ready for sea.

Mordred learned of Arthur's purpose. He cared not though
he came, for peace was not in his heart. He sent letters to
Cheldric of Saxony, praying him to sail to his aid. The Saxon
came with seven hundred galleys, furnished with all manner of
store, and laden with fighting men. Mordred plighted faith
that so Cheldric would help him with all his power, he would
grant him the land from beyond Humber to the marches of
Scotland, besides all the land in Kent that Hengist held of
Vortigern's gift, when the king espoused Rowena. Mordred
and Cheldric gathered together a right fair company. Counting
Saxon pagans and christened men there assembled sixty thousand riders on horses, in coats of mail. Mordred numbered his
army with a quiet mind. He considered he was so strong as
to drive Arthur from any haven. Let come what might he
would never abandon his spoil. For him there was no place for
repentance; yea, so black was his sin that to proffer peace
would be but a jest. Arthur saw to the harness of his men. He
got them on the ships, a multitude whom none could number,
and set forth to Romney, where he purposed to cast anchor.
Arthur and his people had scarcely issued from the galleys,
when Mordred hastened against him with his own men, and
those folk from beyond the sea who had sworn to fight in his
quarrel. The men in the boats strove to get them to shore;
whilst those on the land contended to thrust them deeper in
the water. Arrows flew and spears were flung from one to the
other, piercing heart and bowels and breast of those to whom
they were addressed. The mariners pained themselves mightily
to run their boats aground. They could neither defend themselves, nor climb from the ships; so that those were swiftly
slain who struggled to land. Often they staggered and fell,

crying aloud; and in their rage they taunted those as traitors
who hindered them from coming on shore. Ere the ships could
be unladen in that port, Arthur suffered wondrous loss. Many
a bold sergeant paid the price with his head. There, too, was
Gawain, his nephew, slain; and Arthur made over him marvellous sorrow; for the knight was dearer to his heart than any
other man. Aguisel was killed at Gawain's side; a mighty lord,
and very helpful at need. Many others also were slain, for
whom Arthur, the courteous prince, felt sore dolour. So long
as Mordred kept the shipmen from the sand, he wrought them
much mischief. But when Arthur's sergeants won forth from
the boats, and arrayed them in the open country, Mordred's
meinie might not endure against them. Mordred and his men
had fared richly and lain softly overlong. They were sickly
with peace. They knew not how to order the battle, neither to
seek shelter nor to wield arms, as these things were known to
Arthur's host, which was cradled and nourished in war. Arthur
and his own ravened amongst them, smiting and slaying with
the sword. They slew them by scores and by hundreds, killing
many and taking captive many more. The slaughter was very
grievous, by reason of the greatness of the press. When daylight failed, and night closed on the field, Arthur ceased from
slaughter, and called his war hounds off. Mordred's host continued their flight. They knew not how they went, nor whither;
for there was none to lead them, and none took heed to his
neighbour. Each thought of himself, and was his own physician.
Mordred fled through the night to London, where he hoped to
find succour. He leaned on a reed, for the citizens would not
suffer him to enter in their gates. He turned from the city, and
passing the fair water of the Thames, rode to Winchester without stay. Mordred sought refuge at Winchester, and tarrying
awhile, summoned his friends to his side. He took hostages and
sureties from the citizens, that peace and faith should be observed between them, and that they would maintain his right.

Arthur might find no rest by reason of the hatred he bore to
Mordred. Great grief was his for Aguisel and Gawain, the
friends whom he had lost. He sorrowed heavily above his
nephew, and offered him seemly burial, though in what place I
cannot tell. The chronicles are silent, and meseems there is not
a man who knows where Gawain was laid,[1] nor the name of him
who slew him with the sword. When Arthur had performed
these fitting rites he gave himself over to his wrath, considering

---

[1] The grave of Gawain was fabled to be in Pembrokeshire.

only in what way he could destroy Mordred. He followed after the traitor to Winchester, calling from every part his vassals as he went. Arthur drew near the city, and lodged his host without the walls. Mordred regarded the host which shut him fast. Fight he must, and fight he would, for the army might never rise up till he was taken. Once Arthur had him in his grip well he knew he was but a dead man. Mordred gathered his sergeants together, and bade them get quickly into their armour. He arrayed them in companies, and came out through the gates to give battle to the pursuers. Immediately he issued from the barriers the host ran to meet him. The contention was very grievous, for many were smitten and many overthrown. It proved but an ill adventure to Mordred, since his men were not able to stay against their adversaries. Mordred was persuaded that for him there was only one hope of safety; for his trespass was beyond forgiveness, and much he feared the king. He assembled privily the folk of his household, his familiar friends, and those who cherished against Arthur the deepest grudge. With these he fled over by-ways to Southampton, leaving the rest of his people to endure as they could. At the port he sought pilots and mariners. These he persuaded by gifts and fair promises straightway to put out to sea, that he might escape from his uncle. With a favourable wind the shipmen carried him to Cornwall. Mordred feared exceedingly for his life, and rejoiced greatly to begone.

King Arthur besieged Winchester strictly. At the end he took burgesses and castle. To Yvain, son of Urian, a baron beloved of the court, Arthur granted Scotland as a heritage. Yvain paid homage for the gift. Of old Aguisel claimed lordship in the realm; but he was dead, leaving neither son nor dame to come before Yvain. This Yvain was a right worshipful knight, worthy, and of passing great valour. Very sweetly was he praised of many.

That queen, who was Arthur's wife, knew and heard tell of the war that was waged by Mordred in England. She learned also that Mordred had fled from before the king, because he might not endure against him, and durst not abide him in the field. The queen was lodged at York, in doubt and sadness. She called to mind her sin, and remembered that for Mordred her name was a hissing. Her lord she had shamed, and set her love on her husband's sister's son. Moreover, she had wedded Mordred in defiance of right, since she was wife already, and so must suffer reproach in earth and hell. Better were the dead

than those who lived, in the eyes of Arthur's queen. Passing
heavy was the lady in her thought. The queen fled to Caerleon.
There she entered in a convent of nuns, and took the veil. All
her life's days were hidden in this abbey. Never again was this
fair lady heard or seen; never again was she found or known of
men. This she did by reason of her exceeding sorrow for her
trespass, and for the sin that she had wrought.

Mordred held Cornwall in his keeping, but for the rest the
realm had returned to its allegiance. He compassed sea and
land to gather soldiers to his banner. Saxon and Dane, the
folk of Ireland and Norway, Saracen and pagan, each and all of
them who hated Arthur and loathed his bondage, Mordred
entreated to his aid. He promised everything they would, and
gave what he could, like a man whom necessity drives hard.
Arthur was sick with wrath that he was not avenged of Mordred.
He had neither peace nor rest whilst the traitor abode in his
land. Arthur learned of Mordred's strength in Cornwall, and
this was grievous to him. His spies brought tidings of the snares
that Mordred spread, and the king waxed heavier thereat.
Arthur sent after his men to the very Humber. He gathered
to himself so mighty a host that it was as the sand for multitude.
With this he sought Mordred where he knew he could be found.
He purposed to slay and make an end of the traitor and his
perjury alike. Mordred had no desire to shrink from battle.
He preferred to stake all on the cast, yea, though the throw
meant death—rather than be harried from place to place. The
battle was arrayed on the Camel, over against the entrance to
Cornwall. A bitter hatred had drawn the hosts together, so
that they strove to do each other sore mischief. Their malice
was wondrous great, and the murder passing grim. I cannot
say who had the better part. I neither know who lost, nor
who gained that day. No man wists the name of overthrower
or of overthrown. All are alike forgotten, the victor with him
who died. Much people were slain on either side, so that the
field was strewn with the dead, and crimson with the blood of
dying men. There perished the brave and comely youth Arthur
had nourished and gathered from so many and far lands. There
also the knights of his Table Round, whose praise was bruited
about the whole world. There, too, was Mordred slain in the
press, together with the greater part of his folk; and in the self-
same day were destroyed the flower of Arthur's host, the best
and hardiest of his men. So the chronicle speaks sooth, Arthur
himself was wounded in his body to the death. He caused him

to be borne to Avalon for the searching of his hurts. He is yet in Avalon, awaited of the Britons; for as they say and deem he will return from whence he went and live again. Master Wace, the writer of this book, cannot add more to this matter of his end than was spoken by Merlin the prophet. Merlin said of Arthur—if I read aright—that his end should be hidden in doubtfulness. The prophet spoke truly. Men have ever doubted, and—as I am persuaded—will always doubt whether he liveth or is dead. Arthur bade that he should be carried to Avalon in this hope in the year 642 of the Incarnation. The sorer sorrow that he was a childless man. To Constantine, Cador's son, Earl of Cornwall, and his near kin, Arthur committed the realm, commanding him to hold it as king until he returned to his own. The earl took the land to his keeping. He held it as bidden, but nevertheless Arthur came never again.

LAYAMON'S BRUT

LAYAMON'S BRUT

At Totnes Constantin the fair and all his host came ashore; thither came the bold man—well was he brave!—and with him two thousand knights such as no king possessed. Forth they gan march into London, and sent after knights over all the kingdom, and every brave man, that speedily he should come anon.

The Britons heard that, where they dwelt in the pits; in earth and in stocks they hid them like badgers, in wood and in wilderness, in heath and in fen, so that well nigh no man might find any Briton, except they were in castle, or in burgh inclosed fast. When they heard of this word, that Constantin was in the land, then came out of the mountains many thousand men; they leapt out of the wood as if it were deer. Many hundred thousand marched toward London, by street and by weald all it forth pressed; and the brave women put on them men's clothes, and they forth journeyed toward the army.

When the Earl Constantin saw all this folk come to him, then he was so blithe as he was never before in life. Forth they took their way two nights and a day, so that they came full truly to Melga and Wanis. Together they rushed with stern strength, fought fiercely—the fated fell! Ere the day were gone, slain was Wanis and Melgan, and Peohtes enow, and Scots without number, Danes and Norwegians, Galloways and Irish. The while that the day was light lasted ever this slaughter.

When it came to the eventime, then called the Earl Constantin, and bade that guides should ride to the waters, and active men toward the sea, for to guard them. A man should have seen the game, how the women forth marched over woods and over fields, over hills and over dales. Wheresoever they found any man escaped, that was with Melga the heathen king, the women loud laughed, and tore him all in pieces, and prayed for the soul, that never should good be to it. Thus the British women killed many thousands, and thus they freed this kingdom of Wanis and of Melga.

And Constantin the brave marched to Silchester, and held there his husting of all his British thanes; all the Britons came

to the meeting, and took Constantin the noble, and made him
king of Britain—much was then the mirth that was among
men. And afterwards they gave him a wife, one wondrous fair,
born of the highest, of Britain the best of all. By this noble
wife Constantin had in this land three little sons. The first
son had well nigh his father's name; Constantin hight the king,
Constance hight the child. When this child was waxed, that it
could ride, then his father caused him to be made a monk,
through counsel of wicked men; and the child was a monk in
Winchester. After him was born another, who was the middle
brother; he was named Aurelius, his surname hight Ambrosius.
Then was last of all born a child that was well disposed; he
was named Uther, his virtues were strong; he was the youngest
brother, but he lived longer than the others.

Guencelin the archbishop, who toward God was full good,
took charge of the two children, for love of the king. But
alas! that their father might live no longer!—for he had good
laws the while that he lived; but he was king here but twelve
years, and then was the king dead—hearken now through what
chance. He had in his house a Peoht, fair knight and most
brave; he fared with the king, and with all his thanes by no other
wise but as it were his brother. Then became he so potent, to all
his companions unlike; then thought he to betray Constantin the
powerful. He came before the king, and fell on his knees, and
thus lied the traitor before his lord: "Lord king, come forth-
right, and speak with Cadal thy knight, and I will thee tell of
strange speeches, such as thou never ere on earth heardest."

Then arose the king Constantin, and went forth out with him.
But alas! that Constantin's knights knew it not! They proceeded so long forward that they came in an orchard. Then
said the traitor there: "Lord, be we here." The traitor sat
down, as if he would hold secret discourse, and he approached
to the king, as a man doth in whispering. He grasped a knife
very long, and the king therewith he pierced into the heart;
and he himself escaped—there the king dead lay, and the
traitor fled away.

The tidings came to court, how the king had fared; then was
mickle sorrow spread to the folk. Then were the Britons busy
in thought, they knew not through anything what they might
have for king, for the king's two sons, little they were both.
Ambrosie could scarcely ride on horse, and Uther, his brother,
yet still sucked his mother; and Constance the eldest was
monk in Winchester; monk's clothes he had on, as one of his

companions. Then came to London all this landfolk, to their husting, and to advise them of a king, what wise they might do, and how they might take on, and which one of these children they might have for king. Then chose this people Aurelie Ambrosie, to have for king over them.

That heard Vortiger, a crafty man and most wary; among the earls he stood, and firmly withstood it, and he thus said— sooth though it were not: " I will advise you counsel with the best; abide a fortnight, and come we eft right here, and I will say to you sooth words, so that with your eyes ye shall see, and your while well bestow; this same time we shall abide, and to our land the while ride, and hold amity and hold peace, freely in land."

All the folk did as Vortiger deemed; and he himself went as if he would go to his land, and turned right the way that into Winchester lay. Vortiger had Welshland the half-part in his hand; forty knights good he had in his retinue. He proceeded to Winchester, where he found Constance, and spake with the abbot who governed the monastery where Constance was monk, the king's son of Britain. He went into the monastery with mild speech; he said that he would speak with Constance. The abbot granted it to him, and he led him to the speech-house. Thus spake Vortiger with the monk then there: " Constance, hearken my counsel, for now is thy father dead. There is Ambrosie thy brother, and Uther the other. Now have the elders, the noblest in land, chosen Aurelie—his sur- name is Ambrosie—if they may through all things they will make him king; and Uther, thy brother, yet sucketh his mother. But I have opposed them, and think to withsay, for I have been steward of all Britain's land, and earl I am potent, unlike to my companions, and I have Welshland half-part in my hand; more I have alone than the others all clean. I am come to thee, for dearest of men thou art to me; if thou wilt swear to me oaths, I will take off thee these clothes, if thou wilt increase my land, and thy counsel place in my hand, and make me thy steward over all Britain's land, and through my counsel do all thy deeds, and if thou wilt pledge me in hand, that I shall rule it all, I will through all things make thee Britain's king." This monk sate well still, the speech went to him at his will. Then answered the monk with much delight: " Well worth thee, Vortiger, that thou art come here; if evermore cometh the day that I may be king, all my counsel and all my land I will place in thine hand, and all that thou wilt do, my men shall accept it. And oaths I will swear to thee, that I will not deceive thee." Thus said the monk; he mourned greatly how else it were, that he were monk; for to him were black clothes wondrously odious. Vortiger was crafty and wary—that he made known everywhere—he took a cape of a knight of his, and on the monk he put it, and led him out of the place; he took a swain anon, and the black clothes put on him, and held secret discourse with the swain, as if it were the monk.

Monks passed upward, monks passed downward; they saw by the way the swain with monk's clothes; the hood hanged down as if he hid his crown; they all weened that it were their brother, who there sate so sorry in the speech-house, in the daylight, among all the knights. They came to their abbot, and greeted him in God's name: "Lord, benedicite, we are come before thee, for strange it seemeth to us what Vortiger thinketh in our speech-house, where he holdeth discourse; throughout this day no monk may come therein, except Constance alone, and the knights all clean. Sore we dread, that they him mis-counsel." Then answered the abbot; "Nay, but they counsel him good; they bid him hold his hood (holy order), for now is his father dead." Vortiger there abode the while Constance away rode. Vortiger up arose, from the monastery departed, and all his knight out went forth-right.

The monks there ran thither anon, they weened to find Constance; when they saw the clothes lie by the walls, then each to other lamented their brother. The abbot leapt on horse, and after Vortiger rode, and soon gan overtake the Earl Vortiger. Thus said the abbot to Vortiger where he rode: "Say me, thou mad knight, why dost thou so great wrong? Thou takest from us our brother;—leave him, and take the other. Take Ambrosie the child, and make of him a king, and anger thou not Saint Benedict, nor do thou to him any wrong!"

Vortiger heard this—he was crafty and very wary;—soon he came back, and the abbot he took, and swore by his hand, that he would him hang, unless he him pledged, that he would forth-right unhood Constance the king's son of this land, and for such need he should be king of this country. The abbot durst no other; there he unhooded his brother, and the child gave the abbot in hand twenty ploughlands; and afterwards they proceeded forth into London. Vortiger the high forbade his attendants, that they to no man should tell, what they had in design. Vortiger lay in London, until the same set day came, that the knights of this land should come to husting.

At the day they came, many and numerous; they counselled, they communed, the stern warriors, that they would have Ambrosie, and raise for king; for Uther was too little—the yet he might suck—and Constance was monk, who was eldest of them; and they would not for anything make a monk king. Vortiger heard this, who was crafty and most wary, and leapt on foot as if it were a lion. None of the Britons there knew what Vortiger had done. He had in a chamber Constance the dear, well bathed and clothed, and afterwards hid with twelve knights. Then thus spake Vortiger—he was of craft wary: "Listen, lordings, the while that I speak of kings. I was in Winchester, where I well sped; I spake with the abbot, who is a holy man and good, and said him the need that is come to this nation by Constantin's death—therefore he is uneasy—and of Constance the child, that he had holden. And I bade him for love of God, to take off the child's hood, and for such need he should be king in the country. And the abbot took his counsel, and did all that I bade him; and here I have his monks, who are good and chief, who shall witness bear before you all. Lo! where here is the same child, make we hereof a king, and here I hold the crown that thereto behoveth; and whoso will this withsay, he shall it buy dear!" Vortiger was most strong, the highest man of Britain; was there never any so bold that his words durst deprecate. In the same town was the archbishop dead; and there was no bishop that forth on his way did not pass, nor monk nor any abbot, that he on his way did not ride, for they durst not for fear of God do there the wrong, to take the monk child, and make him Britain's king. Vortiger saw this—of all evil he was well ware; up he gan to stand, the crown he took in hand, and he set it upon Constance—that was to him in thought. Was there never any man that might there do Christendom, that might do blessing upon the king, but Vortiger alone did it clean for all! The beginning was unfair, and also was the end; he deserted God's hood (holy order), therefore he had sorrow! Thus was Constance king of this land, and Vortiger was his steward.

Constance set all his kingdom in Vortiger's hand, and he did all in the land, as he himself would. Then saw Vortiger—of much evil he was ware—that Constance the king knew nothing of land (government?), for he had not learnt ever any learning, except what a monk should perform in his monastery.

Vortiger saw that—the Worse was full nigh him!—oft he
bethought him what he might do, how he might with leasing
please the king. Now thou mayest hear; how this traitor gan
him fare. The best men of Britain were all dead; now were
the king's brothers both full little, and Guencelin the archbishop
therebefore was dead, and this land's king himself of the law
knew nothing. Vortiger saw this, and he came to the king,
with mild speech his lord he gan greet: "Hail be thou, Constance,
Britain's lord! I am come thus nigh thee for much need, for to
say to thee tidings that are come to land, of very great danger.
Now thee behoveth might, now weapons behove thee to defend
thy country. Here are chapmen arrived from other lands, as it
is the custom; they have brought to me toll for their goods,
and they have told me and plighted troth, that the King of
Norway will newly fare hither, and the Danish king these Danes
will seek, and the King of Russia, sternest of all knights, and
the King of Gothland with host most strong, and the King of
Frise—therefore it alarmeth me. The tidings are evil that
are come to land; herefore I am most adread, for I know no
good counsel, unless we may with might send after knights, that
are good and strong, and that are well able in land; and fill
thy castles with keen men, and so thou mightest defend thy
kingdom against foreigners, and maintain thy worship with high
strength. For there is no kingdom, so broad nor so long, that
will not soon be taken if there are too few warriors."

Then answered the king—of land he knew nothing—"Vortiger,
thou art steward over all Britain's land, and thou shalt it
rule after thy will. Send after knights that are good in fight;
and take all in thine hand, my castles and my land, and do all
thy will, and I will be still, except the single thing, that I will
be called king."

Then laughed Vortiger—he was of evil most ware—was he
never so blithe ere in his life! Vortiger took leave, and forth
he gan pass, and so he proceeded through all Britain's land; all
the castles and all the land he set in his own hand, and the
fealty he took ever where he came. And so he took his
messengers, and sent to Scotland, and ordered the Peohtes,
the knights best of all, three hundred to come to him, and he
would well do to them. And the knights came to him thereafter well soon; thus spake the traitorous man: "Knights,
ye are welcome. I have in my hand all this regal land; with
me ye shall go, and I will you love, and I will you bring
before our king; ye shall have silver and gold, the best horses

of this land, clothes, and fair wives; your will I will perform.
Ye shall be to me dear, for the Britons are hateful to me; loud
and still I will do your will, if ye will in land hold me for lord."
Then forth-right answered the knights: "We will do all thy
will;" and they gan proceed to Constance the king.   To the
king came Vortiger—of evil he was well ware—and said him of
his deed, how he had done.—" And here I have the Peohtes, who
shall be household knights; and I have most well stored all thy
castles; and these foreign knights shall before us fight."   The
king commended all as Vortiger purposed, but alas! that the
king knew nothing of his thoughts, nor of his treachery, that
he did soon thereafter! These knights were in court highly
honoured; full two years with the king they dwelt there, and
Vortiger the steward was lord of them all.   Ever he said that
the Britons were not of use, but he said that the Peohtes were
good knights.   Ever were the Britons deprived of goods, and
the Peohtes wielded all that they would.   They had drink, they
had meat, they had eke much bliss.   Vortiger granted them
all that they would, and was to them as dear as their own
life; so that they all spake, where they ate their meat, that
Vortiger were worthy to govern this realm throughout all things,
better than three such kings! Vortiger gave these men very
much treasure.

Then befell it on a day, that Vortiger lay at his inn; he took
his two knights and sent after the Peohtes; bade them come
here, for they all should eat there.   Forth-right the knights
came to him, to his inn; he tried them with words as they sate
at the board, he caused draughts to be brought them of many
kinds of drinks; they drank, they revelled, the day there forth
passed.   When they were so drunk that their shanks weakened,
then spake Vortiger what he had previously thought: " Hearken
now to me, knights, I will say to you forth-right of my mickle
sorrow that I for you have mourned.   The king delivered me this
land for to be his steward.   Ye are to me liefest of all men alive,
but I have not wealth to give my knights, for this king possesses
all this land, and he is young and also strong, and all I must
yield to him that I take of his land; and if I destroy his goods, I
shall suffer the law; and mine own wealth I have spent, because I
would please you.   And now I must depart hence far to some
king, serve him with peace, and gain wealth with him; I may
not for much shame have here this abode, but forth I must go to
foreign lands.   And if the day shall ever come, that I may
acquire wealth, and I may so well thrive, that ye come in the

land where I am, I will well reward you with much worship. And have now all good day, for to-night I will go away; it is a great doubt whether ye see me evermore."—These knights knew not what the traitor thought. Vortiger was treacherous, for here he betrayed his lord, and the knights held it for sooth, what the traitor said. Vortiger ordered his swains to saddle his steeds, and named twelve men to lead with himself; to horse they went as if they would depart from the land.

The Peohtes saw that—the drunken knights—how Vortiger would depart; herefore they had much care; they went to counsel, they went to communing; all they lamented their life exceedingly, because Vortiger was so dear to them. And thus said the Peohtes, the drunken knights: " What may we now in counsel? who shall us now advise? who shall us feed, who shall us clothe, who shall be our lord at court? Now Vortiger is gone, we all must depart;—we will not for anything have a monk for king! But we will do well, forth-right go we to him, secretly and still, and do all our will, into his chamber, and drink of his beer. When we have drunk, loudly revel we; and some shall go to the door, and with swords stand therebefore, and some forth-right take the king and his knights, and smite off the heads of them, and we ourselves have the court; and cause soon our lord Vortiger to be overtaken, and afterwards through all things raise him to be king;—then may we live as to us is liefest of all."

The knights proceeded to the king forth-right; they all went throughout the hall into the king's chamber, where he sate by the fire. There was none that spake a word except Gille Callæt; thus he spake with the king whom he there thought to betray: " Listen to me now, monarch; I will nothing lie to thee. We have been in court highly honoured through thy steward, who hath governed all this land; he hath us well fed, he hath us well clothed. And in sooth I may say to thee, with him we ate now to-day, but sore it us grieveth, we had nought to drink, and now we are in thy chamber, give us drink of thy beer." Then gave the king answer: " That shall be your least care, for ye shall have to drink the while that you think good." Men brought them drink, and they gan to revel; thus said Gille Callæt—at the door he was full active: " Where be ye, knights? Bestir you forth-right! " And they seized the king, and smote off his head, and all his knights they slew forth-right. And took a messenger, and sent toward London, that he should ride quickly after Vortiger, that he should come speedily, and take the kingdom, for that he should know through all things, slain was Constance the king. Vortiger heard that, who was traitor full secret; thus he ordered the messenger back forth-right anon, and bade them "well to keep all our worship, that never one depart out of the place, but all abide me, until that I arrive, and so I will divide this land among us all."

Forth went the messenger, and Vortiger took anon and sent over London, and ordered them quickly and full soon, that they all should come to husting. When the burgh-men were come, who were most bold, then spake Vortiger, who was traitor full secret;—much he gan to weep, and sorrowfully to sigh, but it was in his head, and not in his heart. Then asked him the burgh-men, who were most bold: "Lord Vortiger, what is that thou mournest? Thou art no woman so sore to weep." Then answered Vortiger, who was traitor full secret: "I will tell you piteous speeches, of much calamity that is come to the land. I have been in this realm your king's steward, and spoken with him, and loved him as my life. But he would not at the end any counsel approve; he loved the Peohtes, the foreign knights, and he would not do good to us, nor anywhere fair receive, but to them he was gracious, ever in their lives. I might not of the king have remuneration (or wages); I spent my wealth, the while that it lasted, and afterwards I took leave to go to my land, and when I had my tribute, come again to court. When the Peohtes saw that the king had no knights, nor ever any kind of man that would aught for them do, they took their course into the king's chamber. I say you through all things, they have slain the king, and think to destroy this kingdom and us all, and will forth-right make them king of a Peoht. But I was his steward; avenge I will my lord; and every brave man help me to do that! On I will with my gear, and forth-right I will go."

Thirty hundred knights marched out of London; they rode and they ran, forth with Vortiger, until they approached where the Peohtes dwelt. And he took one of his knights, and sent to the Peohtes, and said to them that he came, if they would him receive. The Peohtes were blithe for their murder (that they had committed), and they took their good gear—there was neither shield nor spear. Vortiger weaponed all his knights forth-right, and the Peohtes there came, and brought the head of the king. When Vortiger saw this head, then fell he full nigh to the ground, as if he had grief most of all men; with his countenance he gan lie, but his heart was full blithe. Then said Vortiger, who was traitor full secret: "Every brave man lay

on them with sword, and avenge well in the land the sorrow of
our lord!" None they captured, but all they them slew; and
proceeded to the inn, into Winchester, and slew their swains, and
their chamber-servants, their cooks, and their boys, all they
deprived of life-day. Thus faired the tidings of Constance the
king.

And the worldly-wise men took charge of the other children;
for they had care of Vortiger they took Ambrosie and Uther,
and led them over sea, into the Less Britain, and delivered them
fairly to Biduz the king. And he them fairly received, for he
was their kin and their friend, and with much joy the children
he brought up; and so well many years with him they were
there.

Vortiger in this land was raised to be king; all the strong
burghs stood in his hand; five-and-twenty years he was king
here. He was mad, he was wild, he was cruel, he was bold; of
all things he had his will, except the Peohtes were never still,
but ever they advanced over the north end, and afflicted this
kingdom with prodigious harm, and avenged their kin enow,
whom Vortiger slew here.

In the meantime came tidings into this land, that Aurelie was
knight, who was named Ambrosie, and also was Uther, good
knight and most wary, and would come to this land, and lead
an army most strong. This was many times a saying oft
repeated; oft came these tidings to Vortiger the king; therefore it oft shamed him, and his heart angered, for men said it
everywhere:—"Now will come Ambrosie and Uther, and will
avenge soon Constance, the king of this land; there is no other
course, avenge they will their brother, and slay Vortiger, and
burn him to dust; thus they will set all this land in their own
hand!" So spake each day all that passed by the way.

Vortiger bethought him what he might do, and thought to
send messengers into other lands, after foreign knights, who
might him defend; and thought to be wary against Ambrosie
and Uther.

In the meantime came tidings to Vortiger the king, that over
sea were come men exceeding strange; in the Thames to land
they were come; three ships good came with the flood, therein
three hundred knights, kings as it were, without (besides) the
shipmen who were there within. These were the fairest men
that ever here came, but they were heathens—that was the
more harm! Vortiger sent to them, and asked how they were
disposed (their business); if they sought peace, and recked of his

friendship? They answered wisely, as well they knew, and said that they would speak with the king, and lovingly him serve, and hold him for lord; and so they gan wend forth to the king. Then was Vortiger the king in Canterbury, where he with his court nobly diverted themselves; there these knights came before the sovereign. As soon as they met him, they greeted him fair, and said that they would serve him in this land, if he would them with right retain. Then answered Vortiger—of each evil he was ware—" In all my life that I have lived, by day nor by night saw I never ere such knights; for your arrival I am blithe, and with me ye shall remain, and your will I will perform, by my quick life! But first I would of you learn, through your sooth worship, what knights ye be, and whence ye are come, and whether ye will be true, old and eke new? "

Then answered the one who was the eldest brother: " Listen to me now, lord king, and I will make known to you what knights we are, and whence we are come. I hight Hengest; Hors is my brother; we are of Alemaine, a land noblest of all, of the same end that Angles is named. In our land are strange tidings; after fifteen years the folk is assembled, all our nation-folk, and cast their lots; upon whom that it falleth, he shall depart from the land. The five shall remain, the sixth shall forth proceed out of the country to a foreign land; be he man ever so loved, he shall forth depart. For there is folk very much, more than they would desire; the women go there with child as the wild deer, every year they bear child there! That is fallen on us, that we should depart; we might not remain, for life nor for death, nor for ever anything, for fear of the sovereign. Thus we fared there, and therefore are we now here, to seek under heaven land and good lord. Now thou hast heard, lord king, sooth of us through all things." Then answered Vortiger— of each evil he was ware—" I believe thee, knight, that thou sayest to me right sooth. And what are your creeds, that ye in believe, and your dear god, whom ye worship? " Then answered Hengest, fairest of all knights—in all this kingdom is not a knight so tall nor so strong:—" We have good gods, whom we love in our mind, whom we have hope in, and serve them with might. The one hight Phebus; the second Saturnus; the third hight Woden, who is a mighty god; the fourth hight Jupiter, of all things he is aware; the fifth hight Mercurius, who is the highest over us; the sixth hight Appolin, who is a god brave; the seventh hight Tervagant, a high god in our land.

Yet (in addition) we have a lady, who is high and mighty, high
she is and holy, therefore courtiers love her—she is named Frea
—well she them treateth. But among all our dear gods whom
we shall serve, Woden had the highest law in our elders' days;
he was dear to them even as their life, he was their ruler, and did
to them worship; the fourth day in the week they gave him
for his honour. To the Thunder (Jupiter) they gave Thursday,
because that it may help them; to Frea, their lady, they gave her
Friday; to Saturnus they gave Saturday; to the Sun they gave
Sunday; to the Moon they gave Monday; to Tidea they gave
Tuesday." Thus said Hengest, fairest of all knights. Then
answered Vortiger—of each evil he was ware—" Knights, ye
are dear to me, but these tidings are loathsome to me; your
creeds are wicked, ye believe not on Christ, but ye believe on
the Worse, whom God himself cursed; your gods are of nought,
in hell they lie beneath. But nevertheless I will retain you in
my power, for northward are the Peohtes, knights most brave,
who oft into my land lead host most strong, and oft do me much
shame, and therefore I have grief. And if ye will me avenge,
and procure me their heads, I will give you land, much silver
and gold." Then answered Hengest, fairest of all knights:
" If Saturnus so will it, and Woden, our lord, on whom we
believe, it shall all thus be! "

Hengest took leave, and gan wend to his ships; there was
many a strong knight; they drew their ships upon the land.
Forth went the warriors to Vortiger the king; Hengest went
before, and Hors, next of all to him; then the Alemainish men,
who were noble in deeds; and afterwards they sent to him
(Vortiger) their brave Saxish knights, Hengest's kinsmen, of his
old race. They came into hall, fairly all; better were clothed
and better were fed Hengest's swains, than Vortiger's thanes!
Then was Vortiger's court held in contempt! the Britons were
sorry for such a sight.

It was no whit long before five knights' sons who had travelled
quickly came to the king; they said to the king new tidings:
" Now forth-right the Peohtes are come; through thy land they
run, and harry, and burn, and all the north end fell to the
ground; hereof thou must advise thee, or we all shall be dead."
The king bethought him what he might do, he sent to the inn,
after all his men. There came Hengest, there came Hors, there
came many a man full brave; there came the Saxish men,
Hengest's kinsmen, and the Alemanish knights, who are good
in fight. The King Vortiger saw this; blithe was he then there.

The Peohtes did, as was their custom, on this side of the
Humber they were come. And the King Vortiger of their
coming was full aware; together they came (encountered),
and many there slew; there was fight most strong, combat
most stern! The Peohtes were oft accustomed to overcome
Vortiger, and so they thought then to do, but it befell then in
other wise, for it was safety to them (the Britons) that Hengest
was there, and the strong knights who came from Saxland, and
the brave Alemainish, who came thither with Hors, for very
many Peohtes they slew in the fight; fiercely they fought, the
fated fell! When the noon was come, then were the Peohtes
overcome, and quickly away they fled, on each side they forth
fled, and all day they fled, many and without number. The
King Vortiger went back to lodging, and ever were nigh to him
Hors and Hengest. Hengest was dear to the king, and to him
he gave Lindesey, and he gave Hors treasures enow, and all
their knights he treated exceeding well, and thus a good time it
stood in the same wise. The Peohtes durst never come into
the land, no robbers nor outlaws, that they were not soon slain;
and Hengest exceeding fairly served the king.

Then befell it on a time, that the king was very blithe,
on a high-day, among his people. Hengest bethought him
what he might do, for he would hold secret discourse with the
king; he went before the king, and gan greet fair. The king
up stood, and set him by himself; they drank, they revelled—
bliss was among them. Then quoth Hengest to the king:
" Lord, hearken tidings, and I will tell thee of secret discourse,
if thou wilt well listen to my advice, and not hold in wrath
what I well teach." And the king answered as Hengest would
it. Then said Hengest, fairest of all knights: " Lord, I have
many a day advanced thy honour, and been thy faithful man
in thy rich court, and in each fight the highest of thy knights.
And I have often heard anxious whisperings among thy courtiers;
they hate thee exceedingly, unto the bare death, if they it durst
show. Oft they speak stilly, and discourse with whispers, of
two young men, that dwell far hence; the one hight Uther, the
other Ambrosie—the third hight Constance who was king in
this land, and he here was slain through traitorous usage. The
others will now come, and avenge their brother, all consume
thy land, and slay thy people, thyself and thy folk drive out of
land. And thus say thy men, where they sit together, because
the twain brothers are both royally born, of Androein's race, these
noble Britons; and thus thy folk stilly condemn thee. But I

will advise thee of thy great need, that thou procure knights
that are good in fight; and give to me a castle, or a royal burgh,
that I may lie in, the while that I live. For I am for thee hated
—therefore I ween to be dead; fare wherever I fare, I am never
without care, unless I lie fast inclosed in a castle. If thou wilt
do this for me, I will it receive with love, and quickly I will send
after my wife, who is a Saxish woman, of wisdom excellent, and
after my daughter Rowenne, who is most dear to me. When
I have my wife, and my kinsmen, and I am in thy land fully
settled, the better I will serve thee, if thou grantest me this."
Then answered Vortiger—of each evil he was ware—"Take
quickly knights, and send after thy wife, and after thy children,
the young and the old, and after thy kin, and receive them with
joy; when they to thee come, thou shalt have riches to feed
them nobly, and worthily to clothe them. But I will not give
to thee any castle or burgh, for men would reproach me in my
kingdom; for ye hold the heathen law that stood in your elders'
days, and we hold Christ's law, and will ever in our days."
The yet spake Hengest, fairest of all knights: "Lord, I will
perform thy will, here and over all, and do all my deeds after
thy counsel. Now will I speedily send after my wife, and after
my daughter, who is to me very dear, and after brave men, the
best of my kin. And thou give me so much land, to stand in
mine own hand, as a bull's hide will each way overspread, far
from each castle, amidst a field. Then nor the poor nor the rich
may blame thee, that thou hast given any noble burgh to a
heathen man." And the king granted him as Hengest yearned.

Hengest took leave, and forth he gan pass, and after his wife
he sent messengers, to his own land; and he himself went over
this land, to seek a broad field whereon he might well spread his
fair hide. He came to a spot, in a fair field; he had obtained a
hide to his need, of a wild bull, that was wondrously strong.
He had a wise man, who well knew of craft, who took this hide,
and laid it on a board, and whet his shears, as if he would shear.
Of the hide he carved a thong, very small and very long; the
thong was not very broad, but as it were a thread of twine;
when the thong was all slit, it was wondrously long, about
therewith he encompassed a great deal of land. He began to
dig a ditch very mickle; there upon a stone wall, that was
strong over all, a burgh he areared, mickle and lofty. When
the burgh was all ready, then shaped he to it a name; he named
it full truly Kaer-Carrai in British, and English knights they
called it Thongchester. Now and evermore the name standeth

there, and for no other adventure had the burgh the name, until that Danish men came, and drove out the Britons; the third name they set there, and Lanecastel (Lancaster) it named; and for such events the town had these three names.

In the meantime arrived hither Hengest's wife with her ships; she had for companions fifteen hundred riders; with her came, to wit, mickle good ships; therein came much of Hengest's kin, and Rowenne, his daughter, who was to him most dear. It was after a while, that that time came, that the burgh was completed with the best of all. And Hengest came to the king, and asked him to a banquet, and said that he had prepared an inn against him (his coming), and bade that he should come thereto, and he should be fairly received. And the king granted him as Hengest it would.

It came to the time that the king gan forth proceed, with the dearest men of all his folk; forth he gan proceed until he came to the burgh. He beheld the wall up and down over all; all it liked him well, that he on looked. He went into the hall, and all his knights with him; trumps they blew, games men gan to call, boards they ordered to be spread, knights sate thereat; they ate, they drank, joy was in the burgh!—when the folk had eaten, then was the better befallen to them.

Hengest went into the inn, where Rowenne dwelt; he caused her to be clad with excessive pride; all the clothes that she had on, they were most excellent, they were good with the best, embroidered with gold. She bare in her hand a golden bowl, filled with wine, that was one wondrous good. High-born men led her into the hall before the king, fairest of all things! Rowenne sate on her knee, and called to the king, and thus first she said in English land: "Lord king, wassail! for thy coming I am glad." The king this heard, and knew not what she said; the King Vortiger asked his knights soon, what were the speech that the maid spake. Then answered Keredic, a knight most admirable; he was the best interpreter that ere came here: "Listen to me now, my lord king, and I will make known to thee what Rowenne saith, fairest of all women. It is the custom in Saxland, wheresoever any people make merry in drink, that friend sayeth to his friend, with fair comely looks, ' Dear friend, wassail!'—the other sayeth, ' Drinchail!' The same that holds the cup, he drinketh it up; another full cup men thither bring, and give to his comrade. When the full cup is come, then kiss they thrice. These are the good customs in Saxland, and in Alemaine they are accounted noble!"

Vortiger heard this—of each evil he was ware—and said it in British, for he knew no English: " Maiden Rouwenne, drink then blithely ! " The maid drank up the wine, and let do (put) other wine therein, and gave to the king, and thrice him kissed. And through the same people the custom came to this land of Wassail and Drinchail—many a man thereof is glad ! Rouwenne the fair sate by the king ; the king beheld her longingly, she was dear to him in heart ; oft he kissed her, oft he embraced her ; all his mind and his might inclined towards the maiden.

The Worse was there full nigh, who in each game is full cruel ; the Worse who never did good, he troubled the king's mood ; he mourned full much, to have the maiden for wife. That was a most loathly thing, that the Christian king should love the heathen maid, to the harm of his people ! The maiden was dear to the king, even as his own life ; he prayed to Hengest, his chieftain, that he should give him the maid-child. Hengest found in his counsel to do what the king asked him ; he gave him Rouwenne, the woman most fair. To the king it was pleasing ; he made her queen, all after the laws that stood in the heathen days ; was there no Christendom, where the king took the maid, nor priest, nor any bishop, nor was God's book ever handled, but in the heathen fashion he wedded her, and brought her to his bed ! Maiden he had her, and ample gift bestowed on her ; when he had disgraced himself on her, he gave her London and Kent.

The king had three sons, who were men exceeding fair ; the eldest hight Vortimer,—Pascent, and Catiger. Garengan was an earl, who possessed Kent long, and his father before him, and he afterwards through his kin (by inheritance) ; when he best weened to hold his land, then had it the queen, and Hengest in his hand ; strange it seemed to the knight, what the king thought. The king loved the heathens and harmed the Christians ; the heathens had all this land to rule under their hand, and the king's three sons oft suffered sorrow and care. Their mother was then dead, therefore they had the less counsel—their mother was a woman most good, and led a life very Christian, and their stepmother was heathen, Hengest's daughter.

It was not long, but a while, that the king made a feast, exceeding great ; the heathens he brought thereto ; he weened most well to do ; thither came thanes, knights and swains. And all that knew of book (the Christians) forsook the feast, for the heathen men were highest in the court, and the Christian fold was held for base ; the heathens were blithe, for the king

loved them greatly.   Hengest bethought him what he might do;
he came to the king, with a hailing (salutation), and drank to the
king.   Then thus spake Hengest, fairest of all knights who lived
of heathen law in those days: " Hearken to me now, lord king,
thou art to me dear through all things; thou hast my daughter,
who is to me very dear, and I am to thee among folk as if I were
thy father.   Hearken to my instruction, it shall be to thee
lief, for I wish chiefly to help counsel thee.   Thy court hate
thee on my account, and I am detested for thee, and thee
hate kings, earls and thanes; they fare in thy land with a
host exceeding strong.   If thou wilt avenge thee with much
worship, and do woe to thy enemies, send after my son Octa, and
after another, Ebissa, his wed-brother.   These are the noblest
men that ever led army; and give them of thy land in the north
end.   They are of mickle might, and strong in fight; they will
defend thy land well with the best; then mightest thou in joy
thy life all spend, with hawks and with hounds court-play love;
needest thou never have care of foreign people."   Then
answered Vortiger—of each evil he was ware—" Send thy
messengers into Saxland, after thy son Octa, and after thy
friends more.   Cause him to know well, that he send his writs
after all the knights that are good in fight, over all Saxland, that
they come to my need; and though he bring ten thousand men,
all they shall be welcome to me."   Hengest heard this, fairest
of all knights; then was he so blithe as he was never in his life.

Hengest sent his messengers into Saxland, and bade Octa
come, and his wed-brother Ebissa, and all of their kindred that
they might gain, and all the knights that they might get.
Octa sent messengers over three kingdoms, and bade each brave
man speedily to come to him, who would obtain land, or silver
or gold.   They came soon to the army, as hail that falleth, that
was to wit, with three hundred ships.   Forth went with Octa
thirty thousand and eke more, brave men and keen; and Ebissa,
his companion, afterwards arrived with numberless folk, and he
led to wit an hundred and fifty ships; thereafter arrived five
and five, by six, by seven, by ten, and by eleven; and thus the
heathen warriors they arrived toward this land, to the court of
this king, so that this land was so full of foreign people, that
there was no man so wise, nor so quick-witted, that might
separate the Christians and the heathens, for the heathens were
so rife; and ever they speedily came!

When the Britons saw that sorrow was in the land, therefore
they were sorry, and in their heart dreary, and proceeded to the

king, the highest of this land, and thus to him said with sorrowful voice: " Listen to us, lord king, of our discourse; thou art
through us (by our means) bold king in this Britain, and thou
hast procured to thee harm and much sin; brought heathen folk
—yet it may thee harm;—and thou forsakest God's law, for
foreign folk, and wilt not worship our Lord, for these heathen
knights.   And we would pray thee, for all God's peace, that thou
leave them, and drive from thy land.   If thou else (otherwise)
mightest not, we will make mickle fight, and drive them from
land, or fell them down, or we ourselves will lie slain, and let
the heathen folk hold this realm, possess it with joy, if they
may it win.   And if they all are heathen, and thou alone
Christian, they will never long have thee for king, except thou
in thy days receive the heathen law, and desert the high God,
and praise their idols.   Then shalt thou perish in this world's
realm, and thy wretched soul sink to hell; then hast thou dearly
bought the love of thy bride!"   Then answered Vortiger—of
each evil he was ware:—" I will not leave them, by my quick
life!   For Hengest is hither come, he is my father, and I his son;
and I have for mistress his daughter Rouwenne, and I have
wedded her, and had in my bed, and afterwards I sent after
Octa, and after more of his companions;—how might I for
shame shun them so soon, and drive from land my dear friends?"
Then answered the Britons, with sorrow bound: "We will
nevermore obey thy commands, nor come to thy court, nor hold
thee for king, but we will hate thee with great strength, and all
thine heathen friends with harm greet.   Be Christ now, that is
God's son, our help!"   Forth went the earls, forth went the lords,
forth went the bishops, and the book-learned men, forth went
the thanes, forth went the swains, all the Britons, until they
came to London.

There was many a noble Briton at the husting, and the king's
three sons they all were come thither; there was Vortimer,
Pascent, and Catiger, and very many others, that came with the
brothers; all the folk came thither, that loved the Christendom.
And all the rich men betook them to counsel, and took the king's
eldest son, who was come to the husting, and with mickle song
of praise elevated him to be king.   Then was Vortimer Christian
king there, and Vortiger, his father, followed the heathens.
All thus it happened, as the counsel was done.

And Vortimer, the young king, was most keen through all
things; he sent Hengest and Hors his brother, unless speedily
they departed from this realm, he would evil do to them, both

blind and hang them; and his own father he would destroy, and
all the heathens, with great strength.   Then answered Hengest,
fairest of all knights: " Here we will dwell winter and summer,
ride and run with the King Vortiger; and all that with Vortimer
go, they shall have sorrow and care!"   Vortimer heard that—
he was wise and most wary—and caused a host to be assembled
over all this land, that all the Christian folk should come to his
court.   Vortimer, the young king, in London held his husting;
the king ordered each man that loved the Christendom, that
they all should hate the heathens, and bring the heads of them
to Vortimer the king, and have twelve pennies for reward, for
his good deed.   Vortimer the young marched out of London,
and Pascent, his brother, and Catiger, the other; to them was
come word, that Hengest lay at Epiford, upon the water that
men name Darwent.   There came together sixty thousand men;
on one half was Vortimer, Pascent, and Catiger, and all the
folk that loved our Lord; on the other half were chiefs with
Vortiger the king, Hengest and his brother, and many thousand
others.   Together they came, and combated with might;
there fell to the ground two and thirty hundred of Hengest's
men; and Hors was wounded.   Catiger came there, and
with his spear ran him through, and Hors forth-right there
wounded Catiger.   And Hengest gan to flee with all his followers,
and Vortiger the king fled forth as the wind; they flew forth
into Kent, and Vortimer went after them; there upon the sea-
shore Hengest suffered pain; there they gan to halt, and fought
very long; five thousand there were slain, and deprived of life-
day, of Vortiger's men, of the heathen race.

Hengest bethought him what he might do; he saw there
beside a haven very large, many good ships there stood in the
sea-flood.   They saw on their right hand an island exceeding
fair, it is called Thanet; thitherward they were brisk; there
the Saxish men sought the sea, and anon gan pass into the
island.   And the Britons followed after them, with many kind
of crafts, and surrounded them on each side; with ships and
with boats they gan to smite and shoot.   Oft was Hengest woe,
and never worse than then; unless he did other counsel he
should there be dead.   He took a spear-shaft, that was long and
very tough, and put on the end a fair mantle, and called to the
Britons, and bade them abide; he would speak with them, and
yearn the king's grace, and send Vortiger with peace to the land,
to make this agreement that he might depart without more
shame into Saxland.

The Britons went to the land, to Vortimer their king, and Hengest spake with Vortiger, in most secret converse. Vortiger went on the land, and bare a wand in his hand. The while that they spake of peace the Saxons leapt into their ships, and drew up high their sails to the top, and proceeded with weather in the wild sea, and left in this land their wives and their children, and Vortiger the king, who loved them through all things. With much grief of mind Vortiger gan away fare; so long they proceeded, that in Saxland they were (arrived). Then were in Britain the Britons most bold; they assumed to them mickle mood, and did all that seemed good to them; and Vortimer, the young king, was doughty man through all things. And Vortiger, his father, proceeded over this Britain, but it was no man so poor, that did not revile him, and so he gan to wander full five years. And his son Vortimer dwelt here powerful king, and all this nation loved him greatly. He was mild to each man, and taught the folk God's law, the young and the old, how they should hold Christendom.

He sent letters to Rome, to the excellent Pope, who was named Saint Romain—all Christendom he made glad.—He took two bishops, holy men they were both, Germain and Louis, of Auxerre and of Troyes; they proceeded out of Rome, so that they hither came. Then was Vortimer so blithe as he was never ere here; he and all his knights went forth-right on their bare feet towards the bishops, and with much mirth mouths there kissed. Now mayest thou hear of the King Vortimer, how he spake with Saint Germain,—for their coming he was glad. "Listen to me, lordings, I am king of this people; I hight Vortimer, my brother hight Catiger; and Vortiger hight our father—miscounsel followeth him! He hath brought into this land heathen people; but we have put them to flight, as our full foes, and felled with weapon many thousands of them, and sent them over sea-stream, so that they never shall come again. And we shall in land worship our Lord, comfort God's folk, and friendly it maintain, and be mild to the land-tillers; churches we shall honour, and heathendom hate. Each good man shall have his right, if God it will grant, and each thral and each slave be set free. And here I give to you in hand each church-land all free; and I forgive to each widow her lord's testament, and each shall love other as though they were brothers. And thus we shall in our day put down Hengest's laws, and him and his heathendom that he hither brought, and deceived my father through his treacherous crafts; through his daughter Rowenne he betrayed my father. And my father so evilly began, that he shunned the Christendom, and loved the heathen laws too much, which we shall avoid the while that we live."

Then answered Saint Germain—for such words he was glad:—" I thank my Lord, who shaped the daylight, that he such mercy sent to mankind ! " These bishops proceeded over this land, and set it all in God's hand, and the Christendom they righted, and the folk thereto instructed; and then soon thereafter they departed to Rome, and said to the Pope, who was named Romain, how they had done here, restored the Christendom. And thus it stood a time in the same wise.

Go we yet to Vortiger—of all kings be he most wretched ! —he loved Rowenne, of the heathen race, Hengest's daughter, she seemed to him well soft. Rowenne bethought her what she might do, how she might avenge her father and her friends' death. Oft she sent messengers to Vortimer the king; she sent him treasures of many a kind, of silver and of gold, the best of any land; she asked his favour, that she might here dwell with Vortiger his father, and follow his counsels. The king for his father's request granted to her her prayer, except that she should do well, and love the Christendom; all that the king yearned, all she it granted. But alas ! that Vortimer was not aware of her thought; alas ! that the good king of her thought knew nothing; that he knew not the treachery that the wicked woman thought !

It befell on a time she betook her to counsel, that she would go to the King Vortimer, and do by his counsel all her need, and at what time she might do well, and receive the Christendom. Forth she gan ride to Vortimer the king; when she him met, fair she greeted him: " Hail be thou, lord king, Britain's darling ! I am come to thee; Christendom I will receive, on the same day that thou thyself deemest fit."

Then was Vortimer the king blithe through all things; he weened that it were sooth what the wretch said. Trumpets there blew, bliss was in the court; forth men brought the water before the king; they sate then at the board with much bliss. When the king had eaten, then went the thanes-men to meat; in hall they drank; harps there resounded. The treacherous Rowenne went to a tun, wherein was placed the king's dearest wine. She took in hand a bowl of red gold, and she gan to pour out on the king's bench. When she saw her time, she filled her vessel with wine, and before all the company she went to the king, and thus the treacherous woman hailed him (drank his

health): " Lord king, wassail, for thee I am most joyful! "
Hearken now the great treachery of the wicked woman, how she
gan there betray the King Vortimer! The king received her
fair, to his own destruction. Vortimer spake British, and
Rowenne Saxish; to the king it seemed game enow, for her
speech he laughed. Hearken how she took on, this deceitful
woman! In her bosom she bare, beneath her teats, a golden
phial filled with poison; and the wicked Rowenne drank (or
drenched) the bowl, until she had half done, after the king's will.
The while that the king laughed, she drew out the phial; the
bowl she set to her chin, the poison she poured in the wine, and
afterwards she delivered the cup to the king; the king drank all
the wine, and the poison therein. The day forth passed, bliss
was in the court, for Vortimer the good king of the treachery
knew nothing, for he saw Rowenne hold the bowl, and drink
half of the same wine that she had put therein. When it came
to the night, then separated the courtiers; and the evil Rowenne
went to her inn, and all her knights with her forth-right. Then
ordered she her swains, and eke the thanes all, that they in
haste their horse should saddle; and they most still to steal
out of the burgh, and proceed all by night to Thwongchester
forth-right, and there most fast to inclose them in a castle,
and lie to Vortiger, that his son would besiege him. And
Vortiger the false king believed the leasing.

Now understood Vortimer, his son, that he had taken poison;
might no leechcraft help him any whit. He took many
messengers, and sent over his land, and bade all his knights to
come to him forth-right. When the folk was arrived, then was
the king exceeding ill; then asked the king their peace, and
thus he spake with them all: " Of all knights are ye best that
serve any king; there is of me no other hap, but that speedily
I be dead. Here I deliver you my land, all my silver and all my
gold, and all my treasures—your worship is the greater. And
ye forth-right send after knights, and give them silver and gold,
and hold ye yourselves your land, and avenge you, if ye can,
of Saxish men; for when as I be departed, Hengest will make
care to you. And take ye my body, and lay in a chest, and
carry me to the sea strand, where Saxish men will come on land;
anon as they know me there, away they will go; neither alive
nor dead dare they abide me! "

Among all this discourse the good king died; there was weeping, there was lament, and piteous cries! They took the king's
body, and carried to London, and beside Belyns-gate buried

him fair; and carried him no whit as the king ordered. Thus lived Vortimer, and thus he ended there.

Then the Britons fell into evil counsel; they took Vortiger anon, and delivered him all this kingdom; there was a well rueful thing, now was eft Vortiger king! Vortiger took his messengers, and sent to Saxland, and greeted well Hengest, fairest of all knights, and bade him in haste to come to this land, and with him should bring here a hundred riders. "—For that know thou through all things, that dead is Vortimer the king, and safe thou mayest hither come, for dead is Vortimer my son. It is no need for thee to bring with thee much folk, least our Britons eft be angry, so that sorrow eft come between you."

Hengest assembled a host of many kind of land, so that he had to wit seven hundred ships, and each ship he filled with three hundred knights; in the Thames at London Hengest came to land. The tidings came full soon to Vortiger the king, that Hengest was in haven with seven hundred ships. Oft was Vortiger woe, but never worse than then, and the Britons were sorry, and sorrowful in heart; they knew not in the worlds-realm counsel that were to them pleasing. Hengest was of evil ware—that he well showed there—he took soon his messengers, and sent to the king, and greeted Vortiger the king with words most fair, and said that he was come as a father should to his son; with peace and with friendship he would dwell in amity; peace he would love, and wrong he would shun; peace he would have, peace he would hold; and all this nation he would love, and love Vortiger the king through all things. But he had brought, in this land, out of Saxland, seven hundred ships of heathen folk, "who are the bravest of all men that dwell under the sun, and I will," quoth Hengest, "lead them all to the king, at a set day, before all his people. And the king shall arise, and choose of the knights two hundred knights, to lead to his fight, who shall guard the king preciously through all things. And afterwards the others shall depart to their land, with peace and with amity, again to Saxland; and I will remain with the best of all men, that is Vortiger the king, whom I love through all things." The tidings came to the Britons how Hengest them promised; then were they fain for his fair words, and set they peace and set amity to such a time that the king on a day would see this folk. Hengest heard that, fairest of all knights; then was he so blithe as he was never ere in life, for he thought to deceive the king in his realm. Here became Hengest

wickedest of knights; so is every man that deceiveth one, who
benefits him. Who would ween, in this worlds-realm, that
Hengest thought to deceive the king who had his daughter!
For there is never any man, that men may not over-reach with
treachery. They took an appointed day, that these people
should come them together with concord and with peace, in a
plain that was pleasant beside Ambresbury; the place was
Ælenge; now hight it Stonehenge. There Hengest the traitor
either by word or by writ made known to the king, that he
would come with his forces, in honour of the king; but he would
not bring in retinue but three hundred knights, the wisest men
of all that he might find. And the king should bring as many
on his side bold thanes, and who should be the wisest of all that
dwelt in Britain, with their good vestments, all without weapons,
that no evil should happen to them, through confidence of the
weapons. Thus they it spake, and eft they it brake; for Hengest
the traitor thus gan he teach his comrades, that each should take
a long sæx (knife), and lay by his shank, within his hose, where
he it might hide. When they came together, the Saxons and
Britons, then quoth Hengest, most deceitful of all knights:
" Hail be thou, lord king, each is to thee thy subject! If ever
any of thy men hath weapon by his side, send it with friendship
far from ourselves, and be we in amity, and speak we of concord;
how we may with peace our lives live." Thus the wicked man
spake there to the Britons. Then answered Vortiger—here he
was too unwary—" If here is any knight so wild, that hath
weapon by his side, he shall lose the hand through his own
brand, unless he soon send it hence." Their weapons they sent
away, then had they nought in hand;—knights went upward,
knights went downward, each spake with other as if he were his
brother.
    When the Britons were mingled with the Saxons, then called
Hengest, of knights most treacherous, " Take your sæxes, my
good warriors, and bravely bestir you, and spare ye none!"
Noble Britons were there, but they knew not of the speech,
what the Saxish men said them between. They drew out the
sæxes, all aside; they smote on the right side, they smote on the
left side; before and behind they laid them to the ground; all
they slew that they came nigh; of the king's men there fell four
hundred and five—woe was the king alive! Then Hengest
grasped him with his grim gripe, and drew him to him by
the mantle, so that the strings brake. And the Saxons set on
him, and would the king kill, and Hengest gan him defend, and

would not suffer it; but he held him full fast, the while the fight lasted. There was many noble Briton bereaved of the life! Some they fled quickly over the broad plain, and defended them with stones, for weapons had they none. There was fight exceeding hard; there fell many a good knight! There was a bold churl of Salisbury come; he bare on his back a great strong club.

Then was there a noble earl, named Aldolf, knight with the best; he possessed Gloucester; he leapt to the churl, as if it were a lion, and took from him the club, that he bare on his back; whomsoever he smote therewith, there forth-right he died; before and behind he laid them to the ground. Three and fifty there he slew, and afterwards drew towards a steed; he leapt upon the steed, and quickly gan him ride; he rode to Gloucester, and the gates locked full fast. And anon forth-right caused his knights to arm, and marched over all the land, and took what they found; they took cattle, they took corn, and all that they found alive, and brought to the burgh with great bliss; the gates they closed fast, and well them guarded.

Let we it thus stand, and speak we of the king. The Saxons leapt towards him, and would kill the king, but Hengest called forth-right, " Stop, my knights, ye shall him not destroy; for us he hath had much care, and he hath for queen my daughter who is fair. But all his burghs he shall deliver to us, if he will enjoy his life, or else is sorrow given to him." Then was Vortiger fast bound; gyves exceeding great they put on his feet; he might not ever bite meat, nor speak with any friend, ere he had to them sworn upon relic that was choice, that he would deliver them all this kingdom, in hand, burghs and castles, and all his kingdoms. And all so he did, as it was deemed. And Hengest took in his hand all this rich kingdom, and divided among his people much of this land. He gave an earl all Kent, as it lay by London; he gave his steward Essex, and on his chamberlain he bestowed Middlesex. The knights received it, and a while they held it, the while Vortiger proceeded over this land, and delivered to Hengest his noble burghs. And Hengest forth-right placed his knights therein; the while much of the baser people lay in Sussex, and in Middlesex much of the race, and in Essex their noblest folk. The meat they carried off, all that they found; they violated the women, and God's law brake; they did in the land all that they would.

The Britons saw that, that mischief was in the land, and how the Saxish men were come to them. The Britons shaped to

the land a name for the shame of Saxish men, and for the
treachery that they had done; and for that cause that they with
knives bereaved them of life, then called they all the land East-
Sex and West-Sex, and the third Middle-Sex.   Vortiger the king
gave them all this land, so that a turf of land did not remain to
him in hand.   And Vortiger himself fled over Severn, far into
Welsh-land, and there he gan tarry, and his retinue with him,
that poor was become.   And he had in hoard treasure most
large; he caused his men to ride wide and far, and caused to be
summoned to him men of each kind, whosoever would yearn
his fee with friendship.   That heard the Britons, that heard the
Scots; they came to him riding, thereafter full soon; on each
side thither they gan ride, many a noble man's son, for gold and
for treasure.   When he had together sixty thousand men, then
assembled he the nobles that well could advise: " Good men,
say me counsel, for to me is great need, where I might in
wilderness work a castle, wherein I might live with my men,
and hold it against Hengest with great strength, until that I
might the better win my burghs, and avenge me of my enemies
who felled my friends, and have all my kingdom wrested out
of my hand, and thus driven me out, my full foes? "   Then
answered a wise man, who well could counsel: " Listen now
to me, lord king, and I will show to thee a good thing; upon
the mount of Reir I will advise, that thou work a castle with
strong stone wall, for there thou mightest dwell, and live with
joy; and yet thou hast in thy hand much silver and gold, to
maintain thy people who shall thee help; and so thou mightest
in life live best of all."   Then answered the king: " Let it be
made known in haste, over my numerous host, that I will go to
the mount of Reir, and rear there a castle."

Forth went the king, and the host with him; when they
thither came, a dyke they began soon; horns there blew,
machines hewed; lime they gan to burn, and over the land to
run; and all west Welsh-land set in Vortiger's hand; all they it
took, that they nigh came.   When the dyke was dug, and
thoroughly deepened, then began they a wall on the dyke over
all, and they laid together lime and stone; of machines there
was plenty—five-and-twenty hundred!   In the day they laid
the wall, in the night it fell over all; in the morrow they reared
it, in the night it gan to tumble!   Full a se'nnight so it them
served; each day they raised it, and each night it gan fall!
Then was the king sorry, and sorrowful through all things; so
was all the host terribly afraid; for ever they looked when
Hengest should come upon them.

The king was full sorry, and sent after sages, after world-wise men, who knew wisdom, and bade them cast lots, and try incantations, try the truth with their powerful craft, on what account it were, that the wall that was so strong might not ever stand a night long. These world-wise men there went in two parties; some they went to the wood, some to the cross-ways; they gan to cast lots with their incantations; full three nights their crafts there they practised; they might never find, through never anything, on what account it were, that the wall that was so strong every night fell down, and the king lost his labour. But there was one sage, he was named Joram, he said that he it found—but it seemed leasing—he said that if men found in ever any land, ever any male-child, that never had father, and opened his breast, and took of his blood, and mingled with the lime, and laid in the wall, that then might it stand to the world's end. The word came to the king, of the leasing, and he it believed, though it were false. Soon he took his messengers, and sent over all the land, so far as they for care (fear) of death durst anyways fare, and in each town hearkened the rumours, where they might find speak of such a child.

These knights forth proceeded wide over the land; two of the number went a way that lay right west, that lay forth-right in where now Caermarthen is. Beside the burgh, in a broad way, all the burgh-lads had a great play. These knights were weary, and in heart exceeding sorry, and sate down by the play, and beheld these lads. After a little time they began striving—as it was ever custom among children's play;—the one smote the other, and he these blows suffered. Then was exceeding wrath Dinabuz toward Merlin, and thus quoth Dinabuz, who had the blow: "Merlin, wicked man, why hast thou thus done to me? Thou hast done me much shame, therefore thou shalt have grief. I am a king's son, and thou art born of nought; thou oughtest not in any spot to have free man's abode; for so was all the adventure, thy mother was a whore, for she knew not ever the man that begat thee on her, nor haddest thou any father among mankind. And thou in our land makest us to be shamed; thou art among us come, and art son of no man; thou shalt therefore in this day suffer death." The knights heard this, where they were aside; they arose up, and went near, and earnestly asked of this strange tale, that they heard of the lad.

Then was in Caermarthen a reve that hight Eli; the knights quickly came to the reve, and thus to him said soon with mouth:

"We are here-right Vortiger's knights, and have found here a
young lad; he is named Merlin; we know no whit his kin.   Take
him in haste, and send him to the king, as thou wilt live, and
thy limbs have, and his mother with him, who bore him to be
man.   If thou this wilt do, the king will receive them, and if
thou carest it not, therefore thou wilt be driven out, and this
burgh all consumed, this folk all destroyed."   Then answered
Eli, the reve of Caermarthen: " Well I wot, that all this land
stands in Vortiger's hand, and we are all his men—his honour is
the more!—and we shall do this gladly, and perform his will."
Forth went the reve, and the burghers his associates, and found
Merlin, and his playfellows with him.   Merlin they took, and
his companions laughed; when that Merlin was led away, then
was Dinabuz full glad; he weened that he were led away for to
lose his limbs, but all another way set the doom, ere it were all
done.

Now was Merlin's mother strangely become in a noble minster
a hooded nun.   Thither went Eli, the reve of Caermarthen, and
took him the good lady, where she lay in the minster, and forth
gan him run to the King Vortiger, and much folk with him, and
led the nun and Merlin.   The word (tidings) was soon made
known to the King Vortiger's mouth, that Eli was come, and
had brought the lady, and that Merlin her son was with her there
come.   Then was Vortiger blithe in life, and received the lady,
with looks most fair and honour promised, and Merlin he
delivered to twelve good knights, who were faithful to the king,
and him should guard.   Then said the King Vortiger, with the
nun he spake there: " Good lady, say to me—well it shall be
to thee—where wert thou born, who begat thee to be child? "
Then answered the nun, and named her father:—" The third
part of all this land stood in my father's hand; of the land he
was king, known it was wide; he was named Conaan, lord of
knights."   Then answered the king, as if she were of his kin:
" Lady, say thou it to me—well it shall be to thee—here is
Merlin thy son, who begat him?   Who was held for father to
him among the folk? "   Then hung she her head, and bent
toward her breast; by the king she sate full softly, and thought
a little while; after a while she spake, and said to the king:
" King, I will tell thee marvellous stories.   My father Conaan
the king loved me through all things; then became I in stature
wondrously fair.   When I was fifteen years of age, then dwelt
I in bower, in my mansion; my maidens with me, wondrously
fair.   And when I was in bed in slumber, with my soft sleep,

then came before me the fairest thing that ever was born, as if it were a tall knight, arrayed all of gold. This I saw in dream each night in sleep. This thing glided before me, and glistened of gold; oft it me kissed, and oft it me embraced; oft it approached me, and oft it came to me very nigh; when I at length looked to myself—strange this seemed to me—my meat to me was loathsome, my limbs unusual; strange it seemed to me, what it might be! Then perceived I at the end that I was with child; when my time came, this boy I had. I know not in this world what his father were, nor who begat him in this worlds-realm, nor whether it were evil-thing, or on God's behalf dight. Alas! as I pray for mercy, I know not any more to say to thee of my son, how he is come to the world." The nun bowed her head down, and covered her features.

The king bethought him what he might do, and drew to him good councillors to counsel; and they said him counsel with the best, that he should send for Magan, who was a marvellous man. —He was a wise clerk, and knew of many crafts; he would advise well, he could far direct; he knew of the craft that dwelleth in the sky (astronomy), he could tell of each history (or language). Magan came to court where the king dwelt, and greeted the king with goodly words: " Hail be thou and sound, Vortiger the king! I am come to thee, show me thy will." Then answered the king, and told the clerk all, how the nun had said, and asked him thereof counsel; from the beginning to the end, all he him told. Then said Magan: " I know full well hereon. There dwell in the sky many kind of beings, that there shall remain until domesday arrive; some they are good, and some they work evil. Therein is a race very numerous, that cometh among men; they are named full truly Incubi Dæmones; they do not much harm, but deceive the folk; many a man in dream oft they delude, and many a fair woman through their craft childeth anon, and many a good man's child they beguile through magic. And thus was Merlin begat, and born of his mother, and thus it is all transacted," quoth the clerk Magan.

Then said Merlin to the king himself: " King, thy men have taken me, and I am to thee come, and I would learn what is thy will, and for what thing I am brought to the king? " Then said the king with quick speech: " Merlin, thou art hither come; thou art son of no man! Much thou longest after loath speech; learn thou wilt the adventure—now thou shalt hear it. I have begun a work with great strength, that hath my treasure well much taken away; five thousand men work each day thereon.

And I have lime and stone, in the world is none better, nor in any land workmen so good. All that they lay in the day—in sooth I may say it—ere day in the morrow all it is down; each stone from the other felled to the ground! Now say my wise and my sage men, that if I take thy blood, out of thy breast, and work my will, and put to my lime, then may it stand to the world's end. Now thou knowest it all, how it shall be to thee." Merlin heard this, and angered in his mood, and said these words, though he were wrath: "God himself, who is lord of men, will it never, that the castle should stand for my heart's blood, nor ever thy stone wall lie still. For all thy sages are exceeding deceitful; they say leasings before thyself—that thou shalt find in this day's space. For Joram said this, who is my full foe; the tidings seem to me sport; I was shapen to his bane! Let Joram thy sage come before thee, and all his companions, forth-right here, who told these leasings to the king; and if I say thee my sooth words of thy wall, and why it down falleth, and with sooth it prove, that their tales are leasing, give me their heads, if I thy work heal." Then answered the king with quick voice: "So help me my hand, this covenant I hold thee!"

To the king was brought Joram the sage, and seven of his companions—all they were fated to die! Merlin angered, and he spake wrathly:—"Say me, Joram, traitor—loathsome to me in heart—why falleth this wall to the ground; say me why it happeneth that the wall falleth, what men may find at the dyke's bottom?" Joram was still; he could not tell. Then said Merlin these words: "King, hold to me covenant! Cause this dyke to be dug anon seven feet deeper than it is now; they shall find a stone wondrously fair; it is fair and broad, for folk to behold." The dyke was dug seven feet deeper; then they found anon there-right the stone. Then said Merlin these words: "King, hold to me covenant! Say to me, Joram, man to me most hateful, and say to this king what kind of thing hath taken station under this stone?" Joram was still; he could not tell.

Then said Merlin a wonder: "A water here is under; do away this stone, the water ye shall find anon." They did away the stone before the king anon; the water they found anon. Then said Merlin: "Ask me Joram, who is my full foe, after a while, to say thee of the bottom, what dwelleth in the water, winter and summer." The king asked Joram, but he knew nought thereof. The yet said Merlin these words: "King, hold to me covenant! Cause this water to be carried off, and away cast; there dwell at the bottom two strong dragons; the one is on the north side, the other on the south side; the one is milk-white, to each beast unlike, the other as red as blood, boldest of all worms! Each midnight they begin to fight, and through their fight thy works fell, the earth began to sink, and thy wall to tumble; and through such wonder thy wall is fallen, that happened in this flood, and not for my blood." This water was all carried off; the king's men were glad, great was the bliss before the monarch, and soon thereafter they were sorry; ere the day came to an end, strange tidings they heard.

When the water was all carried off, and the pit was empty, then came out these two dragons, and made great din, and fought fiercely down in the dyke. Never saw any man any loathlier fight; flames of fire flew from their mouths! The monarch saw this fight, their grim gestures; then was he astonished in this worlds-realm, what this tokening were, that he saw there at the bottom, and how Merlin knew it, that no other man knew. First was the white above, and afterwards he was beneath, and the red dragon wounded him to death; and either went to his hole—no man born saw them afterwards! Thus fared this thing that Vortiger the king saw. And all that were with him loved Merlin greatly; and the king hated Joram, and deprived him of his head, and all his seven comrades that with him were there.

The king went to his house, and led Merlin with him, and said to him with much love: "Merlin, thou art welcome, and I will give thee all that thou desirest, of my land, of silver and of gold." He weened through Merlin to win all the land, but it happened all otherwise ere the day's end came. The king thus asked his dear friend Merlin, "Say me now, Merlin, man to me dearest, what betoken the dragons that made the din, and the stone, and the water, and the wondrous fight? Say me, if thy will is, what betokeneth all this? And afterwards thou must counsel me how I shall guide me, and how I may win my kingdom from Hengest, my wife's father, who hath harmed me greatly." Then answered Merlin to the king that spake with him: "King, thou art unwise, and foolish in counsel; thou askest of the dragons that made the din, and what betokened their fight, and their fierce assaults? They betoken kings that yet are to come, and their fight, and their adventure, and their fated folk! But if thou wert so wise a man, and so prudent in thought, that thou haddest inquired of me of thy many sorrows, of thy great care, that is to come to thee, I would say to thee of thy sorrow." Then quoth Vortiger the king: "Dear friend Merlin, say me of the things that are to come to me." "Blithely," quoth Merlin, with bold voice, "I will say to thee; but ever it will thee rue. King, king, be-see thee (see to thyself), sorrow is to thee given of Constantine's kin!—his son thou killedest; thou causedest Constance to be slain, who was king in this land; thou causedst thy Peohtes to betray (or destroy) him basely; therefore thou shalt suffer sorrows most of all! Afterwards thou drewest upon thee foreign people, the Saxons to this land; therefore thou shalt be destroyed! Now are the barons of Britain arrived; it is, Aurelie and Uther—now thou art thereof aware; —they shall come to-morrow, full truly, in this land at Totnes, I do thee well to wit, with seven hundred ships; and now they sail speedily in the sea. Thou hast much evil done to them, and now thou must the harm receive; thou hast on both sides bane that to thee shall seem; for now thy foes are before thee, and thy enemies behind. But flee, flee thy way, and save thy life—and flee whither that thou fleest, they will pursue after thee! Ambrosie Aurelie he shall have first this kingdom; but he through draught of poison shall suffer death. And afterwards shall Uther Pendragon have this kingdom; but thy kin shall kill him with poison; but ere he suffer death, he shall din (contest) make. Uther shall have a son, out of Cornwall he shall come, that shall be a wild boar, bristled with steel; the boar shall consume the noble burghs; he shall destroy (or devour) all the traitors with authority; he shall kill with death all thy rich kindred; he shall be man most brave, and noble in thought; hence into Rome this same shall rule; all his foes he shall fell to the ground. Sooth I have said to thee, but it is not to thee the softer;—but flee with thine host, thy foes come to thee to thy court!" Then Merlin the wise ceased his words, and the king caused thirteen trumpets to be blown, and marched forth with his army exceeding quickly. There was not forth-right but space of one night, that the brothers came, both together, to the sea-strand full truly, at Dartmouth in Totnes.

The Britons heard this, and were full surely blithe; they drew themselves out of the woods, and out of the wilderness, by sixty, and by sixty, and by seven hundred, by thirty, and by thirty, and by many thousands—when they came together, full good it seemed to them! And the brothers brought to this land a numerous host; and here came before them these bold Britons, a numerous folk, who would it all avenge, that ere were over the woods wondrously scattered, through the mickle dread, and through the great misery, and through the mickle harm that Hengest wrought them, and who had murdered all their chief men with knives, with sæxes cut in pieces the good thanes! The Britons held husting with great wisdom; they took anon Aurelie, the elder brother, in the noble husting, and raised him to be king. Then were the Britons filled with bliss, blithe in mood who ere were mournful. These tidings came to Vortiger the king, that Aurelie was chosen and raised to be king. Then was Vortiger woe, and eft to him was worse! Vortiger proceeded far to a castle, named Genoure, upon a high mount; Cloard hight the mount, and Hergin hight the land, near the Wye, that is a fair water (stream). Vortiger's men took all that they came nigh; they took weapons and meat, on many a wise; to the castle they brought as much as they cared for, so that they had enow, though it little helped them. Aurelie and Uther were aware of Vortiger, where he was upon Cloard, inclosed in a castle. They caused trumpets to be blown, their host to be assembled— a numerous folk of many a land—they marched to Genoure, where Vortiger lay. A king was within, a king was without; knights there fought with fierce encounters; every good man made himself ready. When they saw that they had not the victory, then a wondrous great force went to the wood; they felled the wood down, and drew to the castle, and filled all the dyke that was wondrously deep. And fire they sent in, on every side, and called to Vortiger: "Now thou shalt warm thee there, for thou slewest Constance, who was king of this land, and afterwards Constantine his son. Now is Aurelie come, and Uther his brother, who send thee bale!" The wind wafted the fire, so that it burnt wonderfully; the castle gan to burn, the chambers there were consumed; the halls fell to the ground. Might no man there against the fire make fight; the fire went over all, and burnt house, and burnt wall; and the King Vortiger therein he gan to burn; all it was consumed that therein dwelt! Thus ended there, with mickle harm, Vortiger!

Then Aurelie had all the land in his hand. There was the strong earl, named Aldolf; he was of Gloucester, of all knights skilfullest; there in the land Aurelie made him his steward. Then had Aurelie, and Uther his brother, felled their foes, and were therefore the blither! Hengest heard this, strongest of all knights; then was he afraid exceeding greatly. He marched his host, and fled toward the Scots; and Aurelie the king went after him in haste. And Hengest thought that he would, with

all his army, if men pursued him, flee into Scotland, so that he
might thence with guile escape, if he might not for Aurelie remain
in the land. Aurelie marched forth, and led his host right
north, with all his might, full a se'nnight. The Britons were
bold, and proceeded over the weald. Then had Aurelie a
numerous force; he found ravaged land, the people slain, and
all the churches burnt, and the Britons consumed. Then said
Aurelie the king, Britain's darling: "If I might abide, that
I should back ride; and if the Lord it will, who shaped the
daylight, that I might in safety obtain my right (or country),
churches I will arear, and God I will worship. I will give to
each man his right, and to every person, the old and the young,
I will be gracious, if God will grant to me my land to win!"

Tidings came to Hengest of Aurelie the king, that he brought
an army of innumerable folk. Then spake Hengest, most
treacherous of all knights: "Hearken now, my men—honour
to you is given—here cometh Aurelie, and Uther eke, his brother;
they bring very much folk, but all they are fated! For the
king is unwise, so are his knights, and a knave is his brother,
the one as the other; therefore may Britons be much the
un-bolder; when the head (leader) is bad, the heap (multitude)
is the worse. And well ye may it remember, what I will say;
better are fifty of us, than of them five hundred—that they
many times have found, since they in land sought the people.
For known it is wide, of our bold feats, that we are chosen
warriors with the best! We shall against them stand, and drive
them from land, and possess this realm after our will." Thus
bold Hengest, fairest of all knights, emboldened his host, where
he was in field, but otherwise it was disposed ere came the day
a se'nnight. Forth came the tidings to Aurelie the king, where
Hengest abode upon a mount.

Aurelie had for companions thirty thousand riders, bold
Britons, who made their threat; and eke he had Welsh,
wondrously many. Then caused he his knights to be ever
weaponed, day and night, as if they should go to battle; for
ever he had care of the heathen folk. And Aurelie with his
host marched quickly towards him. When Hengest heard that
Aurelie was near, he took his army, and marched against him.
When Aurelie was aware that Hengest would come there, he
went into a field, well weaponed under shield; he took forth-
right ten thousand knights, that were the best born and chosen
of his force, and set them in the field, on foot under shield. Ten
thousand Welsh he sent to the wood; ten thousand Scots he

sent aside, to meet the heathens by ways and by streets; himself he took his earls and his good warriors, and his faithfullest men, that he had in hand, and made his shield-troop, as it were a wild wood; five thousand there rode, who should all this folk well defend. Then called Aldolf, Earl of Gloucester, "If the Lord, that ruleth all dooms, grant it to me, that I might abide, that Hengest should come riding, who has in this land so long remained, and betrayed my dear friends with his long sæxes beside Ambresbury, with miserable death! But if I might of the earl win to me the country; then might I say my sooth words, that God himself had granted good to me, if I might fell my foes to ground anon, and avenge my dear kindred, whom they have laid adown!"

Scarcely was this speech said to the end, that they saw Hengest approach over the down. With a numerous host they fiercely marched; together soon they came, and terribly they slew; there the stern men together rushed themselves, helms there gan resound, knights there fell; steel went against the bones, mischief there was rife; streams of blood flowed in the ways; the fields were dyed, and the grass changed colour! When Hengest saw that his help failed him, then withdrew he from the fight, and fled aside, and his folk after speedily moved. The Christians pursued after, and laid on them, and called Christ, God's son, to be to them in aid; and the heathen people also called loud, "Our God Tervagant, why failest thou us now?" When Hengest saw the heathens recede, and the Christian men come upon them, then fled Hengest through and through, until he came to Coningsburgh; in the burgh he went, safety to obtain. And the King Aurelie went after him anon, and called to his people with loud voice: "Run ever forth and forth! Hengest is gone northwards!" And they pursued after him until they came to the burgh. When Hengest and his son saw all the host come after them, then said Hengest, of all knights wrathest, "Will I no more flee, but now I will fight, and my son Octa, and his wed-brother Ebissa! And all my army, stir ye your weapons, and march we against them, and make we strong slaughter! And if we fell them not, then be we dead, laid on the field, and deprived of friends!" Hengest marched on the weald, and left all his tents; and made his shield-troop all of his heathen men. Then came Aurelie the king, and many thousands with him, and began there another fight, that was exceeding strong; there was many great stroke dealt in the combat! There were the Christians well nigh overcome. Then approached

there five thousand riders, that Aurelie had on horse to fight;
they smote on the heathens, so that they down fell; there was
fight most strong, combat full stern!

In the fight came the Earl Aldolf of Gloucester, and found
Hengest, wickedest of knights, where he fought fiercely, and
felled the Christians. Aldolf drew his good sword, and upon
Hengest smote; and Hengest cast the shield before him, and
else were his life destroyed; and Aldolf smote on the shield, so
that it was shivered in two. And Hengest leapt to him, as if
it were a lion, and smote upon Aldolf's helm, so that it parted in
two. Then hewed they with swords—the strokes were grim—
fire flew from the steel, oft and well frequent! After a time,
then leapt Aldolf to the ground, and saw by him Gorlois, who
was a keen man full truly; of Cornwall he was earl, he was
widely known. Then was the baron Aldolf much the bolder,
and heaved high his sword, and let it down swing, and smote
Hengest on the hand, so that he let go his good brand; and in
haste grasped him, with his grim looks, by the cuirasses hood
that was on his head, and with great strength struck him down;
and then he him up drew, as if he would crush him, and with
arms embraced him, and forth him led. Now was Hengest taken,
through Aldolf, the brave man! Then called Aldolf, the Earl
of Gloucester: "Hengest, it is not so merry for thee now as it
was whilom by Ambresbury, where thou drewest the sæxes, and
slew the Britons, with much treachery thou slewest my kindred!
Now thou shalt pay retribution, and lose thy friends; with
cruel death perish in the world!" Hengest proceeded still
(without speaking); he saw no help; Aldolf led him to his sovereign, and greeted the sovereign with loving words: "Hail be
thou, Aurelie, of noble race! Here I bring before thee Hengest,
the heathen, who was thy kindred's bane, who hath sought to
us harm; God granted it to me, that I have him grasped!
Now I give him to thee, for dearest of men art thou to me; and
let thy attendants play with this hound; shoot with their
arrows, and his race anon destroy!" Then answered the king
with quick voice: "Blessed be thou, Aldolf, noblest of all earls!
Thou art to me dear as my life, thou shalt be chief of people!"
There men took Hengest, and there men bound Hengest; there
was then Hengest of all knights most wretched! This fight
was overcome, and the heathens fled. Then saw Octa, that his
father was full woe; and with Ebissa, his wed-brother, joined
them together, and fled into York, with harm enow, and made
ready the walls, and pulled down the halls. Some of the

heathens went to the wood, where the folk on foot laid them to ground.

Then was Aurelie the king pleased well through all things; he proceeded into Coningsburgh, with all his folk, and thanked the Lord for such might.   Three days and three nights the king dwelt there forth-right, to heal the wounds of his dear knights, and rest in the burgh their weary bones.   When the third day came, and the folk had made none, then caused the king the trumpets to blow, and summoned his earls, that they should come to husting, to Aurelie the king.   When they came together, the king asked them soon, what they would counsel him, who were his rich men, by what death Hengest should die, and how he might best avenge his dearest friends, who lay buried near Ambresbury.

Then stood up Ældadus, and with the king he spake thus;—towards God he was good, he was a holy bishop, Aldolf the earl's brother, he had no other:—"Lord king, listen now to me, what I will thee tell.   I will make the sentence, how he shall be put to death.   For he is most hateful of men to us in the world, and hath slain our kindred, and deprived of life-day; and he is a heathen hound—hell he shall seek; there he shall sink for his treachery!   Lord king, hearken to me, what I thee will tell. A king was in Jerusalem, who was named Saul; and in heathen-dom was a king of mickle might, who was named Agag—Jerusalem he hated—he was king of the Amalech—the Worse was full nigh to him!   Ever he hated Jerusalem with harm the most; never would he give them peace, but ever he withstood them; he burnt them, he slew them, he did them sorrow enow! It fell on a time that the sun gan to shine; then sate Agag the king on his high chair; his fated blood was troubled, and urged him to march.   He called his knights anon forth-right: ' Quick to your steeds! and forth we shall ride; we shall burn and slay all about Jerusalem!'   Forth went the king, and a great host with him; the land they gan through-run, and the towns to consume.   The men saw that who dwelt in Jerusalem; and they advanced against them, knights and swains, and fought with the king, and with fight him overcame, and slew all his folk, and Agag the king they took; and so they with him came to Saul the king.   Then was Saul the king blithe through all things!   The king asked counsel at his rich knights anon, which he might the better do to him, either slay or up hang. Then leapt up Samuel, a prophet of Israel;—he was a man exceeding holy, high toward the Lord; no man knew in those days man so high in God's law. Samuel took Agag the king, and led him in the market-place, and caused him most fast to a stake to be bound; and took with his right hand a precious brand; and thus called to him Samuel, the good man: ' Thou hightest Agag the king, now thou art in sorrow! Now thou shalt receive the retribution for that thou destroyedest Jerusalem, for that thou hast this noble burgh so greatly injured, and many a good man slain, and deprived of life-day! As I hope for mercy, shalt thou do so no more.' Samuel heaved up the sword, and strongly down struck, and cut the king all in pieces in Jerusalem's market, and threw the pieces wide over the streets. Thus Samuel took-on (acted), and so oughtest thou do to Hengest."

Aldolf heard this, the Earl of Gloucester; toward Hengest he leapt, as if it were a lion, and grasped him by the head, and after him hauled him, and drew him through and through, and throughout all Coningsburgh; and without the burgh he caused him to be bound. Aldolf drew his sword, and smote off Hengest's head; and the king took him forth-right, because he was so brave a knight, and laid him in earth, after the heathen law, and prayed for the soul, that it never were happy.

And now Aurelie the king caused a husting to be summoned, and caused trumpets to be blown, and his army to assemble— there was wondrous folk — and marched right to York, and inclosed Octa with his men there within. The king caused a dyke to be dug, all about York, that no man might there either go out or in. Octa saw that; therefore he was full woe. And his heathen folk, that he had in the burgh, they betook them to counsel, what they might do. And thus spake Octa with his companion Ebissa: " I have now bethought me, what I will do. I and my knights shall forth-right in our bare-breech go out of the burgh, hang on my neck a chain, and come to the king, praying his mercy. We all shall else be dead, except we follow this counsel." And they all did so, as Octa them advised; put off their clothes the careful knights, and proceeded out of the burgh, miserable thanes, twain and twain, twenty hundred! Aurelie beheld this, noblest of kings, strange it seemed to him of the naked knights. Together came the host that lay over the land; they saw Octa naked come, that was Hengest's son. He bare in his hand a long chain; he came to the king, and before his warriors he fell upon the ground, and the king's feet sought; and these words then said Hengest's son Octa: " Mercy, my lord king, through God the mild; for the

love of God Almighty have mercy of my knights! For all our
heathendom is become base, our laws and our people, for loathsome we are to the Lord. For us has failed in hand Appolin,
and Tervagant, Woden, and Mercurius, Jupiter, and Saturnus,
Venus, and Didon, Frea, and Mamilon, and all our beliefs are
now to us odious; but we will believe on thy dear Lord, for all it
faileth us now in hand, that we worshipped. We yearn thy
favour, now and evermore; if thou wilt me grant peace, and if
thou wilt me grant amity, we will draw to thee, and be thy faithful men; love thy people, and hold thy laws; if thou wilt not
that, do thy will, whetherso (whatsoever) thou wilt do, or slay
us or up hang us."

And the king was mild-hearted, and held him still; he
beheld on the right hand, he beheld on the left hand, which of
his wise men first would speak. They all were still, and kept
silence with voice; was there no man so high, that durst a word
utter; and ever lay Octa at the king's feet so; all his knights
lay behind him. Then spake Aldadus, the good bishop, and said
thus: " Ever it was, and ever it shall be, and yet it behoveth
us, when we yearn mercy, that we should have mercy; worthy
is he of mercy, who worthily prayeth for it. And thou thyself,
lord king, thou art chief of the people, pardon thou Octa, and
also his companions, if they will receive Christendom with good
belief; for yet it may befall, in some country that they may
fitly worship the Lord. Now stands all this kingdom in thine
own hand; give them a place, where it shall be agreeable to
thee, and take of them hostages, such as thou wilt require;
and let them be well held in iron bonds; the hostages be
found meat and clothes, be found all that to them shall be lief;
and then mightest thou well hold this people in thy land,
and let them till the land, and live by their tilth. And if
it subsequently shall befall, soon thereafter, that they fail in
hand to hold troth, and weaken in work, and withstand thee,
now I decree to thee the doom, what thou mayest then do.
Cause men to ride to them exceeding quickly, and cause them
all to be destroyed, slain and eke up hung. This I decree to thee;
the Lord it hear!" Then answered the king, with quick voice:
" All I will so do as thou hast deemed." Thus spake the king
then: " Arise up, Octa; thou shalt quickly do well, receive
Christendom." There was Octa baptised, and his companions
also; and all his knights on the spot forth-right. They took
their hostages, and gave to the king, three-and-fifty children
they delivered to the king. And the king sent them beside

Scotland; oaths they swore, that they would not deceive him. The king gave them in hand sixty hides of land; thereon they dwelt well many winters.

The king was in York, good it seemed to him; he took his messengers, and sent over all his land; and ordered his bishops, his book-learned men, earls and thanes, to come towards him, to Aurelie the king, to a great husting. It soon came to pass, that they came together. The king greeted his folk with his fair words, he welcomed earls, he welcomed barons, and the bishops, and the book-learned men.—" I will say to you with sooth words, why I sent after you, and for what thing. Here I give to each knight his land and his right, and to every earl and every baron, what he may win, to possess it with joy; and each man I order to love peace, on his life. And I bid you all to work and build the churches that are fallen, to let the bells ring, to sing God's praise, and each with our might to worship our dear Lord; each man by his might to hold peace and amity, and cause the land to be tilled, now it is all in my hand." When this doom was all said, they all praised this counsel. The king gave them leave to depart thence; each fared homeward, as to them it best seemed.

Full seven nights the king lay there still, and then he gan proceed into London, to gladden the burgh-folk, who oft were busy. He caused walls to be strengthened, he caused halls to be built, and all the works to be righted that ere were broken; and gave them all the laws that stood in their elders' days; and he made there reves, to rule the folk. And thence he gan proceed right to Winchester; and there he caused to be worked halls and churches;—there it seemed to him most pleasant;—and afterwards he went to Ambresbury, to the burial-place of his dear friends, whom Hengest with knives had murdered there. He caused men anon to be inquired for, who could hew stone, and eke good wrights, who could work with axe; he thought to work there a work wondrously fair, that ever should last, the while men lived! Then was in Caerleon a bishop, that hight Tremoriun; he was a man exceeding wise in the worlds-realm; with the king he was, over the weald. And thus Tremoriun, God's servant, spake there with the king, of a good thing: " Listen now to me, Aurelie, what I will make known to thee, and I will say to thee the best of all counsel; if thou wilt it approve, eft it will like to thee. We have a prophet, who is Merlin named; if any man might him find, upon this weald, and bring him to thee, through any kind of thing, and if thou his will wouldest perform, he would say to thee best of all counsel, how thou mightest this work make strong and stark, that ever might last, the while that men lived." Then answered the king —these words were to him agreeable:—" Dear friend Tremoriun, all this I will do." The king in haste sent his messengers over all his kingdom, and bade every man to ask after Merlin; and if men might him find, to bring him to the king; he would give him land, both silver and gold, and in the worlds-realm perform his will. The messengers gan to ride wide and far; some they went right north, and some they went forth south; some they went right east, and some they went right west; some they went anon, so that they came to Alaban, that is a fair well in Welsh land. The well he (Merlin) much loved, and oft therein bathed him; the knights him found where he sate by the strand. So soon as they him met, they greeted him fair; and thus said the two knights to him forth-right: " Hail be thou, Merlin, wisest of men! By us he who is a goodly king, named Aurelie, noblest of all kings, greets thee, and he beseecheth thee courteously, that thou come to him; and he will give land to thee, both silver and gold, if thou in the realm wilt counsel the king." Then answered Merlin, what to the knights was full woe: " I reck not of his land, his silver, nor his gold, nor his clothes, nor his horses; myself I have enow." Then sate he still a long time. These knights were afraid, that he would flee. When it all brake forth, it was good that he spake: " Ye are two knights come right here; yesterday ere noon I knew that ye should come, and if I so would, ye might not have found me. Ye bring me greeting from Aurelie the king. I knew his qualities ere he came to land, and I knew the other, Uther his brother; I knew both ere they were born, though I never saw either with eye. But alas! alas! that it is so ordered, that the monarch may not live long! But now will I go, and be your companion; to the king I will proceed, and perform his will."

Forth went Merlin, and the knights with him, so long that they came to the sovereign. The good tidings came to the king; never ere in his life was the king so blithe, for ever any kind of man that came to him! The king went to his steed, and out gan him ride, and all his knights with him, to welcome Merlin. The king him met, and greeted him fair; he embraced him, he kissed him, he made him his familiar. Great was the mirth among the people, all for Merlin's arrival, who was son of no man. Alas! that in the world was no wise man that ever knew here whose son he were, but the Lord alone, who surveys (or explores) all clean! The king led to chamber Merlin who was dear; and he gan ask him anon with his fair words, that he should cause him to understand of the world's course, and of all the years that were to come; for it were to him greatly in will, that he thereof knew. Merlin then answered, and to the king said thus: " O Aurelie, the king, thou askest me a strange thing; look that thou no more such thing inquire. For my spirit truly is wrathful, that is in my breast; and if I among men would make boast, with gladness, with game, with goodly words, my spirit would wrath himself, and become still, and deprive me of my sense, and my wise words fore-close; then were I dumb of every sentence. But leave all such things," quoth Merlin to the king, " for whensoever need shall come to ever any people, and man will beseech me with mildness, and I may with my will dwell still, then may I say, how it afterwards shall happen. But I will counsel thee of thy nearest need, and say to thee right here what thou hast in heart. A plain is by Ambresbury, that is broad, and exceeding pleasant; there was thy kindred deprived of life with knives, there was many bold Briton betrayed to the death; and thinkest to greet the place with worship, and with surprising works to honour the dead, that there shall ever stand, to the world's end. But thou hast never any man, that knows aught thereon, who can make a work that never will fail. But I will counsel thee at such need, for I know a work with wonder encompassed; far the work standeth in Ireland. It is a most surprising thing, it is named the Giant's Ring; the work is of stone, such another there is none, so wide as is the worlds-realm is no work its like. The stones are great, and virtue they have; the men who are sick they go to the stones, and they wash the stones, and therewith bathe their bones; after a little while they become all sound! But the stones are mickle, and immensely great; for was never any man born, in ever any burgh, who might with strength bring the stones thence." Then answered the king: " Merlin, thou sayest strange thing; that never any man born may bring them thence, nor with any strength carry from the place, how might I then bring them hence? " Then answered Merlin to the king who spake with him: " Yes, yes, lord king, it was of yore said, that better is art, than evil strength; for with art men may hold what strength may not obtain. But assemble thine army, and go to the land, and lead thou with thee a good host; and I will go with thee—thy worship will be the

more! Ere thou back come, thy will thou shalt have, and the
work thou shalt bring with thee to this land, and so thou shalt
carry it to the burial-place, and honour the spot where thy
friends lie. And thou thyself shalt therein thy bones rest;
when thy life endeth, there shalt thou rest." Thus said Merlin,
and afterwards he sate still, as though he would from the world
depart. The king caused him to be brought into a fair chamber,
and dwell therein, after his will.

Aurelie the king caused a husting to be summoned from all the
lands that stood in his hand; he bade them counsel him at such
need. And his noble barons they well advised him, that he
should do the counsel that Merlin had said to him. But they
would not lead the king out of this land, but they chose them
for chief Uther the good, and fifteen thousand knights, weaponed
fair, of bold Britons, who thither should go. When this army
was all ready, then began they to fare with all the best ships
that by the sea stood, and voyaged so long that they came to
Ireland. And the brave knights took the haven; they went
upon the sea-strand, and beheld Ireland. Then spake Merlin,
and discoursed with words: " See ye now, brave men, the great
hill, the hill so exceeding high, that to the welkin it is full high?
That is the marvellous thing, it is named the Giant's Ring, to
each work unlike — it came from Africa. Pitch your tents
over all these fields; here we shall rest for the space of three
days; on the fourth day we shall march hence toward the hill,
where our will is. But we shall first refresh us, and assemble
our warriors; make ready our weapons, for well they behove
us (we shall need them)." Thus it remained, and there lay the
army.

Then possessed Ireland a king that was most strong; he hight
Gillomaur, he was lord of the people; the tidings came to him
that the Britons were in the land; he caused forces to be
summoned over all Ireland's territory, and he gan to threaten
greatly, that he would all drive them out. When the word
came to him, what the Britons would do there, and that they
came for that only, to fetch the stones, then the King Gillomar
made mickle derision and scorn, and said that they were foolish
fellows, who over the broad sea were thither arrived, to seek
there stones, as if none were in their land; and swore by
Saint Brandan:—" They shall not carry away one stone, but
for love of the stones they shall abide the most of all mischiefs;
spill their blood out of their bellies—and so men shall teach
them (they shall be taught) to seek stones! And afterwards

I will go into Britain, and say to the King Aurelie, that my stones
I will defend; and unless the king be still, and do my will, I will
in his land with fight withstand; make him waste paths, and
wildernesses many; widows enow—there husbands shall die!"
Thus the unwise king played with words, but it all happened
another wise, other than he weened. His army was ready, and
forth they gan march, so long that they came whereon the
Britons lay. Together they came, and hardily encountered,
and fought fiercely—the fated fell! But the Irish were bare,
and the Britons in armour; the Irish fell, and covered all the
fields. And the King Gillomar gan him to flee there, and fled
forth-right, with twenty of his knights, into a great wood—of
worship bereaved—his Irish folk was felled with steel. Thus
was the king shamed, and thus he ended his boast, and thus
went to the wood, and let his folk fall! The Britons beheld the
dead over the fields; seven thousand there lay deprived of life.
The Britons went over the fields to their tents, and worthily
looked to (or took care of) their good weapons, and there they
gan to rest, as Merlin counselled them.

On the fourth day then gan they to march, and proceeded to
the hill, all well weaponed, where the marvellous work stood,
great and most strong! Knights went upward, knights went
downward, knights went all about, and earnestly beheld it; they
saw there on the land the marvellous work stand. There
were a thousand knights with weapons well furnished, and all
the others to wit guarded well their ships. Then spake Merlin,
and discoursed with the knights: " Knights, ye are strong; these
stones are great and long; ye must go nigh, and forcibly take
hold of them; ye must wreathe them fast with strong sail-
ropes; shove and heave with utmost strength trees great and
long, that are exceeding strong; and go ye to one stone, all
clean, and come again with strength, if ye may it stir." But
Merlin wist well how it should happen. The knights advanced
with mickle strength; they laboured full greatly, but they had
not power, so that they ever any stone might stir! Merlin
beheld Uther, who was the king's brother, and Merlin the
prophet said these words: " Uther, draw thee back, and assemble
thy knights, and stand ye all about, and diligently behold, and
be ye all still, so that no man there stir ere I say to you now
anon how we shall commence, ' Take ye each a stone.' " Uther
drew him back, and assembled his knights, so that none there
remained near the stones, as far as a man might cast a stone.
And Merlin went about, and diligently gan behold; thrice he

went about, within and without, and moved his tongue as if he sung his beads. Thus did Merlin there; then called he Uther: " Uther, come quickly, and all thy knights with thee, and take ye these stones all; ye shall not leave one; for now ye may heave them like feather balls; and so ye shall with counsel carry them to our ships." These stones they carried away, as Merlin counselled them, and placed them in their ships, and sailed forth to wit, and so they gan proceed into this land, and brought them on a plain that is wondrously broad; broad it is and most pleasant, near Ambresbury, where Hengest betrayed the Britons with sæxes. Merlin gan rear them, as they ere stood, so never any other man could do the craft, nor ever ere there-before was any man so wise born, that could the work raise, and the stones dispose.

The tidings came to the king in the north end, of Merlin's proceeding, and of Uther, his brother, that they were with safety come to this land, and that the work was all disposed, and set up right. The king was in breast wondrously blithe; and caused a husting to be summoned, so wide as was all his land, that all his merry folk so very joyous should come to Ambresbury, all his people, at Whitsunday, and the king would be there, and honour the place. Thither came Aurelie the king, and all his folk with him; on Whitsunday he there made a feast, as I will thee tell in this book-story. There were on the weald tents raised, on the broad plain, nine thousand tents. All the Whitsunday the king on the plain lay; ordered the place to be hallowed, that hight Stonehenge. Full three days the king dwelt still; on the third day, his people he highly honoured; he made two bishops, wondrously good, Saint Dubriz at Kaerleon, and Saint Samson at York; both they became holy, and with God high. On the fourth day people separated, and so a time it stood in the same wise.

The yet there was a wicked man, Pascent, Vortiger's son; was the same Pascent gone into Welsh land, and there in the same days was become outlaw. But he durst not long dwell there, for Aurelie and for Uther; but he procured good ships, and went by the sea-flood; into Germany he proceeded, with five hundred men, and there he won much folk, and made a fleet, and voyaged so long that he came to this land, into the Humber, where he harm wrought. But he durst not long remain in the territory. The king marched thitherward, and Pascent fled awayward, by sea so long that he came to Ireland.

Soon he found there the king of the land; his heart was very sore, he greeted the King Gillomar with God's greeting: "Hail be thou, Gillomar, chief of men! I am to thee come; I was Vortiger's son; my father was Britain's king, he loved thee through all things. And if thou wouldest now be my companion, as we shall agree, and my father well avenge, and well avenge thy folk that Uther here killed, and thy marvellous work, that he hence drew. And eke I heard say, where I voyaged in the sea, that the King Aurelie is become sick, and lieth in Winchester, in bed full fast. Thou mayest believe me enow, for this is verily sooth." Thus Pascent and Gillomar made their compact there; oaths they swore, many and innumerable, that they would set all this land in their two (joint) hands; the oaths were sworn, but eft they were broken! The king gathered a host wide over his land; to the sea they are gone, Gillomar and Pascent; into the ships they went, and forth let them glide. Forth they proceeded quickly, so that they came to Meneve, that was in that time a town exceeding fair, that men now truly call Saint David's. There they took haven with great bliss; the ships went on the strand, the knights went on the land. Then said Pascent—toward Gillomar he went—"Say me, King Gillomar, now we are come here; now I set to thee in hand half-part this kingdom; for there is from Winchester come to me a knight's son, and saith to me such advice, that Aurelie will be dead; the sickness is under his ribs, so that he may not live. Here we shall well avenge our kindred, and win his territories, as to us shall be best of all."

To the king came the word, into Winchester, that Pascent and Gillomar were come here with an army. The king called Uther, who was his dear brother:—"Uther, summon forces over all this land, and march to our enemies, and drive them from land; either thou them disperse, either thou them fell. And I would eke fare, if I were not so sick; but if I may be sound I will come after thee soon." Uther did all as the king said to him there. And Pascent at Saint David's wrought thereby much sorrow; and to the king Gillomar much sorrow he did there; Britain they through-ran, harried and burnt. And Uther in this land assembled his host, and it was long time ere he might march aright. And Pascent set in his own hand all West Welsh land.

It was on a day, his people were blithe, there arrived Appas —the fiends him conveyed! To Pascent he quoth thus: " Come hither to us. I will thee tell of a joyful tiding. I was at Winchester, with thine adversaries, where the king

lieth sick, and sorrowful in heart. But what shall be my
meed, if I thither ride, and I so gratify thee, that I kill
him?" Then answered Pascent, and toward Appas he went:
"I promise thee to-day a hundred pounds, for I may, if thou
me so gratifiest, that thou kill him." Troth they plight this
treachery to contrive. Appas went to his chamber, and this
mischief meditated; he was a heathen man, out of Saxland
come. Monk's clothes he took on, he shaved his crown upon;
he took to him two companions, and forth he gan proceed, and
went anon right into Winchester, as if it were a holy man—the
heathen devil! He went to the burgh-gate, where the king lay
in chamber, and greeted the door-keeper with God's greeting;
and bade him in haste go into the king, and say to him in sooth,
that Uther his brother had sent him thither a good leech; the
best leech that dwelt in any land, that ever any sick man
out of sickness can bring. Thus he lied, the odious man, to
the monarch, for Uther was gone forth with his army, nor
ever him saw Uther, nor thither him sent! And the king
weened that it were sooth, and believed him enow. Who
would ween that he were traitor!—for on his bare body he wore
a cuirass, thereupon he had a loathly hair-cloth, and then a
cowl of a black cloth; he had blackened his body, as if smutted
with coal! He kneeled to the king, his speech was full mild:
"Hail be thou, Aurelie, noblest of all kings! Hither me sent
Uther, that is thine own brother; and I all for God's love am
here to thee come. For I will heal, and all whole thee make,
for Christ's love, God's son; I reck not any treasure, nor meed
of land, nor of silver nor of gold, but to each sick person I do it
for love of my Lord." The king heard this, it was to him most
agreeable;—but where is ever any man in this middle-earth, that
would this ween, that he were traitor! He took his glass vessel
anon, and the king urined therein; a while after that, the glass
vessel in hand he took, and viewed it forth-right before the
king's knights; and thus said anon Appas, the heathen man:
"If ye will me believe, ere to-morrow eve this king shall be all
whole, healed at his will." Then were blithe all that were in
chamber. Appas went in a chamber, and the mischief meditated,
and put thereto poison, that hight scamony, and came out
forth-right among the chamber-knights, and to the knights he
gan to distribute much canel, and gingiver and liquorice he gave
them lovingly. They all took the gift, and he deceived them
all. This traitor fell on his knees before the monarch, and thus
said to him: "Lord, now thou shalt receive this, of this drink

a part, and that shall be thy cure." And the king up drank, and there the poison he drank. Anon as he had drank, the leech laid him down. Thus said Appas to the chamber-knights: "Wrap now the king well, that he lie in sweating; for I say to you through all things, all whole shall your king be. And I will go to my inn, and speak with my men, and at the midnight I will come again forth-right, with other leechcraft, that shall be to him healing." Forth went—while the king lay in slumber—the traitor Appas to his inn, and spake with his men; and with stilly counsel stole from the town.

At the midnight then sent the chamber-knights six of their men to Appas's inn; they weened to find him, and bring him to the king. Then was he flown, and the fiends him carried! The men came back where the king dwelt, and made known in the chamber of Appas's departure. Then might men see sorrow enow be! Knights fell down, and yearned their deaths; there was mickle lamentation and heart-groaning, there was many a piteous speech, there was yell of men! They leapt to the bed, and beheld the king; the yet he lay in slumber, and in great sweat. The knights with weeping awakened the king, and they called to him with mild voice: "Lord, how is it with thee? how is thy harm? For now is our leech departed without leave, gone out of court, and left us as wretches." The king gave them answer: "I am all over swollen, and there is no other hap, now anon I shall be dead. And I bid forth-right, ye who are my knights, that ye greet Uther, who is my own brother, and bid him hold my land in his sway. God himself through all things let him be a good king! And bid him be keen, and always deem right, as a father to the poor folk, to the destitute for comfort; —then may he hold the land in power. And now to-day, when I be dead, take ye all one counsel, and cause me to be brought right to Stonehenge, where lie much of my kindred, by the Saxons killed. And send for bishops, and book-learned men; my gold and silver distribute for my soul, and lay me at the east end, in Stonehenge." There was no other hap—there was the king dead! And all so his men did as the king directed. Uther was in Wales, and hereof was nothing ware, never through any art hereof nothing wist; nevertheless he had with him the prophet Merlin, he proceeded towards the army that was come to the land.

Uther lay in Wales, in a wilderness, and prepared to march, to fight with Pascent. Then in the eventime, the moon gan to shine, well nigh all as bright as the sunlight. Then they saw afar a marvellous star; it was broad, it was large, it was immense! From it came gleams terribly shining; the star is named in Latin, comet. Came from the star a gleam most fierce; at this gleam's end was a dragon fair; from this dragon's mouth came gleams enow! But twain there were mickle, unlike to the others; the one drew toward France, the other toward Ireland. The gleam that toward France drew, it was itself bright enow; to Munt-Giu was seen the marvellous token! The gleam that stretched right west, it was disposed in seven beams. Uther saw this—but he was not hereof wary— sorrow was to him in heart, and strangely he was frightened; so was all the great folk that was in the host. Uther called Merlin, and bade him come to him, and thus said to him with very soft words: " Merlin, Merlin, dear friend, prove thyself, and say to us of the token that we have seen; for I wot not in the worlds-realm to what end it shall befall; unless thou us counsel, back we must ride."

Merlin sate him still, a long time, as if he with dream full greatly laboured. They said who saw it with their own eyes, that oft he turned him, as if it were a worm! At length he gan to awake, then gan he to quake, and these words said Merlin the prophet: " Walaway! Walaway! in this worlds-realm, much is the sorrow that is come to the land! Where art thou, Uther? Set before me here, and I will say to thee of sorrows enow. Dead is Aurelie, noblest of kings; so is the other, Constance, thy brother, whom Vortiger betrayed with his treachery. Now hath Vortiger's kin killed Aurelie; now art thou alone of thy noble kindred. But hope not thou for counsel of them that lie dead, but think of thyself—prosperity shall be given to thee;— for seldom he faileth, who to himself thinketh. Thou shalt become good king, and lord of men. And thou at the midnight weapon thy knights, that we in the morning-light may come forth-right, before Meneve—there thou shalt fight; ere thou thence depart, slaughter thou shalt make; for thou shalt both slay there, Pascent and Gillomar, and many thousands of the men that are with them hither come. The token of the star, that we saw so far, sooth it is, Uther dear, that betokened thy brother's death. Before the star was the dragon, to each worm unlike; the token was on thy half, that was thou, Uther, thyself! Thou shalt have this land, and thy authority be great and strong. Such tokens are marvellous that came of the dragon's mouth; two gleams proceeded forth that were wondrously light. The one stretched far south, out over France—that signifies a powerful son, that of thy body shall come, who shall win many kingdoms with conflict, and in the end he shall rule many a nation. The other gleam that stretched west, wondrously light, that shall be a daughter, that to thee shall be exceeding dear. The gleams that gan to spread in seven fair strings, are seven fair sons, who shall come of thy daughter, who shall win to their own hand many a kingdom; they shall be well strong, on water and on land. Now thou hast of me heard what will thee help, quickly forth-right march to thy fight." And Merlin gan to slumber, as if he would sleep.

Up arose Uther, now he was wise and wary, and ordered his knights forth-right to horse, and ordered them quickly to proceed to Meneve; and all their expedition (or forces) to prepare, as if they should fight. In the troop before he had knights well chosen; seven thousand knights, brave men and active. He had in the middle knights well beseen, other seven thousand good thanes. He had behind brave knights eighteen thousand, brave warriors, and of folk on foot so many thousands, that in no speech might any man tell them! Forth they marched quickly, until they came to Meneve.

There saw Gillomar where Uther came to him, and commanded his knights to weapon them forth-right. And they very speedily grasped their knives, and off with their breeches—strange were their looks—and grasped in their hands their long spears, and hung on their shoulders great battle-axes. Then said Gillomar the king a thing very strange:—" Here cometh Uther, Aurelie's brother; he will ask my peace, and not fight with me. The foremost are his swains; march we against them; ye need never reek, though ye slay the wretches! For if Uther, Constantine's son, will here become my man, and give to Pascent his father's realm, I will him grant peace, and let him live, and in fair bonds lead him to my land." The king spake thus, the while worse him befell!

Uther's knights were in the town forth-right, and laid fire in the town, and fought sharply; with swords rushed towards them; and the Irish were naked. When the Irish men saw, that the Britons were in conflict, they fought fiercely, and nevertheless they fell; they called on their king: " Where art thou, nithing! why wilt thou not come hither? thou lettest us here be destroyed;—and Pascent, thy comrade, saw us fall here;—come ye to us to help, with great strength!" Gillomar heard this; therefore his heart was sore; with his Irish knights he came to the fight, and Pascent forth with him—both they

were fated! When Uther saw, that Gillomar was there come,
to him he gan ride, and smote him in the side, so that the spear
through pierced, and glided to the heart. Hastily he passed
by him, and overtook Pascent; and said these words Uther
the good: "Pascent, thou shalt abide; here cometh Uther
riding!" He smote him upon the head, so that he fell down,
and the sword put in his mouth—such meat to him was strange
—so that the point of the sword went in the earth. Then said
Uther: "Pascent, lie now there; now thou hast Britain all
won to thy hand! So is now hap to thee; therein thou art
dead; dwell ye shall here, thou, and Gillomar thy companion,
and possess well Britain! For now I deliver it to you in hand,
so that ye may presently dwell with us here; ye need not ever
dread who you shall feed!" Thus said Uther, and afterwards
he there ran, and drove the Irish men over waters and over
fens, and slew all the host that with Pascent came to land.
Some to the sea fled, and leapt into their ships; with weather
and with water there they perished! Thus they sped here,
Pascent and Gillomar. Now was this fight done; and Uther
back came, and forth-right marched into Winchester.

In a broad way he gan meet three knights and their swains,
who came toward him. Anon as they met him, fair they him
greeted: "Hail be thou, Uther; these territories are thine own.
Dead is Aurelie, noblest of kings; he hath set to thee in hand
all his regal land; he bade thee be in prosperity, and think of
his soul." Then wept Uther wondrously much there. Uther
proceeded forth-right into Winchester; then were before him,
without the burgh, all the burghers with piteous cries. So
soon as they saw him, they said to him: "Uther, thy favour,
now and evermore! Our king we have lost, woe is to us therefore. Thou wert his brother—he had no other, nor he had no
son, who might become king. But take thou the crown, it is
thy right, and we will help thee, and hold for lord, with weapons
and with goods, and with all our might." Uther heard this;
he was wise and he was aware, that there was no other course,
since his brother was dead. He took the crown, that came to
him exceeding well, and he worthily became king, and held
good laws, and loved his folk. Whilst that he was king, and
chose his ministers, Merlin disappeared; he knew not ever
whither he went, nor ever in the worlds-realm what became
of him. Woe was the king, so was all his people, and all
his courtiers were therefore mourning. The king caused men
to ride wide and far; he offered gold and treasure to each

travelling man, whosoever might find Merlin in the land;
thereto he laid mickle praise, but he heard no whit of him.
Then bethought Uther, what Merlin said to him ere, in the expedition into Welsh land, where they saw the dragon, to each worm
incomparable; and he thought of the tokens that Merlin taught
him. The king was exceeding sorry, and sorrowful in heart,
for he lost never a dearer man, since he was alive, never any
other, not even Aurelie, his brother. The king caused to be
worked two images, two golden dragons, all for Merlin's love—
so greatly he desired his coming. When the dragons were ready,
the one was his companion; wheresoever he in the land led his
army, it was his standard, in every hap; the other he worthily
gave into Winchester, into the bishop's see, where he stead
holdeth. Thereto he gave his good spear, wherewith men
should bear the dragon, when men should carry relics at pro-
cessions. The Britons saw this, these dragons that were thus
made; ever since they called Uther, who for a standard bare the
dragon, the name they laid on him, that was Uther Pendragon;
Pendragon in British, Dragon's-head in English.

Now was Uther their good king, but of Merlin he had
nothing. This word heard Octa, where he dwelt northward,
and Ebissa his wed-brother, and Ossa the other, that Aurelie sent
thither, and set them there in his peace, and gave them in hand
sixty hides of land. Octa heard full truly all how it was transacted, of Aurelie's death, and of Uther's kingdom. Octa called
to him his kin that was nearest; they betook them to counsel,
of their old deeds, that they would by their life desert Christendom. They held husting, and became heathens; then came
there together, of Hengest's kindred, five and sixty hundred of
heathen men. Soon was the word reported and over the land
known, that Octa, Hengest's son, was become heathen, and all
these same men to whom Aurelie had granted peace. Octa
sent his messengers into Welsh land, after the Irish that from
Uther were fled, and after the Alemains (Germans), that away
were drawn, that were gone to the wood, the while men slew
Pascent, and hid them well everywhere, the while men slew
Gillomar; the folk out of the wood drew, and toward Scotland
proceeded. There came ever more and more, and proceeded
toward Octa; when they together were all come, then were
there thirty thousand, without the women, of Hengest's kin.
They took their host, and forth gan to fare, and set all in their
hand beyond the Humber, and the people, where they gan
march; there was a marvellous host! And they proceeded

right to York, and on each side the heathen people gan ride
about the burgh, and the burgh besieged; and took it all in their
hand, forth into Scotland; all that they saw they accounted
their own. But Uther's knights who were in the castle, defended
the town within, so that they might never get within; in no
place heard any one, of few men that did so well!

So soon as Uther of this thing was aware, he assembled a
strong army, over all his kingdom, and he very speedily marched
toward York; proceeded forth-right anon, where Octa him lay.
Octa and his forces marched against them; encountered them
together with grim strength; hewed hardily; helms resounded;
the fields were dyed with the blood of the slain, and the heathen
souls hell sought! When the day's end arrived, then was it so
evilly done, that the heathen folk had the upper hand, and with
great strength routed the Britons, and drove them to a mount
that was exceeding strong. And Uther with his men drew to
the mount, and had lost in the fight his dear knights, full seven
hundred—his hap was the worse! The mount hight Dunian,
that Uther was upon; the mount was overgrown with a fair
wood. The king was there within with very many men, and
Octa besieged him with the heathen men night and day—
besieged him all about, woe was to the Britons! Woe was the
King Uther, that he was not ere aware, that he had not in land
better understood. Oft they went to counsel of such need,
how they might overcome Octa, Hengest's son.

There was an earl Gorlois, bold man full truly—knight he was
good, he was Uther's man,—Earl of Cornwall, known he was
wide—he was a very wise man, in all things excellent. To him
said Uther, sorry in heart: "Hail be thou, Gorlois, lord of
men! Thou art mine own man, and very well I thee treat;
thou art knight good, great is thy wisdom; all my people I put
in thy counsel, and all we shall work after thy will." Then hung
he his brows down, the King Uther Pendragon, and stood him
full still, and bade Gorlois say his will. Then answered Gorlois,
who was courteous full truly; "Say me, Uther Pendragon,
why bowest thou thy head down? Knowest thou not that
God alone is better than we all clean? He may to whomsoever he will give worship. Promise we him in life that we will
not him deceive; and let we counsel us of our misdeeds. Each
man forth-right take shrift of all his sins; each man shrive
other, as if it were his brother, and every good knight take on
him much shrift, and God we shall promise to amend our sins.
And at the midnight prepare us to fight; these heathen hounds

account us all here bound. Octa, Hengest's son, weeneth that we are all taken; they lie in these fields covered in their tents, they are very weary of carrying their weapons; now anon they shall slumber, and afterwards sleep; of us they have no care, that we will march against them. At the midnight we shall forth-right go exceeding still, down from this hill; be no knight so mad, that he ask any word, nor ever any man be so mad, that he blow horn. But we shall step to them as if we would steal; ere they are aware, we shall destroy them; we shall approach to them, and tell them tidings. And let every brave man strongly lay on them; and so we shall drive the foreigners from the land, and with the might of our Lord, win our rights." All this host did as Gorlois had bid them; each man forth-right put him under shrift; promised to do good; and Uther Pendragon fore-most went down, and all his knights, exceeding still; and smote in the wealds, among all the tents, and slew the heathens with great strength; slew over the fields the yellow locks; of folk it was most wretched, they drew along their bowels; with much destruction they fell to the ground!

And there was forth-right captured Octa, Hengest's son, and his wed-brother Ebissa, and his comrade Ossa. The king caused them to be bound with iron bands, and delivered them to sixty knights, who were good in fight, fast to hold over the weald. And he himself drove him forth, and made much din; and Gorlois the fair, forth on the other side; and all their knights ever forth-right slew downright all that they came nigh. Some they crept to the wood on their bare knees, and they were on the morrow most miserable of all folk. Octa was bound, and led to London, and Ebissa, and Ossa—was never to them such woe!

This fight was all done, and the king forth marched into Northumberland with great bliss; and afterwards to Scotland, and set it all in his own hand. He established peace, he estab-lished quiet, that each man might journey with from land to land, though he bare gold in his hand; of peace he did such things, that no king might ever ere, from that time that the Britons here arrived. And then, after a time, he proceeded to London; he was there at Easter, with his good folk; blithe was the London's town, for Uther Pendragon. He sent his messengers over all his kingdom; he bade the earls, he bade the churls, he bade the bishops, and the book-learned men, that they should come to London, to Uther the king, into London's town, to Uther Pendragon. Rich men soon to London came; they brought wife, they brought child, as Uther the king commanded. With much goodness the king heard mass, and Gorlois, the Earl of Cornwall, and many knights with him: much bliss was in the town, with King Uther Pendragon. When the mass was sung, to the hall they crowded; trumpets they blew, boards they spread; all the folk ate and drank, and bliss was among them.

There sate Uther the king in his high chair; opposite to him Gorlois, fair knight full truly, the Earl of Cornwall, with his noble wife. When they were all seated, the earls to their meat, the king sent his messengers to Ygærne the fair, Gorlois the earl's wife, woman fairest of all. Oft he looked on her, and glanced with his eyes; oft he sent his cup-bearers forth to her table; oft he laughed at her, and made glances to her; and she him lovingly beheld—but I know not whether she loved him. The king was not so wise, nor so far prudent, that among his folk he could his thoughts hide. So long the king this practised, that Gorlois became him wrath, and angered him greatly with the king, because of his wife. The earl and his knights arose forth-right, and went forth with the woman, knights most wrath. King Uther saw this, and herefore was sorry, and took him forth-right twelve wise knights, and sent after Gorlois, chieftain of men, and bade him come in haste to the king, and do the king good right, and acknowledge his fault, that he had disgraced the king, and from his board had departed; he, and his knights, with mickle wrong, for the king was cheerful with him, and for he hailed (drank health) to his wife. And if he would not back come, and acknowledge his guilt, the king would follow after him, and do all his might; take from him all his land, and his silver, and his gold. Gorlois heard this, lord of men, and he answer gave, wrathest of earls: "Nay, so help me the Lord, that formed the daylight, will I never back come, nor yearn his peace; nor shall he ever in life disgrace me of my wife! And say ye to Uther the king, at Tintaieol he may find me; if he thither will ride, there will I abide him, and there he shall have hard game, and mickle world's shame." Forth proceeded the earl, angry in his mood; he was wrath with the king wondrously much, and threatened Uther the king, and all his thanes with him. But he knew not what should come subsequently, soon thereafter.

The earl proceeded anon into Cornwall; he had there two castles inclosed most fast; the castles were good, and belonged to the race of his ancestors. To Tintaieol he sent his mistress

who was so fair, named Ygærne, best of all women; and he
inclosed her fast in the castle. Ygærne was sorry, and sorrowful in heart, that so many men for her should there have destruction. The earl sent messengers over all Britain, and bade each
brave man, that he should come to him, for gold and for silver,
and for other good gifts, that they full soon should come to
Tintaieol; and bade his own knights to come forth-right.
When they were together, the good thanes, then had he full
fifteen thousand, and they fast inclosed Tintaieol. Upon the
sea-strand Tintaieol standeth; it is with the sea cliffs fast
inclosed, so that it may not be won, by no kind of man,
but if hunger come therein under. The earl marched thence
with seven thousand men, and proceeded to another castle, and
inclosed it full fast, and left his wife in Tintaieol, with ten
thousand men. For it needed the knights, day or night, only
to guard the castle gate, and lie careless asleep; and the earl
kept the other, and with him his own brother.

Uther heard this, who was king most stark, that Gorlois, his
earl, had gathered his forces, and would hold war, with much
wrath. The king summoned his host over all this territory,
over all the land that stood in his hand; people of many kind
marched them together, and came to London to the sovereign.
Out of London's town fared Uther Pendragon; he and his knights
proceeded forth-right, so long, that they came into Cornwall, and
over the water they passed, that Tambres hight, right to the
castle, where they knew Gorlois to be. With much enmity the
castle they besieged; oft they assaulted it with fierce strength;
together they leapt, people there fell. Full seven nights the
king with his knights besieged the castle; his men there had
sorrow; he might not of the earl anything win, and all the
se'nnight lasted the marvellous fight. When Uther the king
saw that nothing sped to him; oft he bethought him what he
might do; for Ygærne was so dear to him, even as his own life,
and Gorlois was to him in the land of all men most loathsome;
and in each way was woe to him in this world's realm; because
he might not have anything of his will.

Then was with the king an old man exceeding well-informed;
he was a very rich thane, and skilful in each doom; he was
named Ulfin; much wisdom was with him. The king drew up
his chin, and looked on Ulfin; greatly he mourned; his mood
was disturbed. Then quoth Uther Pendragon to Ulfin the
knight: "Ulfin, say me some counsel, or I shall be full soon
dead, so much it longeth me after the fair Ygærne, that I may

not live. This word hold to me secret; for Ulfin the dear, thy good counsels, loud and still I will do them." Then answered Ulfin to the king who spake with him: " Now hear I a king say great marvel! Thou lovest Ygærne, and holdest it so secret; the woman is to thee dear, and her lord all loath; his land thou consumest, and makest him destitute, and threatenest himself to slay, and his kin to destroy. Weenest thou with such harm to obtain Ygærne? She should do then as no woman doth, with dread unmeet hold love sweet. But if thou lovest Ygærne, thou shouldest hold it secret, and send her soon of silver and of gold, and love her with art, and with loving behest. The yet it were a doubt, whether thou mightest possess her; for Ygærne is chaste, a woman most true; so was her mother, and more of the kin. In sooth I thee say, dearest of all kings, that otherwise thou must begin, if thou wilt win her. For yesterday came to me a good hermit, and swore by his chin, that he knew Merlin, where he each night resteth under heaven; and oft he spake with him, and stories him told. And if we might with art get Merlin, then mightest thou thy will wholly obtain."

Then was Uther Pendragon the softer in his mood, and gave answer: " Ulfin, thou hast well said counsel; I give thee in hand thirty ploughs of land, so that thou get Merlin, and do my will." Ulfin went through the folk, and sought all the host, and he after a time found the hermit, and in haste brought him to the king. And the king set to him in hand seven ploughs of land, if he might find and bring Merlin to the king. The hermit gan wend in the west end, to a wilderness, to a mickle wood, where he had dwelt well many winters; and Merlin very oft sought him there. So soon as the hermit came in, then found he Merlin, standing under a tree, and sore gan for him long; he saw the hermit come, as whilom was his custom; he ran towards him, both they rejoiced for this; they embraced, they kissed, and familiarly spake. Then said Merlin—much wisdom was with him—" Say thou, my dear friend, why wouldest thou not say to me, through no kind of thing, that thou wouldest go to the king? But full quickly I it knew anon as I thee missed, that thou wert come to Uther the king; and what the king spake with thee, and of his land thee offered, that thou shouldest bring me to Uther the king. And Ulfin thee sought, and to the king brought, and Uther Pendragon forth-right anon, set him in hand thirty ploughs of land; and he set thee in hand seven ploughs of land. Uther is desirous after Ygærne the fair, wondrously much, after Gorlois's wife. But so long as is

eternity, that shall never come, that he obtain her, but through
my stratagem; for there is no woman truer in this world's
realm. And nevertheless he shall possess the fair Ygærne; and
he shall beget on her what shall widely rule; he shall beget on
her a man exceeding marvellous. So long as is eternity, he
shall never die; the while that this world standeth, his glory
shall last; and he shall in Rome rule the thanes. All shall bow
to him that dwelleth in Britain; of him shall gleemen goodly
sing; of his breast noble poets shall eat; of his blood shall men
be drunk; from his eyes shall fly fiery embers; each finger on
his hand shall be a sharp steel brand; stone walls shall before
him tumble; barons shall give way, and their standards fall!
Thus he shall well long fare over all the lands, people to conquer,
and set his laws. These are the tokens of the son, that shall
come of Uther Pendragon and of Ygærne. This speech is full
secret; for yet neither it knoweth, Ygærne nor Uther, that of
Uther Pendragon such a son shall arise; for yet he is unbegot,
that shall govern all the people. But, Lord," quoth Merlin,
" now it is thy will, that forth I shall go to the host of the king;
thy words I will obey, and now I will depart, and proceed I will
for thy love to Uther Pendragon. And thou shalt have the
land that he set thee in hand."

Thus they then spake: the hermit gan to weep; dearly he
him kissed; there they gan to separate. Merlin went right
forth south, the land was well known to him; forth-right he
proceeded to the king's host. So soon as Uther him saw, so he
approached towards him; and thus quoth Uther Pendragon:
" Merlin, thou art welcome! Here I set thee in hand all the
counsel of my land, and that thou must me advise, at my great
need." Uther told him all that he would, and how Ygærne
was to him in the land dearest of women, and Gorlois, her lord,
most odious of all men.—" And unless I have thy counsel, full
soon thou wilt see me dead." Then answered Merlin: " Let
Ulfin now come in, and give him in hand thirty ploughs of land,
and give to the hermit what thou him promisedest; for I will not
possess any land, neither silver nor gold; for I am in counsel
most skilful of all men, and if I wished for possessions, then
should I become worse in craft. But all thy will well shall
come to pass; for I know such leech-craft, that shall be to thee
lief, so that all thy appearance shall become as the earl's; thy
speech, thy deeds among thy people; thy horse and thy weeds
(garments); and so shalt thou ride. When Ygærne shall see
thee, in mood shall it be well to her; she lieth in Tintaieol, fast

inclosed. There is no knight so well born, of no land chosen, that might with strength unfasten the gates of Tintaieol, unless they were burst with hunger and with thirst. But that is the sooth that I will say to thee; through all things thou shalt be as if thou wert the earl; and I will be every bit as Britael he is, who is a knight most hardy, he is this earl's steward; Jurdan is his chamber-knight, he is exceeding well dight; I will make Ulfin anon such as Jurdan is. Then wilt thou be lord, and I be Britael, thy steward, and Ulfin be Jurdan, thy chamber-knight. And we shall go now to-night; and fare thou shalt by counsel, whither soever I lead thee. Now to-night shall half a hundred knights with spear and with shield be about thy tents, so that never any man alive come there near; and if ever any man come there, that his head be taken from him. For the knights shall say—thy good men—that thou art let blood, and restest thee in bed."

These things were forth-right thus dight. Forth went the king; it was nothing known; and forth went with him Ulfin and Merlin; they proceeded right the way that lay into Tintaieol; they came to the castle-gate, and called familiarly: "Undo this gate-bolt; the earl is come here, Gorlois the lord, and Britael his steward, and Jordan the chamber-knight; we have journeyed all night!" The gateward made it known over all, and knights ran upon the wall, and spake with Gorlois, and knew him full surely. The knights were most alert, and weighed up the castle-gate, and let him come within—the less was then their care;—they weened certainly to have much bliss. Then had they with stratagem Merlin there within, and Uther the king within their possession, and led there with him his good thane Ulfin. These tidings came quickly unto the lady, that her lord was come, and with him his three men. Out came Ygærne forth to the earl, and said these words with winsome speech: "Welcome, lord, man to me dearest; and welcome, Jordan, and Britael is also;—be ye in safety parted from the king?" Then quoth Uther full truly as if it were Gorlois: "Mickle is the multitude that is with Uther Pendragon; and I am all by night stolen from the fight, for after thee I was desirous, woman thou art to me dearest. Go into the chamber, and cause my bed to be made, and I will rest me for this night's space, and all day to-morrow, to gladden my people." Ygærne went to chamber, and caused a bed to be made for him; the kingly bed was all overspread with a pall. The king viewed it well, and went to his bed; and Ygærne lay down by Uther Pendragon.

Now weened Ygærne full truly, that it were Gorlois; through
never any kind of thing knew she Uther the king. The king
approached her as man should do to woman, and had him to do
with the dearest of women; and he begat on her a marvellous
man, keenest of all kings, that ever came among men, and he
was on earth named Arthur. Ygærne knew not who lay in her
arms; for ever she weened full surely, that it were the Earl
Gorlois.

There was no greater interval but until it was daylight, there
forth-right the knights understood, that the king was departed out
of the host. Then said the knights, sooth though it were not,
that the king was flown, filled with dread; but it all was leasing
that they said of the king; they held hereof much converse upon
Uther Pendragon. Then said the earls and the highest barons;
" Now when Gorlois shall know it, how it is passed, that our king
is departed, and has left his host, he will forth-right weapon his
knights, and out he will to fight, and fell us to ground, with his
furious thanes make mickle slaughter; then were it better for
us, that we were not born. But cause we the trumpets to be
blown, and our army to assemble; and Cador the brave shall
bear the king's standard; heave high the Dragon before this
people, and march to the castle, with our keen folk. And the
Earl Aldolf shall be our chief, and we shall obey him, as if he
were the king; and so we shall with right with Gorlois fight; and
if he will speak with us, and yearn this king's peace, set amity
with soothfast oath, then may we with worship go hence; then
our underlings will have no upbraidings, that we for any timidity
hence fled." All the nation-folk praised this same counsel.
Trumpets they blew, and assembled their host; up they heaved
the Dragon, by each standard unmatched; there was many a
bold man, that hung shield on shoulder, many a keen thane; and
proceeded to the castle, where Gorlois was within, with his keen
men. He caused trumpets to be blown, and his host to assemble;
they leapt on steed; knights gan to ride. These knights were
exceeding active, and went out at the gate; together they came
soon, and quickly they attacked; fell the fated men; the ground
they sought; there was much blood shed, harm was among the
folk; amidst the fight full certainly men slew the Earl Gorlois.
Then gan his men to flee, and the others to pursue after; they
came to the castle, and within they thrust. Soon it came
within, both the two hosts; there lasted the fight throughout
the daylight; ere the day were all gone, the castle was won;
was there no swain so mean, that he was not a well good thane.

The tidings came into Tintageol in haste, forth into the castle wherein Uther was, that the good earl their lord Gorlois was slain full truly, and all his soldiers, and his castle taken. The king heard this, where he lay in amorous play, and leapt out of bower, as if it were a lion. Then quoth the King Uther, of this tiding he was ware: "Be still, be still, knights in hall! Here I am full truly, your lord Gorlois; and Jordan, my chamberlain, and Britael, my steward. I and these two knights leapt out of the fight, and in hither we are arrived—we were not there slain. But now I will march, and assemble my host; and I and my knights shall all by night proceed into a town, and meet Uther Pendragon, and unless he speak of reconciliation, I will worthily avenge me! And inclose ye this castle most fast, and bid Ygærne that she mourn not. Now go I forth-right; have ye all good night!" Merlin went before, and the thane Ulfin, and afterwards Uther Pendragon, out of Tintageol's town; ever they proceeded all night, until it was daylight.

When he came to the spot where his army lay, Merlin had on the king set his own features through all things; then his knights knew their sovereign; there was many a bold Briton filled with bliss; then was in Britain bliss enow; horns there blew, gleemen gan chant, glad was every knight, all arrayed with pall! Three days was the king dwelling there; and on the fourth day he went to Tintaieol. He sent to the castle his best thanes, and greeted Ygærne, noblest of women, and sent her token what they spake in bed; and ordered her that she should yield the castle quickly—there was no other counsel, for her lord was dead. Yet Ygærne weened that it were sooth, that the dead earl had sought his people, and she all believed, that it were false, that the King Uther had ever come down. Knights went to counsel, knights went to communing; they resolved that they would not hold the castle any longer; their bridge they let down and delivered it to Uther Pendragon. Then stood all this kingdom eft in Uther's own hand.

There Uther the king took Ygærne for queen; Ygærne was with child by Uther the king, all through Merlin's craft, before she was wedded. The time came that was chosen, then was Arthur born. So soon as he came on earth, elves took him; they enchanted the child with magic most strong, they gave him might to be the best of all knights; they gave him another thing, that he should be a rich king; they gave him the third, that he should live long; they gave to him the prince virtues most good, so that he was most generous of all men alive. This the elves gave him, and thus the child thrived. After Arthur, the blessed lady was born, she was named Anna, the blessed maiden; and afterwards she took (married) Loth, who possessed Leoneis (Lothian); she was in Leoneis lady of the people. Long lived Uther with mickle bliss here, with good peace, with much quiet, free in his kingdom.

When that he was an old man, then came illness on him; the illness laid him down, sick was Uther Pendragon; so he was here sick seven years. Then became the Britons much emboldened; they did oft wickedly, all for absence of dread. The yet lay Octa, Hengest's son, bound in the prison of London, who was taken at York, and his comrade Ebissa, and his other Ossa. Twelve knights guarded them day and night, who were wearily oppressed with watching, in London. Octa heard say of the sickness of the king, and spake with the guardsmen, who should keep him: "Hearken to me now, knights, what I will make known to you. We lie here in London fast bound, and ye many a long day have watched over us. Better were it for us to live in Saxland, with much wealth, than thus miserably here lie asleep. And if ye would in all things accomplish this, and do my will, I would give you land, much silver and gold, so that ever ye might richly rule in the land, and live your life as to you shall be liefest of all. For ye shall never have good gifts of Uther, your king, for now full soon he will be dead, and his people all desert; then will ye have neither, the one nor the other. But bethink you, brave men, and give to us your compassion, and think what were lief to you, if ye thus lay bound, and might in your land live in joy." Very oft Octa spake so with these knights. The knights gan to commune, the knights gan to counsel; and to Octa they said full still: "We shall do thy will." Oaths they swore, that they would not deceive. It was on a night that the wind went right; forth went the knights at the midnight, and led forth Octa, and Ebissa, and Ossa; along the Thames they proceeded forth into the sea; forth they passed into Saxland. Their kindred came towards them with great flocks (forces); they marched over all the land, as to them was liefest; men gave them gifts and land; men gave them silver and gold. Octa bethought him what he might do; he thought to come hither, and avenge his father's wounds. They procured a host of innumerable folk; to the sea they proceeded with great threats; they came to Scotland; soon they pushed on land, and greeted it with fire; the Saxons were cruel, the Scots they slew; with fire they down laid thirty hundred towns; the Scots they slew, many and innumerable.

The tidings came to Uther the king. Uther was exceeding woe, and wonderfully grieved, and sent in to Loeneis, to his dear friends; and greeted Loth, his son-in-law, and bade him be in health, and ordered him to take in his own hand all his royal land; knights and freemen, and freely hold them, and lead them in a host, as the laws are in the land. And he ordered his dear knights to be obedient to Loth, with loving looks, as if he were sovereign. For Loth was very good knight, and had held many fight, and he was liberal to every man, he delivered to him the government of all this land. Octa held much war, and Loth often fought with him, and oft he gained possessions, and oft he them lost. The Britons had mickle mood, and immoderate pride, and were void of dread, on account of the king's age; and looked very contemptuously on Loth the earl, and did very evilly all his commands, and were all two counsels—their care was the more! This was soon said to the sick king, that his high men Loth all despised.

Now will I tell thee, in this history, how Uther the king disposed himself. He said that he would go to his host, and see with his eyes who would there do well. He caused there to be made a good horse-litter, and caused an army to be assembled over all his kingdom; that each man by (on pain of) his life should come to him quickly, by their lives and by their limbs, to avenge the king's shame.—"And if there is any man, who will not come hastily, I will speedily destroy him, either slay either hang." All full soon to the court (or to the army) they came; durst there none remain, nor the fat nor the lean. The king forthright took all his knights, and marched him anon to the town of Verulam; about Verolam's town came him Uther Pendragon; Octa was within with all his men. Then was Verulam a most royal town; Saint Alban was there slain, and deprived of lifeday; the burgh was subsequently destroyed, and much folk there was slain. Uther lay without, and Octa within. Uther's army advanced to the wall; the powerful thanes fiercely assaulted it; they might not of the wall one stone detach, nor with any strength the wall injure.

Well blithe was then Hengest's son Octa, when he saw the Britons recede from the walls, and go sorrowful again to their tents. Then said Octa to his comrade Ebissa: "Here is come to Verulam Uther, the lame man, and will with us here fight in his litter; he weened with his crutch to thrust us down!

But to-morrow when it is day, the people shall arise, and open our castle-gate, and this realm we shall all win; shall we never lie here for one lame man! Out we shall ride upon our good steeds, and advance to Uther, and fell his folk; for all they are fated (shall die) that hither are ridden; and take the lame man, and lay in our bonds, and hold the wretch until that he dies; and so men shall leach his limbs that are sore, and heal his bones with bitter steel!" Thus spake him Octa with his comrade Ebissa; but all it happened otherwise than they weened. On the morrow when it dawned, they unfastened the doors; up arose Octa, Ebissa, and Ossa, and ordered their knights to prepare them for fight, to undo their broad gates, and unfasten the burgh. Octa rode him out, and much folk followed after him; with his bold warriors there he bale found! Uther saw him this, that Octa approached to them, and thought to fell his host to the ground.

Then called Uther with quick voice there: "Where be ye, Britons, my bold thanes? Now is come that day, that the Lord may help us;—that Octa shall find, in that he threatened me to bind. Think of your ancestors, how good they were in fight; think of the worship that I have to you well given; nor let ye ever this heathen enjoy your homes, or these same raging hounds possess your lands. And I will pray to the Lord who formed the daylight, and to all the hallows, that sit high in heaven, that I on this field may be succoured. Now march quickly to them,—may the Lord aid you, may the all-ruling God protect my thanes!" Knights gan to ride, spears gan to glide, and broad spears brake, shivered shields—helms there were severed, men fell! The Britons were bold, and busy in fight, and the heathen hounds fell to the ground. There was slain Octa, Ebissa, and Ossa; there seventeen thousand sunk into hell; and many there escaped toward the north end. And all the daylight Uther's knights slew and captured all that they came nigh; when it was even, then was it all won. Then sung the soldiers with great strength, and said these words in their merry songs: "Here is Uther Pendragon come to Verulam's town; and he hath so beaten Octa, and Ebissa, and Ossa, and given them in the land laws most strong, so that men may tell their kin in story, and thereof make songs in Saxland!" Then was Uther blithe, and exceeding glad, and spake with his people, that was dear to him in heart, and these words said Uther the old: "Saxish men have accounted me for base; my sickness they twitted me with their scornful words, because I was led here in a horse-litter; and said that I was dead, and my folk asleep. And now is much wonder come to this realm, that now this dead king hath killed these quick; and some he hath them driven forth with the weather! Now hereafter be done the Lord's will!"

The Saxish men fled exceeding fast, that had aside retreated from the fight; forth they gan proceed into Scotland; and took to them for king Colgrim the fair. He was Hengest's relation, and dearest of men to him; and Octa loved him, the while that he lived. The Saxish men were greatly discouraged, and proceeded them together into Scotland; and they made Colgrim the fair for king, and assembled a host, wide over the land, and said that they would with their wicked craft in Winchester town kill Uther Pendragon. Alas, that it should so happen! Now said the Saxish men in their communing together: "Take we six knights, wise men and active, and skilful spies, and send we to the court, in almsman's guise, and dwell in the court, with the high king, and every day pass through all the people; and go to the king's dole, as if they were infirm, and among the poor people hearken studiously if man might with craft, by day or by night, in Winchester's town come to Uther Pendragon, and kill the king with murder;"—then were (would be) their will wholly accomplished, then were they careless of Constantine's kin. Now went forth the knights all by daylight, in almsman's clothes—knights most wicked—to the king's court —there they harm wrought. They went to the dole, as if they were infirm, and hearkened studiously of the king's sickness, how men might put the king to death. Then met they with a knight, from the king he came forth-right; he was Uther's relation, and dearest of men to him. These deceivers, where they sate along the street, called to the knight with familiar words: "Lord, we are wretched men in this world's realm; whilom we were in land accounted for good men, until Saxish men set us adown, and bereaved us of all, and our possessions took from us. Now we sing beads (prayers) for Uther the king; each day in a meal our meat faileth; cometh never in our dish neither flesh nor any fish, nor any kind of drink but a draught of water, but water clean—therefore we are thus lean."

The knight heard this; back he went forth-right, and came to the king, where he lay in chamber, and said to the king: "Lord, be thou in health! Here out sit six men, alike in hue; all they are companions, and clothed with hard hair-cloth. Whilom they were in this world's realm goodly thanes,

and filled with goods; now have Saxish men set them to ground,
so that they are in the world accounted for wretches; they have
not at board but bread alone, nor for their drink but water
draughts. Thus they lead their life in thy people, and bid their
beads, that God will let thee long live." Then quoth Uther the
king: "Let them come in hither; I will them clothe, and I will
them feed, for the love of my Lord, the while that I live." The
treacherous men came into the chamber; the king caused them
to be fed, the king caused them to be clothed, and at night each
laid them on his bed. And each on his part aspied earnestly
how they might kill the king with murder; but they might not
through anything kill Uther the king, nor through any craft
might come to him.

Then happened it on a time, the rain it gan to pour; then
called there a leech, where he lay in the chamber, to a chamber-
knight, and ordered him forth-right to run to the well, that was
near the hall, and set there a good swain, to keep it from the
rain.—"For the king may not enjoy no draught in the world
but the cold well stream, that is to him pleasant; that is for his
sickness best of all draughts." This speech forth-right heard
these six knights—to harm they were prompt—and went
out by night forth to the well—there they harm wrought.
Out they drew soon fair phials, filled with poison, of all liquids
bitterest; six phials full they poured in the well; then was
the well anon with poison infected. Then were full blithe
the traitors in their life, and forth they went; they durst
not there remain. Then came there forth-right two chamber-
knights; they bare in their hands two bowls of gold. They
came to the well, and filled their bowls; back they gan wend
to Uther the king, forth into the chamber, where he lay in
bed.—"Hail be thou, Uther! Now we are come here, and we
have brought thee, what thou ere bade, cold well water; receive
it with joy." Up arose the sick king, and sate on his bed; of the
water he drank, and soon he gan to sweat; his heart gan to
weaken, his face began to blacken, his belly gan to swell, the
king gan to burst. There was no other hap, but there was
Uther the king dead; and all they were dead, who drank of the
water.

When the attendants saw the calamity of the king, and of the
king's men, who with poison were destroyed, then went to the well
knights that were active, and destroyed the well with painful
labour, with earth and with stones made a steep hill. Then
the people took the dead king—numerous folk—and forth him

carried the stiff-minded men into Stonehenge, and there buried him, by his dear brother; side by side there they lie both.

Then came it all together, that was highest in the land, earls and barons, and book-learned men; they came to London, to a mickle husting, and the rich thanes betook them all to counsel, that they would send messengers over sea into Britanny, after the best of all youth that was in the worlds-realm in those days, named Arthur the strong, the best of all knights; and say that he should come soon to his kingdom; for dead was he Uther Pendragon, as Aurelie was ere, and Uther Pendragon had no other son, that might after his days hold by law the Britons, maintain with worship, and rule this kingdom. For yet were in this land the Saxons settled; Colgrim the keen, and many thousands of his companions, that oft made to our Britons evil injuries. The Britons full soon took three bishops, and seven riders, strong in wisdom; forth they gan proceed into Britanny, and they full soon came to Arthur.—" Hail be thou, Arthur, noblest of knights! Uther thee greeted, when he should depart, and bade that thou shouldest thyself in Britain hold right laws, and help thy folk, and defend this kingdom, as good king should do; defeat thy enemies, and drive them from land. And he prayed the mild Son of God to be to thee now in aid, that thou mightest do well, and the land receive from God. For dead is Uther Pendragon, and thou art Arthur, his son; and dead is the other, Aurelie his brother." Thus they gan tell, and Arthur sate full still; one while he was wan, and in hue exceeding pale; one while he was red, and was moved in heart. When it all brake forth, it was good that he spake; and thus said he there right, Arthur the noble knight: " Lord Christ, God's Son, be to us now in aid, that I may in life hold God's laws! "

Arthur was fifteen years old, when this tiding was told to him, and all they were well employed, for he was much instructed. Arthur forth-right called his knights, and bade every man get ready his weapons, and saddle their horses very speedily, for he would go to this Britain. To the sea proceeded the good thanes, at Michael's mount, with a mickle host; the sea set them on the strand, at Southampton they came ashore. Forth he gan ride, Arthur the powerful, right to Silchester; there it seemed good to him; there was the host of Britons boldly assembled. Great was the bliss when Arthur came to the burgh; then was blast of trumpets, and men most glad; there they raised to be king Arthur the young.

When Arthur was king—hearken now a marvellous thing;—
he was liberal to each man alive, knight with the best, wondrously
keen! He was to the young for father, to the old for comforter,
and with the unwise wonderfully stern; wrong was to him
exceeding loathsome, and the right ever dear. Each of his
cupbearers, and of his chamber-thanes, and his chamber-
knights, bare gold in hand, to back and to bed, clad with gold
web. He had never any cook, that he was not champion most
good; never any knight's swain, that he was not bold thane!
The king held all his folk together with great bliss; and with
such things he overcame all kings, with fierce strength and with
treasure. Such were his qualities, that all folk it knew. Now
was Arthur good king; his people loved him; eke it was known
wide, of his kingdom.

The king held in London a mickle husting; thereto were
arrived all his knights, rich men and poor, to honour the king.
When that it was all come, a numerous folk; up arose Arthur
noblest of kings, and caused to be brought before him reliques
well choice; and thereto the king gan soon to kneel thrice;—
his people knew not what he would pronounce. Arthur held
up his right hand, an oath he there swore, that never by
his life, for no man's lore, should the Saxons become blithe
in Britain, nor be landholders, nor enjoy worship; but he
would drive them out, for they were at enmity with him.
For they slew Uther Pendragon, who was son of Constance;
so they did the other, Aurelie, his brother; therefore they
were in land loathest of all folk. Arthur forth-right took his
wise knights; were it lief to them were it loath to them, they
all swore the same oath, that they would truly hold with
Arthur, and avenge the King Uther, whom the Saxons killed
here. Arthur sent his writs wide over his land, after all the
knights that he might obtain; that they full soon should come
to the king, and he would in land lovingly maintain them;
reward them with land, with silver and with gold. Forth went
the king with a numerous host; he led a surprising multitude,
and marched right to York. There he lay one night; on the
morrow he proceeded forth-right where he knew Colgrim to be,
and his comrades with him.

Since Octa was slain, and deprived of life-day, who was
Hengest's son, out of Saxland come, Colgrim was the noblest
man that came out of Saxland, after Hengest, and Hors, his
brother, and Octa, and Ossa, and their companion Ebissa. At
that day Colgrim ruled the Saxons by authority, led and coun-

selled, with fierce strength; mickle was the multitude that marched with Colgrim! Colgrim heard tiding of Arthur the king, that he came toward him, and would do to him evil. Colgrim bethought him what he might do, and assembled his host over all the North land. There came together all the Scottish people; Peohtes and Saxons joined them together, and men of many kind followed Colgrim. Forth he gan to march with an immense force, against Arthur, noblest of kings; he thought to kill the king in his land, and fell his folk to the ground, and set all this kingdom in his own hand, and fell to the ground Arthur the young. Forth marched Colgrim, and his army with him, and proceeded with his host until he came to a water; the water is named Duglas; people it destroyed!

There came Arthur against him, ready with his fight; on a broad ford the hosts them met; vigorously their brave champions attacked; the fated fell to the ground! There was much blood shed, and woe there was rife; shivered shafts; men there fell! Arthur saw that; in mood he was uneasy; Arthur bethought him what he might do, and drew him backward on a broad field. When his foes weened that he would fly, then was Colgrim glad, and all his host with him; they weened that Arthur had with fear retreated there, and passed over the water, as if they were mad. When Arthur saw that, that Colgrim was so nigh to him, and they were both beside the water, thus said Arthur, noblest of kings: " See ye not, my Britons, here beside us, our full foes—Christ destroy them!— Colgrim the strong, out of Saxland? His kin in this land killed our ancestors; but now is the day come, that the Lord hath appointed, that he shall lose the life, and lose his friends, or else we shall be dead; we may not see him alive! The Saxish men shall abide sorrow, and we avenge worthily our friends." Up caught Arthur his shield, before his breast, and he gan to rush as the howling wolf, when he cometh from the wood, behung with snow, and thinketh to bite such beasts as he liketh. Arthur then called to his dear knights: " Advance we quickly, brave thanes! all together towards them; we all shall do well, and they forth fly, as the high wood, when the furious wind heaveth it with strength! " Flew over the wealds thirty thousand shields, and smote on Colgrim's knights, so that the earth shook again. Brake the broad spears, shivered shields; the Saxish men fell to the ground! Colgrim saw that, therefore he was woe—the fairest man of all that came out of Saxland. Colgrim gan to flee, exceeding quickly; and his horse bare him

with great strength over the deep water, and saved him from
death. The Saxons gan to sink—sorrow was given to them!
Arthur hastened speedily to the water, and turned his spear's
point, and hindered to them the ford; there the Saxons were
drowned, full seven thousand. Some they gan wander, as the
wild crane doth in the moorfen, when his flight is impaired, and
swift hawks pursue after him, and hounds with mischief meet
him in the reeds; then is neither good to him, nor the land nor
the flood; the hawks him smite, the hounds him bite, then is the
royal fowl at his death-time! Colgrim fled him over the fields
quickly, until he came to York, riding most marvellously; he
went into the burgh, and fast it inclosed; he had within ten
thousand men, burghers with the best; that were beside him.
Arthur pursued after him with thirty thousand knights, and
marched right to York with folk very numerous, and besieged
Colgrim at York, who defended it against him.

Seven nights therebefore Baldolf the fair, Colgrim's brother,
was gone southward, and lay by the sea-side, and abode Childric.
Childric was in those days a kaiser of powerful authority; the
land in Alemaine was his own. When Baldolf heard, where
he lay by the sea, that Arthur had inclosed Colgrim in York,
Baldolf had assembled seven thousand men, bold fellows, who
by the sea lay; they took them to counsel, that back they
would ride, and leave Childric, and proceed into York, and
fight with Arthur, and destroy all his people. Baldolf swore
in his anger, that he would be Arthur's bane, and possess all
this realm, with Colgrim his brother. Baldolf would not wait
for the kaiser Childric, but thence he marched forth, and drew
him forth right north, from day to day, with his bold folk,
until he came into a wood, into a wilderness, full seven miles
from Arthur's host. He had thought by night with seven
thousand knights to ride upon Arthur, and fell his folk, and
himself kill.

But all it otherwise happened, other than he weened; for
Baldolf had in his host a British knight; he was Arthur's relative,
named Maurin. Maurin went aside to the wood, through woods
and through fields, until he came to Arthur's tents; and thus
said soon to Arthur the king: " Hail be thou, Arthur, noblest
of kings! I am hither come; I am of thy kindred. Here is
Baldolf arrived with warriors most hardy, and thinketh in this
night to slay thee and thy knights, to avenge his brother, who
is greatly discouraged; but God shall prevent him, through his
mickle might. And send now forth Cador, the Earl of Cornwall,

and with him bold knights, good and brave, full seven hundred good thanes; and I will counsel them, and I will lead them, how they may Baldolf slay as if a wolf." Forth went Cador and all these knights, so that they came aside where Baldolf lay in tents; they advanced to him on each side; they slew, they captured all that they came nigh;—there were killed nine hundred all out told.

Baldolf was gone aside to save himself, and fled through the wilderness, wondrously fast; and had his dear men with sorrow deserted; and fled him so far north, that he came so forth, where Arthur lay on the weald, with his powerful host, all about York—king most surprising! Colgrim was within with the Saxish men, and Baldulf bethought him what he might do; with what kind of stratagem he might come within, into the burgh, to Colgrim his brother, who was to him the dearest of all men alive. Baldulf caused to be shaved to the bare skin his beard and his chin, and made him as a fool; he caused half his head to be shorn, and took him in hand a long harp. He could harp exceeding well in his childhood; and with his harp he went to the king's host, and gan there to play, and much game to make. Oft men him smote with wands most smart; oft men him struck as men do fool; each man that met him, greeted him with derision; so never any man knew of Baldulf's appearance, but that it were a fool come to the folk! So long he went upward, so long he went downward, that they were aware, who were there within, that it was Baldulf without, Colgrim's brother. They cast out a rope, and Baldulf grasped it fast, and they drew up Baldulf, so that he came within; with such kind of stratagem Baldulf came within. Then was Colgrim blithe, and all his knights with him, and greatly they gan to threaten Arthur the king. Arthur was beside, and saw this game, and wrathed himself wondrously much; and ordered anon all his brave folk to weapon them; he thought to win the burgh with strength.

As Arthur was about to assault the wall, then came there riding Patrick, the rich man, who was a Scottish thane, fair in his land; and thus began to call to the king anon: " Hail be thou, Arthur the king, noblest of Britons! I will tell thee new tiding, of the kaiser Childric, the furious and the powerful, the strong and the bold. He is in Scotland arrived in a haven, and the homes consumeth, and wieldeth all our land in his own hand. He hath a host brave; all the strength of Rome; he saith with his boast, when men pour to him the wine, that thou darest not in any spot his attacks abide, neither in field, nor in wood, nor in ever any place. And if thou him abidest, he will thee bind; destroy thy people, and possess thy land."

Oft was Arthur woe, but never worse than then; and he drew him backward, beside the burgh; called to counsel knights at need, barons and earls, and the holy bishops; and bade that they should him counsel, how he might in the realm with his army his honour maintain, and fight with Childric, the strong and the powerful, who hither would come, to help Colgrim. Then answered the Britons, that were there beside: "Go we right to London, and let him come after; and if he cometh riding, sorrow he shall abide; he himself and his host shall die!" Arthur approved all that his people counselled; forth he gan march until he came to London.

Colgrim was in York, and there he abode Childric. Childric gan proceed over the North end, and took in his hand a great deal of land. All Scotland he gave to a thane of his, and all Northumberland he set in the hand of his brother; Galloway and Orkney he gave to an earl of his; himself he took the land from Humber into London. He thought never more of Arthur to have mercy, unless he would become his man, Arthur, Uther's son.

Arthur was in London, with all the Britons; he summoned his forces over all this land, that every man, that good would grant to him, quickly and full soon to London should come. Then was England filled with harm; here was weeping and here was lament, and sorrow immoderate; mickle hunger and strife at every man's gate! Arthur sent over sea two good knights, to Howel his relation, who was to him dearest of men, who possessed Britanny, knight with the best; and bade him full soon, that he hither should come, sail to land, to help the people; for Childric had in hand much of this land, and Colgrim and Baldulf were come to him, and thought to drive Arthur the king out of the land; take from him his right, and his kingdom;—then were his kindred disgraced with shameful injury; their worship lost in this worlds-realm; then were it better for the king, that he were not born! Howel heard this, the highest of Britanny; and he gan to call his good knights anon, and bade them to horse exceeding speedily, and go into France, to the free knights, and should say to them that they should come, quickly and full soon, to Michael's Mount, with mickle strength, all who would of silver and of gold, win worship in this worlds-realm. To Poitou he sent his good thanes; and some toward Flanders, exceeding quickly; and to Touraine, two there proceeded; and into Gascony, knights eke good; and ordered them to come with strength toward Michael's Mount; and ere they went to flood (embarked), they should have gifts good, that they might the blither depart from their land, and with Howel the fair come to this land, to help Arthur, noblest of kings. Thirteen days were passed since the messengers came there; then advanced they toward the sea, as the hail doth from the welkin; and two hundred ships were there well prepared; men filled them with folk, and forth they voyaged; the wind and the weather stood after their will; and they came to land at Hamtone. Up leapt from the ships the furious men; bare to the land helms and burnies; with spears and with shields they covered all the fields. There was many a bold Briton that threat had raised; they threatened greatly, by their quick life, that they would greet Childric the powerful, the bold kaiser, with much harm there. And if he would not flee away, and toward Alemaine proceed, and if he would in the land with fight resist; with his bold people the barks abide; here they should leave what to them were dearest of all, their heads and hands, and their white helms; "and so they shall in this land lose their friends, and fall into hell—the heathen hounds!"

Arthur was in London, noblest of kings, and heard say sooth relation, that Howel the strong was come to land, forth-right to Hamtone, with thirty thousand knights, and with innumerable folk, that followed the king; Arthur towards him marched, with great bliss; with a mickle host, towards his relation. Together they came—bliss was among the folk—and they kissed and embraced, and spake familiarly; and anon forth-right assembled their knights. Then were there together two good armies; of whom Howel should command thirty thousand knights, and Arthur had in land forty thousand in hand. Forth-right they marched toward the North end, toward Lincoln night and day, that Childric the kaiser besieged. But he the yet had nought won; for there were within seven thousand men, brave men and active, by day and night.

Arthur with his forces marched toward the burgh; and Arthur fore-ordered his knights, by day and night, that they should proceed as still, as if they would steal; pass over the country, and cease any noise; horns and trumpets, all should be relinquished. Arthur took a knight, that was a brave man and active; and sent him to Lincoln to his dear men, and he said

to them in sooth, with mouth, that Arthur would come, noblest
of kings, at the midnight, and with him many a good knight.—
" And ye within, then be ye ware, that when ye hear the din, that
ye the gates unfasten; and sally out of the burgh, and fell your
foes; and smite on Childric, the strong and the powerful; and
we shall tell them British tales! "

It was at the midnight, when the moon shone right south,
Arthur with his host marched to the burgh; the folk was as still
as if they would steal; forth they proceeded until they saw
Lincoln. Thus gan he call, Arthur the keen man: "Where be
ye, my knights, my dear-worthy warriors? See ye the tents,
where Childric lieth on the fields; Colgrim and Baldulf, with
bold strength; the Alemainish folk, that us hath harmed, and
the Saxish folk, that sorrow to us promiseth; that all hath
killed the highest of my kin; Constance and Constantine, and
Uther, who was my father, and Aurelie Ambrosie, who was my
father's brother, and many thousand men of my noble kindred?
Go we out to them, and lay to the ground, and worthily avenge
our kin and their realm; and all together forth-right now ride
every good knight! " Then Arthur gan to ride, and the army
gan to move, as if all the earth would be consumed; and smote
in the fields among Childric's tents. That was the first man,
that there gan to shout—Arthur the noble man, who was
Uther's son—keenly and loud, as becometh a king: "Now aid us,
Mary, God's mild mother! And I pray her son, that he be to us
in succour! " Even with the words they turned their spears;
pierced and slew all that they came nigh. And the knights out
of the burgh marched against them (the enemy); if they fled
to the burgh, there they were destroyed; if they fled to the wood,
there they slaughtered them; come wherever they might come,
ever they them slew. It is not in any book indited, that ever
any fight were in this Britain, that mischief was so rife; for
folk it was most miserable, that ever came to the land! There
was mickle blood-shed, mischief was among the folk; death
there was rife; the earth there became dun!

Childric the kaiser had a castle here, in Lincoln's field, where
he lay within, that was newly wrought, and exceeding well
guarded; and there were with him Baldulf and Colgrim, and saw
that their folk suffered death. And they anon forth-right, on
with their burnies, and fled out of the castle, of courage bereft;
and fled forth-right anon to the wood of Calidon. They had
for companions seven hundred riders; and they left forty
thousand slain, and deprived of life-day, felled to the ground;

Alemainish men, with mischief destroyed, and the Saxish men,
brought to the ground!

Then saw Arthur, noblest of kings, that Childric was flown,
and into Calidon gone, and Colgrim and Baldulf with him were
gone into the high wood, into the high holm. And Arthur
pursued after with sixty thousand knights of British people; the
wood he all surrounded; and on one side they it felled, full
seven miles, one tree upon another, truly fast; on the other side
he surrounded it with his army, three days and three nights;—
that was to them mickle harm.

Then saw Colgrim, as he lay therein, that there was without
meat sharp hunger, and strife; nor they nor their horses help
had any. And thus called Colgrim to the kaiser: "Say me,
Lord Childric, sooth words; for what kind of thing lie we thus
herein? Why should we not go out, and assemble our host, and
begin fight with Arthur and with his knights? For better it is
for us on land with honour to lie, than that we thus here perish
for hunger; it grieveth us sore, to the destruction of the folk.
Either send we again and again, and yearn Arthur's peace, and
pray thus his mercy, and hostages deliver him, and make friendship with the free king." Childric heard this, where he lay
within the dyke, and he answered with sorrowful voice: " If
Baldulf it will, who is thine own brother, and more of our
comrades, who with us are here, that we pray Arthur's peace,
and make amity with him, after your will I will do it. For
Arthur is esteemed very noble man in land; dear to all his
men, and of royal kindred, all come of kings; he was Uther's
son. And oft it befalleth, in many kind of land, where the good
knights come to stern fight, that they who first gain, afterwards
they it lose. And thus to us now is befallen here, and eft to us
better will happen, if we may live." Soon forth-right answered
all the knights: " We all praise this counsel, for thou hast well
said!"

They took twelve knights, and sent forth-right, where he was
in tent, by the wood's end; and the one called anon with quick
voice: " Lord Arthur, thy peace! We would speak with thee;
hither the kaiser sent us, who is named Childric, and Colgrim
and Baldulf, both together. Now and evermore they pray thy
mercy; thy men they will become, and thy honour advance,
and they will give to thee hostages enow, and hold thee for
lord, as to thee shall be liefest of all, if they may depart hence
with life into their land; and bring evil tidings. For here
we have found sorrows of many kind; at Lincoln left our

dear relatives; sixty thousand men, that there are slain. And if it were to thee will in heart, that we might pass over sea with sail, we would nevermore eft come here; for here we have lost our dear relatives. So long as is ever, here come we back never!"

Then laughed Arthur, with loud voice:—"Thanked be the Lord, that all dooms wieldeth, that Childric the strong is tired of my land! My land he hath divided to all his knights; myself he thought to drive out of my country; hold me for base, and have my realm, and my kin all put to death, my folk all destroy. But of him it is happened, as it is of the fox, when he is boldest over the weald, and hath his full play, and fowls enow; for wildness he climbeth, and rocks he seeketh; in the wilderness holes to him worketh. Fare whosoever shall fare, he hath never any care; he weeneth to be of power the boldest of all animals. But when come to him the men under the hills, with horns, with hounds, with loud cries; the hunters there hollow, the hounds there give tongue, they drive the fox over dales and over downs, he fleeth to the holm, and seeketh his hole; in the furthest end in the hole he goeth; then is the bold fox of bliss all deprived, and men dig to him on each side; then is there most wretched the proudest of all animals! So was it with Childric, the strong and the rich; he thought all my kingdom to set in his own hand; but now I have driven him to the bare death, whether so (whatsoever) I will do, either slay or hang. Now will I give him peace, and let him speak with me; I will not him slay, nor hang, but his prayer I will receive. Hostages I will have of the highest of his men; their horses and weapons, ere they hence depart; and so they shall as wretches go to their ships; sail over sea to their good land, and there worthily dwell in their realm, and tell tidings of Arthur the king, how I them have freed, for my father's soul, and for my freedom solaced the wretches." Hereby was Arthur the king of honour deprived; was there no man so bold that durst him advise;—that repented him sore, soon thereafter!

Childric came from covert to Arthur the king; and he there became his man, with all his knights. Four-and-twenty hostages Childric there delivered; all they were chosen, and noble men born; they delivered their horses, and their burnies, spears and shields, and their long swords; all they relinquished that they there had. Forth they gan to march until they came to the sea, where their good ships by the sea stood. The wind stood at will, the weather most favourable, and they shoved from the strand ships great and long; the land they all left, and

floated with the waves, that no sight of land they might see.
The water was still, after their will; they let together their sails
glide, board against board, the men there discoursed and said
that they would return eft to this land, and avenge worthily
their relatives, and waste Arthur's land, and kill his folk, and
win the castles, and work their pleasure.

So they voyaged on the sea even so long, that they came
between England and Normandy; they veered their luffs, and
came toward land, so that they came full surely to Dartmouth
at Totnes; with much bliss they approached to the land. So
soon as they came on land, the folk they slew; the churls they
drove off, that tilled the earth there; the knights they hung,
that defended the land; all the good wives they sticked with
knives; all the maidens they killed with murder; and all the
learned men (clerics) they laid on embers. All the domestics (or
baser sort) they killed with clubs; they felled the castles, the
land they ravaged; the churches they consumed—grief was
among the folk!—the sucking children they drowned in the
water. The cattle that they took, all they slaughtered; to
their inns they carried it, and boiled it and roasted; all they
it took, that they came nigh. All day they sung of Arthur
the king, and said that they had won homes, that they should
hold in their power; and there they would dwell winter and
summer. And if Arthur were so keen, that he would come
to fight with Childric, the strong and the rich, they would
of his back make a bridge, and take all the bones of the noble
king, and tie them together with golden ties, and lay them in
the hall door, where each man should go forth, to the worship
of Childric, the strong and the rich! This was all their game,
for Arthur the king's shame; but all it happened in other
wise, soon thereafter; their boast and their game befell to themselves to shame; and so doth well everywhere the man that so
acteth.

Childric the kaiser won all that he looked on with eyes; he took
Somerset, and he took Dorset, and in Devonshire the folk all destroyed, and Wiltshire with hostility he greeted; he took all the
lands unto the sea strand. Then at the last, then caused he horns
and trumpets to be blown, and his host to be assembled, and
forth he would march, and Bath all besiege, and eke Bristol about
berow. This was their threat, ere they to Bath came. To Bath
came the kaiser, and belay the castle there; and the men within
bravely began; they mounted upon the stone walls, well
weaponed over all, and defended the place against Childric the

strong. There lay the kaiser, and Colgrim his companion, and Baldulf his brother, and many another.

Arthur was by the North, and knew nought hereof; he proceeded over all Scotland, and set it in his own hand; Orkney and Galloway, Man and Moray, and all the lands that lay thereto. Arthur it weened to be certain thing, that Childric had departed to his own land, and that he never more would come here. When the tidings came to Arthur the king, that Childric the kaiser was come to land, and in the South end sorrow there wrought, then said Arthur, noblest of kings: "Alas! alas! that I spared my foe! that I had not with hunger destroyed him in the wood, or with sword cut him all to pieces! Now he yields to me meed for my good deeds. But so held me the Lord, who formed the daylight, he shall therefore abide bitterest of all bales—hard games;—his bane I will be! And Colgrim and Baldulf both I will kill, and all their people shall suffer death. If the Ruler of Heaven will grant it, I will worthily avenge all his hostile deeds; if the life in my breast may last to me, and the Power that formed moon and sun will grant it to me, never shall Childric eft deceive me!"

Now called Arthur, noblest of kings:—"Where be ye, my knights, brave men and active! To horse, to horse, good warriors; and we shall march toward Bath speedily! Let high gallows be up raised, and bring here the hostages before our knights, and they shall hang on high trees!" There he caused to be destroyed four-and-twenty children, Alemainish men of very noble race.

Then came tidings to Arthur the king, that Howel, his relation, was sick lying in Clud—therefore he was sorry—and there he left him. Forth he gan to push exceeding hastily, until he beside Bath approached to a plain; there he alighted, and all his knights; and on with their burnies the stern men, and he in five divisions separated his army.

When he had duly set all, and it all beseemed, then he put on his burny, fashioned of steel, that an elvish smith made, with his excellent craft; he was named Wygar, the witty wright. His shanks he covered with hose of steel. Caliburn, his sword, he hung by his side; it was wrought in Avalon, with magic craft. A helm he set on his head, high of steel; thereon was many gemstone, all encompassed with gold; it was Uther's, the noble king's; it was named Goswhit, each other unlike. He hung on his neck a precious shield; its name was in British called Pridwen; therein was engraved with red gold tracings a precious image of God's mother. His spear he took in hand, that was named Ron. When he had all his weeds, then leapt he on his steed. Then might he behold, who stood beside, the fairest knight, that ever host should lead; never saw any man better knight none, than Arthur he was, noblest of race! Then called Arthur with loud voice: " Lo! where here before us the heathen hounds, who slew our ancestors with their wicked crafts; and they are to us in land loathest of all things. Now march we to them, and starkly lay on them, and avenge worthily our kindred, and our realm, and avenge the mickle shame by which they have disgraced us, that they over the waves should have come to Dartmouth. And all they are forsworn, and all they shall be destroyed; they shall be all put to death, with the Lord's assistance! March we now forward, fast together, even all as softly as if we thought no evil; and when we come to them, myself I will commence; foremost of all the fight I will begin. Now we shall ride, and over the land glide; and no man on pain of his life make noise, but fare quickly; the Lord us aid!" Then Arthur the rich man gan to ride; he proceeded over the weald, and Bath would seek.

The tiding came to Childric, the strong and the rich, that Arthur came with host all ready to fight. Childric and his brave men leapt them to horse, and grasped their weapons— they knew themselves to be hateful!

Arthur saw this, noblest of kings; he saw a heathen earl advance against him, with seven hundred knights, all ready to fight. The earl himself approached before all his troop, and Arthur himself rode before all his host. Arthur the bold took Ron in hand; he extended (couched) the stark shaft, the stiff-minded king; his horse he let run, so that all the earth dinned. His shield he drew to his breast—the king was incensed—he smote Borel the earl throughout the breast, so that the heart sundered. And the king called anon, " The foremost is dead! Now help us the Lord, and the heavenly queen, who the Lord bore!" Then called Arthur, noblest of kings: "Now to them! now to them! The commencement is well done!" The Britons laid on them, as men should do on the wicked; they gave bitter strokes with axes and with swords. There fell of Childric's men full two thousand, so that never Arthur lost ever one of his men; there were the Saxish men of all folk most wretched, and the Alemainish men most miserable of all people! Arthur with his sword wrought destruction; all that he smote at, it was soon destroyed! The king was all enraged as is the wild boar, when

he in the beech-wood meeteth many swine. Childric saw this,
and gan him to turn, and bent him over the Avon, to save himself. And Arthur approached to him, as if it were a lion, and
drove them to the flood; there many were slain; they sunk to
the bottom five-and-twenty hundred, so that all Avon's stream
was bridged with steel! Childric over the water fled, with
fifteen hundred knights; he thought forth to push, and sail over
the sea. Arthur saw Colgrim climb to the mount, retreat to
the hill that standeth over Bath; and Baldulf went after him,
with seven thousand knights; they thought on the hill to withstand nobly, defend them with weapons, and do injury to
Arthur.

When Arthur saw, noblest of kings, where Colgrim withstood,
and eke battle wrought, then called the king, keenly loud:
"My bold thanes, advance to the hills! For yesterday was
Colgrim of all men keenest, but now it is to him all as to the goat,
where he guards the hill; high upon the hill he fighteth with
horns, when the wild wolf approacheth toward him. Though
the wolf be alone, without each herd, and there were in a fold five
hundred goats, the wolf to them goeth, and all them biteth. So
will I now to-day Colgrim all destroy; I am the wolf and he is
the goat; the man shall die!" The yet called Arthur, noblest
of kings: "Yesterday was Baldulf of all knights boldest, but
now he standeth on the hill, and beholdeth the Avon, how the
steel fishes lie in the stream! Armed with sword, their life is
destroyed; their scales float like gold-dyed shields; there float
their fins, as if it were spears. These are marvellous things come
to this land; such beasts on the hill, such fishes in the stream!
Yesterday was the kaiser keenest of all kings; now is he become
a hunter, and horns him follow; he flieth over the broad weald;
his hounds bark; he hath beside Bath his hunting deserted;
from his deer he flieth, and we it shall fell, and his bold threats
bring to nought; and so we shall enjoy our rights gained."
Even with the words that the king said, he drew his shield high
before his breast; he grasped his long spear, his horse he gan
spur. Nigh all so swift as the fowl flieth, five-and-twenty thousand of brave men, mad under arms, followed the king; they
proceeded to the hill with great strength, and smote upon
Colgrim with exceeding smart strokes. And Colgrim them
there received, and felled the Britons to ground; in the foremost attack fell five hundred.

Arthur saw that, noblest of kings, and wrathed him
wondrously much; and thus gan to call Arthur, the noble man:

"Where be ye, Britons, my bold men! Here stand before us our foes all chosen; my good warriors, lay we them to the ground!" Arthur grasped his sword right, and he smote a Saxish knight, so that the sword that was so good at the teeth stopt; and he smote another, who was this knight's brother, so that his helm and his head fell to the ground; the third blow he soon gave, and a knight in two clave. Then were the Britons greatly emboldened, and laid on the Saxons laws (blows) most strong with their long spears and with swords most strong; so that the Saxons there fell, and made their death-time, by hundreds and hundreds sank to the ground, by thousands and thousands fell there ever on the ground! When Colgrim saw where Arthur came toward him, Colgrim might not for the slaughtered flee on any side; there fought Baldulf beside his brother. Then called Arthur with loud voice: "Here I come, Colgrim! to the realm we two shall reach; now we shall divide this land, as shall be to thee loathest of all!" Even with the words that the king said, his broad sword he up heaved, and hardily down struck, and smote Colgrim's helm, so that he clove it in the midst, and clove asunder the burny's hood, so that it (the sword) stopt at the breast. And he smote toward Baldulf with his left hand, and struck off the head, forth with the helm.

Then laughed Arthur, the noble king, and thus gan to speak with gameful words: "Lie thou there, Colgrim; thou wert climbed too high; and Baldulf, thy brother, lie by thy side; now set I all this kingdom in your own hands; dales and downs, and all my good folk! Thou climbed on this hill wondrously high, as if thou wouldst ascend to heaven; but now thou shalt to hell, and there thou mayest know much of thy kindred. And greet thou there Hengest, that was fairest of knights, Ebissa, and Ossa, Octa, and more of thy kin, and bid them there dwell winter and summer; and we shall here in land live in bliss; pray for your souls, that happiness never come to them; and here shall your yones lie, beside Bath!"

Arthur, the king, called Cador, the keen;—of Cornwall he was earl, the knight was most keen:—"Hearken to me, Cador, thou art mine own kin. Now is Childric flown, and awayward gone; he thinketh with safety again to come hither. But take of my host five thousand men, and go forth-right, by day and by night, until thou come to the sea, before Childric; and all that thou mayest win, possess it with joy; and if thou mayest with evil kill there the kaiser, I will give thee all Dorset to meed." All as the noble king these words had said, Cador

sprang to horse, as spark it doth from fire; full seven thousand
followed the earl. Cador the keen, and much of his kindred,
proceeded over wealds, and over wilderness, over dales and
over downs, and over deep waters. Cador knew the way
that toward his country lay, by the nearest he proceeded full
surely right toward Totnes, day and night, until he came there
forth-right, so that Childric never knew any manner of his
coming. Cador came to the country before Childric, and caused
to advance before him all the folk of the land; churls full
sagacious, with clubs exceeding great, with spears and with
great staves, chosen for the purpose; and placed them all clean
into the ships' holds, and ordered them there to stoop low,
that Childric were not aware of them; and when his folk came,
and in would climb, to grasp their bats, and bravely on smite;
with their staves and with their spears to murder Childric's host.
The churls did all, as Cador them taught. To the ships proceeded the valiant churls; in every ship a hundred and half.
And Cador the keen withdrew, in toward a wood high, five
miles from the place where the ships stood; and hid him a while,
wondrously still. And Childric soon approached, over the
weald; and would flee to the ships, and push from land. So
soon as Cador saw this, who was the earl keen, that Childric was
in land, between him and the churls, then called Cador, with
loud voice: " Where be ye, knights, brave men and active?
Bethink ye what Arthur, who is our noble king, at Bath besought
us, ere we went from the host. Lo! where Childric wendeth,
and will flee from the land; and thinketh to pass to Alemaine,
where his ancestors are; and will obtain an army, and eft come
hither, and will fare in hither; and thinketh to avenge Colgrim,
and Baldulf, his brother, who rest at Bath. But he never shall
abide the day; he shall not, if we may prevent him! "
Even with the speech, that the powerful earl spake, and
promptly he gan ride, that was stern in mood; the warriors most
keen advanced out of the wood-shaw, and after Childric pursued,
the strong and the rich. Childric's knights looked behind them;
they saw over the weald the standards wind; approach over the
fields five thousand shields. Then became Childric careful in
heart, and these words said the powerful kaiser: " This is
Arthur the king, who will us all kill; flee we now quickly, and
into ship go, and voyage forth with the water, reck we never
whither! " When Childric the kaiser had said these words,
then gan he to flee exceeding quickly; and Cador the keen came
soon after him. Childric and his knights came to ship forth-

right; they weened to shove the strong ships from the land. The churls with their bats were there within; the bats they up heaved, and adown right swung; there was soon slain many a knight with their clubs; with their pitch-forks they felled them to ground, and Cador and his knights slew them behind. Then saw Childric, that it befell to them evilly; that all his mickle folk fell to the ground; now saw he there beside a hill exceeding great; the water floweth there under, that is named Teine; the hill is named Teinewic; thitherward fled Childric, as quickly as he might, with four-and-twenty knights. Then Cador saw, how it then fared there, that the kaiser fled, and toward the hill retreated; and Cador pursued after him, as speedily as he might, and came up to him, and overtook him soon. Then said Cador, the earl most keen: "Abide, abide, Childric! I will give thee Teinewic!" Cador heaved up his sword, and he Childric slew. Many that there fled, to the water they drew; in Teine the water, there they perished; Cador killed all that he found alive; and some they crept into the wood, and all he them there destroyed. When Cador had overcome them all, and eke all the land taken, he set peace most good, that thereafter long stood; though each man bare in hand rings of gold, durst never any man greet another evilly.

Arthur was forth marched into Scotland; for Howel lay in Clud, fast inclosed. The Scots had besieged him with their wicked crafts; and if Arthur were not the earlier come, then were Howel taken, and all his folk there slain, and deprived of life-day. But Arthur came soon, with good strength, and the Scots gan to flee far from the land, into Moray, with a mickle host. And Cador came to Scotland, where he Arthur found. Arthur and Cador proceeded into Clud, and found Howel there, with great bliss in health, of all his sickness whole he was become; great was the bliss that then was in the burgh! The Scots were in Moray, and there thought to dwell, and with their bold words made their boast, and said that they would rule the realm, and Arthur there abide, with bold strength; for Arthur durst never for his life come there. When Arthur heard, void of fear, what the Scots had said with their scornful words, then said Arthur, noblest of kings: "Where art thou, Howel, highest of my kindred, and Cador the keen, out of Cornwall? Let the trumpets blow, and assemble our host, and at the midnight we shall march forth-right toward Moray, our honour to win. If the Lord will it, who shaped the daylight, we shall them tell sorrowful tales, and fell their boast, and themselves kill." At the midnight Arthur forth-right arose; horns men gan to blow with loud sound; knights gan arise, and stern words to speak. With a great army he marched into Moray; forth gan press thirteen thousand in the foremost flock, men exceeding keen. Afterwards came Cador, the Earl of Cornwall, with seventeen thousand good thanes. Next came Howel, with his champions exceeding well, with one-and-twenty thousand noble champions. Then came Arthur himself, noblest of kings; with seven-and-twenty thousand followed them afterward; the shields there glistened, and light it gan to dawn.

The tidings came to the Scots, there where they dwelt, how Arthur the king came toward their land, exceeding quickly, with innumerable folk. Then were they fearfullest, who ere were boldest, and gan to flee exceeding quickly into the water, where wonders are enow! That is a marvellous lake, set in middle-earth, with fen, and with reed, and with water exceeding broad; with fish, and with fowl, with evil things! The water is immeasurably broad; nikers therein bathe; there is play of elves in the hideous pool. Sixty islands are in the long water; in each of the islands is a rock high and strong; there nest eagles, and other great fowls. The eagles have a law by every king's day; whensoever any army cometh to the country, then fly the fowls far into the sky, many hundred thousands, and mickle fight make. Then is the folk without doubt, that sorrow is to come to them from people of some kind, that will seek the land. Two days or three thus shall this token be, ere foreign men approach to the land. Yet there is a marvellous thing to say of the water; there falleth in the lake, on many a side, from dales and from downs, and from deep valleys, sixty streams, all there collected; yet never out of the lake any man findeth that thereout they flow, except a small brook at one end, that from the lake falleth, and wendeth very stilly into the sea. The Scots were dispersed with much misery, over all the many mounts that were in the water. And Arthur sought ships, and gan to enter them; and slew there without number, many and enow; and many a thousand there was dead, because all bread failed them. Arthur the noble was on the east side; Howel the good was on the south half; and Cador the keen guarded them by the north; and his inferior folk he set all by the west side. Then were the Scots accounted for sots, where they lay around the cliffs, fast inclosed; there were sixty thousand with sorrow destroyed.

Then was come into haven the King of Ireland; twelve miles

from Arthur, where he lay with an army, to help the Scots, and
Howel to destroy. Arthur heard this, noblest of kings, and
took one host of his, and thitherward marched; and found the
King Gillomar, who was come there to land. And Arthur
fought with him, and would give him no peace (quarter), and
felled the Irish men exceedingly to the ground. And Gillomar
with twelve ships departed from the land, and proceeded to
Ireland, with harm most strong. And Arthur in the land slew
all that he found; and afterwards he went to the lake, where
he left his relation Howel the fair, noblest of Britain, except
Arthur, noblest of kings. Arthur found Howel, where he was
by the haven, by the broad lake, where he had abode. Then
rejoiced greatly the folk in the host, of Arthur's arrival, and of
his noble deeds; there was Arthur forth-right, two days and two
nights. The Scots lay over the rocks, many thousands dead,
with hunger destroyed, most miserable of all folk!

On the third day, it gan to dawn fair; then came toward the
host all that were hooded, and three wise bishops, in book well
learned; priests and monks, many without number; canons
there came, many and good, with all the reliques that were
noblest in the land, and yearned Arthur's peace, and his compassion. Thither came the women, that dwelt in the land;
they carried in their arms their miserable children; they wept
before Arthur wondrously much, and their fair hair threw to
the earth; cut off their locks, and there down laid at the king's
feet, before all his people; set their nails to their face, so that
afterwards it bled. They were naked nigh (nearly) all clean;
and sorrowfully they gan to call to Arthur the king, and together
thus said, where they were in affliction: " King, we are on
earth most wretched of all folk; we yearn thy mercy, through
the mild God! Thou hast in this land our people slain, with
hunger and with strife, and with many kind of harms; with
weapon, with water, and with many mischiefs our children made
fatherless and deprived of comfort. Thou art a Christian man,
and we are also; the Saxish men are heathen hounds. They
came to this land, and this folk here killed; if we obeyed them,
that was because of our harm, for we had no man that might
accord us with them. They did us much woe, and thou dost
to us also; the heathens us hate, and the Christians make
us sorrowful;—whereto and what shall become of us!"—quoth
the women to the king. " Give us yet the men alive, who
lie over these rocks; and if thou givest grace to this multitude, thy honour will be the greater, now and evermore. Lord

Arthur our king, loosen our bonds! Thou has taken (conquered) all this land, and all this folk is overcome; we are under thy foot; in thee is all the remedy."

Arthur heard this, noblest of kings; this weeping and this lament, and immoderate sorrow; then took he to counsel, and had pity in heart; he found in his counsel to do what they him prayed; he gave them life, he gave them limb, and their land to hold. He caused the trumpets to be blown, and the Scots to be summoned; and they came out of the rocks to the ships; on every side approached toward land. They were greatly harmed by the sharp hunger; and oaths they swore, that they would not deceive; and they then gave hostages to the king, and all full soon became the king's men. And then they gan depart; the folk there separated, each man to the end, where he was dwelling; and Arthur there set peace, good with the best.

Then said Arthur: "Where art thou, Howel, my relation, dearest of men to me? Seest thou this great lake, where the Scots are harmed; seest thou these high trees, and seest thou these eagles fly? In this fen is fish innumerable. Seest thou these islands, that stand over this water?" Marvellous it seemed to Howel, of such a sight, and he wondered greatly by the water-flood; and thus there spake Howel, of noble race: "Since I was born man of my mother's bosom, saw I in no land things thus wonderful, as I here before me behold with eyes!" The Britons wondered wondrously much. Then spake Arthur, noblest of kings: "Howel, mine own relative, dearest to me of men, listen to my words, of a much greater wonder that I will tell to thee in my sooth speech. By this lake's end, where this water floweth, is a certain little lake, to the wonder of men! It is in length four-and-sixty palms; it is in measure in breadth five-and-twenty feet; five feet it is deep; elves it dug! Four-cornered it is, and therein is fish of four kinds, and each fish in his end where he findeth his kind; may there none go to other, except all as belongeth to his kind. Was never any man born, nor of so wise craft chosen, live he ever so long, that may understand it; what letteth (hindereth) the fish to swim to the others; for there is nought between but water clean!" The yet spake Arthur, noblest of kings: "Howel, in this land's end, nigh the sea-strand, is a lake exceeding great—the water is evil—and when the sea floweth, as if it would rage, and falleth in the lake exceeding quickly, the lake is never the more increased in water. But when the sea falleth in (ebbs), and the ground becomes fair, and in it is all in its old seat, then swelleth the lake, and the waves darken; out the waves there leap, exceeding great, flow out on the land, and the people soon terrify. If any man cometh there, that knoweth nought thereof, to behold the marvel by the sea-strand; if he turneth his face toward the lake, be he nought (never) so low born, full well he shall be saved; the water glideth him beside, and the man there remaineth easy; after his will he dwelleth there full still, so that he is not because of the water anything injured!" Then said Howel, noble man of Brittany: "Now I hear tell a wonderful story, and marvellous is the Lord that it all made!"

Then said Arthur, noblest of kings: "Blow ye my horns with loud noise, and say ye to my knights, that I will march forth-right." Trumpets there were blown, horns there resounded; bliss was in the host with the busy king; for each was solaced, and proceeded toward his land. And the king forbade them, by their bare life, that no man in the world should be so mad, nor person so unwise, that he should break his peace; and if any man did it, he should suffer doom. Even with the words the army marched; there sung warriors marvellous songs of Arthur the king, and of his chieftains, and said in song, to this world's end never more would be such a king as Arthur, through all things, king nor caiser, in ever any realm!

Arthur proceeded to York, with folk very surprising (numerous), and dwelt there six weeks with much joy. The burgh walls were broken and fallen down, that Childric all consumed, and the halls all clean. Then called the king a distinguished priest, Piram;—he was an exceeding wise man, and learned in book:—"Piram, thou art mine own priest, the easier it shall be for thee." The king took a rood, holy and most good, and gave to Piram in hand, and therewith very much land; and the archbishop's staff he there gave to Piram;—ere was Piram a good priest, now is he archbishop! Then bade him Arthur, noblest of kings, that he should arear churches, and restore the hymns, and take charge of God's folk, and rule them fair. And he bade all his knights to deem right (just) dooms; and the earth-tillers to take to their craft; and every man to greet other. And what man soever did worse than the king had ordered, he would drive him to a bare burning, and if it were a base man, he should for that hang. The yet spake Arthur, noblest of kings; ordered that each man who had lost his land by whatsoever kind of punishment he were bereaved, that he should come again, full quickly and full soon—the rich and the low— and should have eft his own, unless he were so foully con-

ditioned, that he were traitor to his lord, or toward his lord
forsworn, whom the king should deem lost (beyond the limit of
pardon). There came three brethren, that were royally born,
Loth, and Angel, and Urien;—well are such three men! These
three chieftains came to the king, and set on their knees before
the casier:—" Hail be thou, Arthur, noblest of kings, and thy
people with thee; ever may they well be! We are three
brethren, born of kings. All our rightful land is gone out of
our hand; for the heathen men have made us poor, and wasted
us all Leoneis, Scotland, and Moray. And we pray thee, for
God's love, that thou be to us in aid, and for thy great honour,
that thou be mild to us, and give us our rightful land; and we
shall love thee, and hold thee for lord, in each land-wise."
Arthur heard this, noblest of kings, how these three knights fair
besought him; he had compassion in heart, and be gan speak,
and said these words—best of all kings:—" Urien, become my
man; thou shalt to Moray again; thereof thou shalt be called
king of the land, and high in my court (or host), with thy forces.
And to Angel I set in hand Scotland altogether; to have it in
hand, and be king of the land, from the father to the son; thereof
thou shalt my man become. And thou, Loth, my dear friend
—God be to thee mild!—thou hast my sister to wife; the better
it shall be for thee. I give thee Leoneis, that is a land fair;
and I will lay (add) thereto lands most good, beside the Humber,
worth an hundred pounds. For my father Uther, the while
that he was king here, loved well his daughter, who was his
desire esteemed; and she is my sister, and sons she hath
twain; they are to me in land dearest of all children." Thus
spake Arthur the king. Then was Walwain a little child; so
was the other, Modred his brother. But alas! that Modred was
born; much harm therefore came! Arthur proceeded to
London, and with him his people; he held in the land a mickle
husting, and established all the laws that stood in his elders'
days; all the good laws that ere here stood; he set peace, he
set protection, and all freedoms.

From thence he marched to Cornwall, to Cador's territory;
he found there a maid extremely fair. This maiden's mother
was of Romanish men, Cador's relative; and the maid Cador on
him bestowed, and he received her fair, and softly her fed. She
was of noble race, of Romanish men; was in no land any maid
so fair, of speech and of deeds, and of manners most good; she
was named Wenhaver, fairest of women. Arthur took her to
wife, and loved her wondrously much; this maiden he gan wed,

and took her to his bed. Arthur was in Cornwall all the winter there; and all for Wenhaver's love, dearest of women to him.

When the winter was gone, and summer came there anon, Arthur bethought him what he might do, that his good folk should not lie there inert. He marched to Exeter, at the mid-feast (St. John Baptist?), and held there his husting of his noble folk, and said that he would go into Ireland, and win all the kingdom to his own hand; unless the King Gillomar the sooner came ere to him, and spake with him with good will, and yearned Arthur's peace, he would waste his land, and go to him evilly in hand, with fire and with steel work hostile game, and the land-folk slay, who would stand against him. Even with the words that the king said, then answered the folk, fair to the king: "Lord king, hold thy word, for we are all ready, to go and to ride over all at thy need." There was many a bold Briton that had boar's glances; heaved up their brows, enraged in their thought. They went toward their inns, knights with their men: they got ready burnies, prepared helms, they wiped their dear horses with linen cloths; they sheared, they shod— the men were bold! Some shaped (or shaved) horn; some shaped bone; some prepared steel darts; some made thongs, good and very strong; some bent spears, and made ready shields. Arthur caused to be bidden over all his kingdom, that every good knight should come to him forth-right, and every brave man should come forth-right anon; and whoso should remain behind, his limbs he should lose, and whoso should come gladly, he should become rich.

Seven nights after Easter, when men had fasted, then came all the knights to ship forth-right; the wind stood to them in hand (favourably), that drove them to Ireland. Arthur marched in the land, and the people destroyed; much folk he there slew, and he took cattle enow; and ever he ordered each man church-peace to hold. The tiding came to the king, who was lord of the land, that Arthur the king was come there, and much harm there wrought. He assembled all his people, over his kingdom; and his Irish folk marched to the fight, against Arthur the noble king. Arthur and his knights they weaponed them forth-right, and advanced against them, a numerous folk. Arthur's men were with arms all covered, the Irish men were nearly naked, with spears and with axes, and with sæxes exceeding sharp. Arthur's men let fly at them numerous darts, and killed the Irish folk; and greatly it felled; they might not this sustain, through any kind of thing, but fled away quickly, very many thousands. And Gillomar the king fled, and awayward drew, and Arthur pursued after him, and caught the king; he took by the hand the king of the land.

Arthur the noble sought lodging; in his mood it was the easier to him, that Gillomar was so nigh him. Now did Arthur, noblest of kings, very great friendship before all his folk; he caused the king to be clothed with each pride (richly); and eke by Arthur he sate, and eke with himself ate; with Arthur he drank wine—that to him was mickle unthank. Nevertheless when he saw that Arthur was most glad, then said Gillomar to him—in his heart he was sore: "Lord Arthur, thy peace! Give me limb and give me life, and I will become thy man, and deliver thee my three sons, my dear sons, to do all thy will. And yet I will do more, if thou wilt give me grace; I will deliver thee hostages exceeding rich, children some sixty, noble and most mighty. And yet I will more, if thou givest me grace; each year of my land seven thousand pounds; and send them to thy land, and sixty marks of gold. And yet I will more, if thou wilt give me grace; and all the steeds, with all their trappings, the hawks, and the hounds, and my rich treasures I give thee in hand, of all my land. And when thou hast this done, I will take the reliques of Saint Columkille, who did God's will, and Saint Brandan's head, that God himself hallowed, and Saint Bride's right foot, that is holy and most good, and reliques enow, that came out of Rome, and swear to thee in sooth, that I will thee not deceive; but I will love thee, and hold thee for lord, hold thee for high king, and myself be thy underling."

Arthur heard this, noblest of kings, and he gan laugh with loud voice, and he gan answer with gracious words: "Be now glad, Gillomar; be not thy heart sore; for thou art a wise man—the better therefore shall it be to thee, for ever one ought worthily a wise man to greet;—for thy wisdom shall it not be the worse for thee; much thou me offerest, the better it shall be to thee. Here forth-right, before all my knights, I forgive thee the more, all the half-part, of gold and of treasure; but thou shalt become my man, and half the tribute send each year into my land. Half the steeds, and half the weeds (garments), half the hawks, and half the hounds, that thou me offerest, I will relinquish to thee; but I will have the children of thy noble men, who are to them dearest of all; I may the better believe thee. And so thou shalt dwell in thy honour in thy kingdom, in thy right territory; and I will give to thee, that the king shall not do wrong to thee, unless he pay for it with his bare back!" Thus it said Arthur, noblest of kings. Then had he all Ireland all together in his own hand; and the king became his man, and delivered him his three sons.

Then spake Arthur to his good knights: "Go we to Iceland, and take we it in our hand." The host there marched, and to Iceland came. The king was named Ælcus, high man of the land; he heard the tiding of Arthur the king; he did all as a wiseman, and marched against him anon; anon forth-right, with sixteen knights; he bare in his hand a mickle wand (sceptre) of gold. So soon as he saw Arthur, he bent him on his knees, and quoth these words to him—the king was afraid: —"Welcome, sir Arthur! welcome, lord! Here I deliver thee in hand all together Iceland; thou shalt be my high king, and I will be thy underling. I will obey thee, as man shall do his master, and I will become here thy man, and deliver thee my dear son, who is named Escol; and thou shalt him honour (or reward), and dub him to knight, as thine own man. His mother I have to wife, the king's choice daughter of Russia. And eke each year I will give thee money, seven thousand pounds of silver and gold; and in every counsel be ready at thy need. This I will swear to thee, upon my sword; the relique is in the hilt, the noblest of this land; like as me shall like, will I never be false to thee!"

Arthur heard this noblest of kings. Arthur was winsome where he had his will, and he was exceeding stern with his enemies. Arthur heard the mild words of the monarch; he granted him all that he yearned; hostages and oaths, and all his proffers. Then heard say sooth words the King of Orkney, exceeding keen, who was named Gonwais, a heathen warrior, that Arthur the king would come to his land; with a mickle fleet sail to his country. Gonwais proceeded towards him, with his wise thanes, and set to Arthur in hand all Orkney's land, and two-and-thirty islands, that thither in lieth, and his homage, with much reverence. And he had (made) to him in covenant, before all his people, each year to wit, full sixty ships at his own cost to bring them to London, filled truly with good sea-fish. This covenant he confirmed, and hostages he found; and oaths he swore good, that he would not deceive. And afterwards he took leave, and forth he gan wend:—"Lord, have well good day! I will come when I may; for now thou art my lord, dearest of all kings."

When Arthur had done this, the yet he would more undertake;

he took his good writs, and sent to Gutlond; and greeted the King Doldanim, and bade him soon come to him, and himself become his man, and bring with him his two sons.—" And if thou wilt not that, do what thou wilt, and I will send thee sixteen thousand noble warriors, to thy mickle harm, who shall waste thy land, and slay thy people, and set the land as to them best seemeth, and thyself bind, and to me bring." The king heard this, the threat of the kaiser, and he speedily took his fair weeds, hounds and hawks, and his good horses; much silver, much gold; his two sons in his hand. And forth he gan wend to Arthur the king; and said these words Doldanim the good: " Hail be thou, Arthur, noblest of kings! Here I bring twain, my sons both; their mother is of king's race, she is mine own queen; I won her with spoil, out of Russia. Here I deliver thee my dear sons, and myself I will become thy man. And I will send thee tribute of my land; every year as thing bestowed, I will send thee into London seven thousand pounds. That I will swear, that I will never be false, but here I will become thy man—thy honour is the greater—so long as is ever, I will deceive thee never!"

Arthur took his messengers, and sent to Winetland, to Rumareth the king, and bade him know in haste, that he had in his hand Britain and Scotland, Gutland and Ireland, Orcany and Iceland. He ordered Rumareth to come, and bring him his eldest son; and if he would not do that, he would drive him from land; and if he might him capture, he would slay him or hang, and destroy all his land; his people exterminate. Rumareth heard this, the rich King of Winet; greatly he was afraid, all as the others were ere; loath to him were the tidings from Arthur the king. Nevertheless the King Rumareth hearkened counsels; he took his eldest son, and twelve good earls, and proceeded to Arthur the noble king, and sate at his feet, and gan him fair greet: " Hail be thou, Arthur, noblest of Britons! I hight Rumareth, the King of Winetland; enow I have heard declared of thy valour; that thou art wide known, keenest of all kings. Thou hast won many kingdom all to thine own hand; there is no king in land that may thee withstand, king nor kaiser, in ever any combat; of all that thou beginnest, thou dost thy will. Here am I to thee come, and brought thee my eldest son; here I set thee in hand myself and my kingdom, and my dear son, and all my people, my wife and my weeds, and all my possessions, on condition that thou give me protection against thy fierce attacks. And be thou my

high king, and I will be thy underling, and send thee to hand
five hundred pounds of gold; these gifts I will thee find, every
year."

Arthur granted him all that the king yearned, and afterwards
he held communing with his good thanes, and said that he would
return again into this land, and see Wenhaver, the comely queen
of the country. Trumpets he caused to be blown, and his army
to assemble; and to ship marched the thanes wondrous blithe.
The wind still stood them at will; weather as they would; blithe
they were all therefore; up they came to Grimesby. That
heard soon the highest of this land, and to the queen came
tiding of Arthur the king, that he was come in safety, and his
folk in prosperity. Then were in Britain joys enow! Here
was fiddling and song, here was harping among; pipes and trumps
sang there merrily. Poets there sung of Arthur the king, and
of the great honour, that he had won. Folk came in concourse of
many kind of land; wide and far the folk was in prosperity.
All that Arthur saw, all it submitted to him, rich men and poor,
as the hail that falleth; was there no Briton so wretched, that
he was not enriched!

Here man may tell of Arthur the king, how he afterwards
dwelt here twelve years, in peace and in amity, in all fairness.
No man fought with him, nor made he any strife; might never
any man bethink of bliss that were greater in any country than
in this; might never man know any so mickle joy, as was with
Arthur, and with his folk here!

I may say how it happened, wondrous though it seem. It
was on a yule-day, that Arthur lay in London; then were come
to him men of all his kingdoms, of Britain, of Scotland, of
Ireland, of Iceland, and of all the lands that Arthur had in hand;
and all the highest thanes, with horses and with swains. There
were come seven kings' sons, with seven hundred knights;
without the folk that obeyed Arthur. Each had in heart proud
thoughts, and esteemed that he were better than his companion.
The folk was of many a land; there was mickle envy; for the one
accounted himself high, the other much higher. Then blew men
the trumpets, and spread the tables; water men brought on
floor, with golden bowls; next soft clothes, all of white silk.
Then sate Arthur down, and by him Wenhaver the queen; next
sate the earls, and thereafter the barons; next the knights, all
as men them disposed. And the high-born men bare the meat
even forth-right then to the knights; then toward the thanes,
then toward the swains, then toward the porters, forth at the

board. The people became angered, and blows there were rife;
at first they threw the loaves, the while that they lasted, and the
silver bowls, filled with wine, and afterwards with the fists
approached to necks. Then leapt there forth a young man,
who came out of Winetland; he was given to Arthur to hold
as hostage; he was Rumareth's son, the King of Winet. Thus
said the knight there to Arthur the king: "Lord Arthur, go
quickly into thy chamber, and thy queen with thee, and thy
known relatives, and we shall decide this combat against these
foreign warriors." Even with the words he leapt to the board
where lay the knives before the sovereign; three knives he
grasped, and with the one he smote the knight in the neck,
that first began the same fight, so that his head on the floor fell
to the ground. Soon he slew another, this same thane's brother;
ere the swords came, seven he felled. There was fight exceeding great; each man smote other; there was much blood shed,
mischief was among the folk!

Then approached the king out of his chamber; with him an
hundred nobles, with helms and with burnies; each bare in his
right hand a white steel brand. Then called Arthur, noblest of
kings: "Sit ye, sit ye quickly, each man on his life! And
whoso will not that do, he shall be put to death. Take ye me
the same man, that this fight first began, and put withy on his
neck, and draw him to a moor, and put him in a low fen; there he
shall lie. And take ye all his dearest kin, that ye may find, and
strike off the heads of them with your broad swords; the women
that ye may find of his nearest kindred, carve ye off their noses,
and let their beauty go to destruction; and so I will all destroy
the race that he of came. And if I evermore subsequently hear,
that any of my folk, of high or of low, eft arear strife on account
of this same slaughter, there shall ransom him neither gold
nor any treasure, fine horse nor war-garment, that he should
not be dead, or with horses drawn in pieces—that is of each
traitor the law! Bring ye the reliques, and I will swear thereon;
and so, knights, shall ye, that were at this fight, earls and barons,
that ye will not it break." First swore Arthur, noblest of kings;
then swore earls, then swore barons; then swore thanes, then
swore swains, that they nevermore the strife would arear. Men
took all the dead, and carried them to burial-place. Afterwards
men blew the trumpets, with noise exceeding merry; were he
lief, were he loath, each there took water and cloth, and then
sate down reconciled to the board, all for Arthur's dread, noblest
of kings. Cupbearers there thronged, gleemen there sung;

harps gan resound, the people was in joy. Thus full seven nights was all the folk treated.

Afterwards it saith in the tale, that the king went to Cornwall; there came to him anon one that was a crafty workman, and met the king, and fair him greeted:—" Hail be thou, Arthur, noblest of kings! I am thine own man; through many land I have gone; I know of tree-works (carpentry) wondrous many crafts. I heard say beyond the sea new tidings, that thy knights gan to fight at thy board; on a midwinter's day many there fell; for their mickle mood wrought murderous play, and for their high lineage each would be within. But I will thee work a board exceeding fair, that thereat may sit sixteen hundred and more, all turn about, so that none be without; without and within, man against man. And when thou wilt ride, with thee thou mightest it carry, and set it where thou wilt, after thy will; and then thou needest never fear, to the world's end, that ever any moody knight at thy board may make fight, for there shall the high be even with the low." Timber was caused to be brought, and the board to be begun; in four weeks' time the work was completed.

At a high day the folk was assembled, and Arthur himself approached soon to the board, and ordered all his knights to the board forth-right. When all were seated, knights to their meat, then spake each with other, as if it were his brother; all they sate about; was there none without. Every sort of knight was there exceeding well disposed; all they were one by one (seated), the high and the low; might none there boast of other kind of drink other than his comrades, that were at the board. This was the same board that Britons boast of, and say many sorts of leasing, respecting Arthur the king. So doth every man, that another can love; if he is to him too dear, then will he lie, and say of him more honour than he is worth; no man is he so wicked, that his friend will not act well to him. Eft if among folk enmity areareth, in ever any time between two men, men can say leasing of the hateful one, though he were the best man that ever ate at board; the man that to him were loath, he can him last find! It is not all sooth nor all falsehood that minstrels sing; but this is the sooth respecting Arthur the king. Was never ere such king, so doughty through all things! For the sooth stands in the writings how it is befallen, from beginning to the end, of Arthur the king, no more nor less but as his laws (or acts) were.

But Britons loved him greatly, and oft of him lie, and say

many things respecting Arthur the king that never was transacted in this worlds-realm! Enow may he say, who the sooth
will frame, marvellous things respecting Arthur the king. Then
was Arthur most high, his folk most fair; so that there was no
knight well esteemed, nor of his manners (or deeds) much assured,
in Wales nor in England, in Scotland nor in Ireland, in Normandy
nor in France, in Flanders nor in Denmark, nor in ever any land,
that on this side of Muntgiu standeth, that were esteemed good
knight, nor his deeds accounted (brave or aught), unless he
could discourse of Arthur, and of his noble court, his weapons,
and his garments, and his horsemen; say and sing of Arthur
the young, and of his strong knights, and of their great might,
and of their wealth, and how well it them became. Then were
he welcome in this worlds-realm, come whereso he came, and
though he were at Rome; all that heard of Arthur tell, it
seemed to them great marvel of the good king!

And so it was foreboded, ere he were born; so said him
Merlin, that was a prophet great, that a king should come of
Uther Pendragon; that gleemen should make a board of this
king's breast, and thereto should sit poets most good, and eat
their will, ere they thence departed, and wine-draughts out
draw from this king's tongue, and drink and revel day and night;
this game should last them to the world's end.

And yet said him Merlin more that was to come, that all that
he looked on to his feet to him should bow. The yet said him
Merlin, a marvel that was greater, that there should be immoderate care (sorrow) at this king's departure. And of this
king's end will no Briton believe it, except it be the last
death, at the great doom, when our Lord judgeth all folk.
Else we cannot deem of Arthur's death; for he himself said to
his good Britons, south in Cornwall, where Walwain was slain,
and himself was wounded wondrously much, that he would fare
into Avalon, into the island, to Argante the fair; for she would
with balm heal his wounds; and when he were all whole, he
would soon come to them. This believed the Britons, that he
will thus come, and look ever when he shall come to his land, as
he promised them, ere he hence went.

Arthur was in the world wise king and powerful; good man
and peaceful; his men him loved. Knights he had proud, and
great in their mood; and they spake to the king of marvellous
thing; and thus the assemblage said to the high king: " Lord
Arthur, go we to the realm of France, and win all the land to
thine own hand; drive away all the French, and their king

slay; all the castles occupy, and set (garrison) them with Britons; and rule in the realm with fierce strength." Then answered Arthur, noblest of kings: " Your will I will do, but ere (previously) I will go to Norway; and I will lead with me Loth my brother-in-law; he who is Walwain's father, whom I well love. For new tidings are come from Norway, that Sichelin the king is there dead, his people has left; and he hath ere bequeathed all his kingdom to Loth. For the king is of all bereaved, son and eke daughter; and Loth is his sister's son—the better to him shall it befall—for I will make him new king in Norway, and well instruct him to govern well the people. And when I have done thus, I will afterwards come home, and get ready my army, and pass into France; and if the king withstandeth me, and will not yearn my peace, I will fell him with fight to the ground."

Arthur caused to be blown horns and trumpets, and caused to be summoned to the sea the Britons most bold. Ships he had good by the sea-flood; fifteen hundred pushed from the land, and flew along the sea, as if they had flight (wings), and bent their course into Norway, with bold strength. So soon as they came, they took haven; with mickle strength they stept (disembarked) on the realm. Arthur sent his messengers wide over the land, and ordered them to come soon, and have Loth for king; and if they would not that, he would slay them all. Then they took their messengers, the Norwegian earls, and sent to the king, and bade him back go—"And if thou wilt not depart, thou shalt have here sorrow and care; for so long as is ever, that shall never come to pass, that we shall raise a foreign man for king. For if Sichelin is departed (dead), here are others choice, whom we may by our will raise to be king. And this is the sooth; there is no other; either move thee awayward, and turn thee right homeward, either to-day a se'nnight, thou shalt have great fight."

The Norwegian earls betook them to counsel, that a king they would have of their own race; for all Sichelin's words they held to be folly.—" And so long as is ever, it shall not ever stand! But we shall take Riculf, who is an earl exceeding powerful, and raise him to be king—this is to us pleasing—and assemble our forces over all this country, and march towards Arthur, and defeat him with fight; and Loth we shall chase, and drive from land, or else we shall fell him with fight." They took Riculf, the Earl of Norway, and raised him to be king, though it were not to him by right; and they assembled their

host over Norway's land. And Arthur on his part, over the
land gan march; the land he through passed, and the burghs he
consumed; goods he took enow, and much folk he there slew.
And Riculf gan him ride against Arthur anon; together they
came, and fight they began. The Britons advanced to them—
woe there was rife! Swords exceeding long they plucked out
of sheath; heads flew on the field; faces paled; man against
man set shaft to breast; burnies there brake; the Britons were
busy; shivered shields, warriors there fell! And so all the
daylight lasted this great fight; moved they east, moved they
west, there was it the worse to the Norwegians; moved they
south, moved they north the Norwegians there fell. The
Britons were bold, the Norwegians they killed; the Norwegian
men there fell, five-and-twenty thousand; and Riculf the king
was there slain, and deprived of life-day; little there remained
of the folk; whoso had the wretched life, they yearned Arthur's
peace. Arthur looked on Loth, who was to him well dear, and
thus gan to him to call, Arthur the rich man: "Loth, wend
hither to me, thou art my dear relative. Here I give to thee
all this kingdom; of me thou shalt it hold, and have me for
protector."

Then was Walwain thither come, Loth's eldest son; from the
pope of Rome, who was named Supplice, who long had him
brought up, and made him knight. Full well was it bestowed,
that Walwain was born to be man, for Walwain was full
noble-minded, in each virtue he was good; he was liberal,
and knight with the best. All Arthur's folk was greatly emboldened, for Walwain the keen, that was come to the host;
and for his father Loth, who was chosen to be king. Then spake
Arthur with him, and bade him hold good peace, and bade him
love his peaceful people, and those that would not hold peace,
to fell them to ground.

The yet called Arthur, noblest of kings: "Where be ye, my
Britons? March ye now forth-right; prepare ye by the flood
my good ships." All did the knights as Arthur them ordered.
When the ships were ready, Arthur gan to the sea fare; with
him he took his knights, his Norwegian thanes, and his bold
Britons; and proceeded forth with the waves; and the doughty
king came into Denmark; he caused his tents to be pitched,
wide over the fields; trumpets he caused to be blown, and his
coming to be announced.

Then was in Denmark a king of much might; he was named
Æscil, the highest over the Danes; he saw that Arthur won all

that was to him in will. Æscil the king bethought him what he might do; loath it was to him to lose his dear people. He saw that with strength he might not stand against Arthur, with ever any combat. He sent greeting to Arthur the king; hounds and hawks, and horses exceeding good; silver and red gold, with prudent words. And yet he did more, Æscil the great; he sent to the highest of Arthur's folk, and prayed them to intercede for him with the noble king; that he might his man become, and deliver his son for hostage, and each year send him tribute of his land, a boat of gold and of treasure, and of rich garments, filled from the top to the bottom, in safety. And afterwards he would swear, that he would not prove false. Arthur heard this, noblest of kings, that Æscil, King of the Danes, would be his underling, without any fight, he and all his knights. Then was gladdened Arthur the rich, and thus answered with mild words: " Well worth the man, that with wisdom obtaineth to him peace and amity, and friendship to hold! When he seeth that he is bound with strength, and his dear realm ready all to destruction, with art he must slacken his odious bonds." Arthur ordered the king to come, and bring his eldest son; and he so did soon, the King of Denmark. Arthur's will soon he gan to fulfill; together they came, and were reconciled.

The yet said Arthur, noblest of kings: " Fare I will to France, with my mickle host. I will have of Norway nine thousand knights; and of Denmark I will lead nine thousand of the people; and of Orkney eleven hundred; and of Moray three thousand men; and of Galloway five thousand of the folk; and of Ireland eleven thousand; and of Britain my knights bold shall march before me, thirty thousand; and of Gutland I will lead ten thousand of the people; and of Frisland five thousand men; and of Little Britain Howel the bold; and with such folk France I will seek. And as I expect God's mercy, yet I will promise more; that of all the lands, that stand in my hand, I will order each brave man, that can bear his weapons, as he would wish to live, and have his limbs, that he go with me, to fight with Frolle, who is King of the French—slain he shall be!—he was born in Rome, of Romanish kin." Forth proceeded Arthur, until he came to Flanders; the land he gan conquer, and set it with his men. And next he marched thence, into Boulogne, and all Boulogne's land took it in his own hand.

And afterwards he took the way that in toward France lay. Then bade he his command to all his men, that fare wheresoever they should fare, they should take no whit, unless they might

it obtain with right; with just purchase, in the king's host.
Frolle heard that, where he was in France, of Arthur's speed
(success), and of all his deeds; and how he all won that he
looked on, and how it all to him submitted that he saw with
eyes; then was the King Frolle horribly afraid! At the same
time that this was transacted, the land of the French was named
Gaul; and Frolle was from Rome come into France, and each
year sent tribute of the land, ten hundred pounds of silver and
of gold. Now heard Frolle, who was chief of France, of the
great sorrow that Arthur did in the land. He sent messengers
soon the nearest way toward Rome, and bade the Romanish
folk advise them between, how many thousand knights they
thither would send, that he might the easier fight with Arthur,
and drive from the land Arthur the strong. Knights gan to ride
out of Rome-land; five-and-twenty thousand proceeded toward
France. Frolle heard this, with his mickle host, that the
Romanish folk rode toward the land. Frolle and his host
marched against them, so that they came together, keen men
and brave, of all the earth an immense force.

Arthur heard that, noblest of kings, and assembled his army,
and advanced against them. But never was there any king,
that was alive on earth, that ever ere on land such folk (multitude) commanded; for from all the kingdoms that Arthur had
in hand, forth he led with him all the keenest men, so that
he knew never in the world how many thousands there were.
So soon as they came together, Arthur and Frolle; hardily
they greeted all that they met. Knights most strong grasped
long spears, and rushed them together, with fierce strength.
All day there were blows most rife; the folk fell to ground, and
wrought destruction; the angry warriors sought the grass-bed;
the helms resounded, murmured earls; shields there shivered,
warriors gan fall. Then called Arthur, noblest of kings:
"Where be ye, my Britons, my bold thanes? The day it forth
goeth; this folk against us standeth. Cause we to glide to them
sharp darts enow, and teach them to ride the way toward
Rome!" Even with the words that Arthur then said, he sprang
forth on steed, as spark doth of fire. Fifty thousand were
following him; the hardy warriors rushed to the fight, and
smote upon Frolle, where he was in the flock, and brought him
to flight, with his mickle folk; there slew Arthur much folk and
innumerable.

Then fled into Paris Frolle the powerful, and fastened the
gates, with grief enow; and these words said, sorrowful in heart:

"Liefer were it to me, that I were not born!" Then were in Paris grievous speeches, full surely, sorrowful cries; burghmen gan to tremble; the walls they gan repair, the gates they gan to form; meat they took, all that they came nigh; on each side they carried it to the burgh; thither came they all, that held with Frolle. Arthur heard that, noblest of kings, that Frolle dwelt in Paris, with an immense force, and said that he would Arthur withstand. To Paris marched Arthur, of fear void, and belay the walls, and areared his tents; on four sides he belay it (the city), four weeks and a day. The people that were there within were sore afraid; the burgh was within filled with men; and they ate soon the meat that was there gathered.

When four weeks were gone, that Arthur was there stationed, then was in the burgh sorrow extreme, with the wretched folk that lay there in hunger; there was weeping, there was lament, and distress great. They called to Frolle, and bade him make peace; become Arthur's man, and his own honour enjoy, and hold the kingdom of Arthur the keen; and let not the wretched folk perish all with hunger. Then answered Frolle—free he was in heart:—" Nay, so help me God, that all dooms wieldeth, shall I never his man become, nor he my sovereign! Myself I will fight; in God is all the right!"

The yet spake Frolle, free man in heart: "Nay, so help me the Lord that shaped the daylight, will I nevermore yearn Arthur's grace; but fight I will, without any knight's aid, body against body, before my people; hand against hand, with Arthur the king! Whetherso of us is the weaker, soon he will be the loather; whetherso of us there may live, to his friends he will be the liefer; and whether of us that may of the other obtain the better (superiority), have he all this other's land, and set it in his own hand. This I will yearn, if Arthur will it grant; and this I will swear upon my sword. And hostages I will find, three kings' sons, that I will hold firmly this covenant; that I will it not violate, by my quick life! For liefer it is to me to lie dead, before my people, than that I should see them on the ground perish with hunger. For we have with fight destroyed our knights—men felled fifty thousand; and many a good woman have made miserable widow, many a child fatherless, and bereaved of comfort; and now this folk with hunger have wondrously harmed. It is better therefore betwixt ourselves to deal and to dispose of this kingdom with fight; and have it the better man, and possess it in joy!" Frolle took twelve knights, with these words forth-right, and sent them in

message to Arthur the king, to know if he would hold this
covenant, and with his own hand win the kingdom, or lie dead
before, to the harm of his people; and if he it won, should have
it in his power.

Arthur heard that, noblest of kings; was he never so blithe
ere in his life, for the tiding liked to him from Frolle the king;
and these words said Arthur the good: " Well saith Frolle, who
is King of France; better it is that we two contest this realm,
than there should be slain our brave thanes.   This covenant I
approve, before my people, at an appointed day to do what he
me biddeth; that shall be to-morrow, before our men, that fight
we shall by ourselves, and fall the worst of us!   And whether
(which) of us that goeth aback, and this fight will forsake, be he
in each land proclaimed for a recreant!   Then may men sing of
one such king, that his brag (or threat) hath made, and his
knighthood forsaken! "

Frolle heard that, who was King of France, that Arthur would
fight himself, without any knight.   Strong man was Frolle, and
stark man in mood; and his boast he had made, before all his
people, and he might not for much shame disgrace himself;
quit his bold bragging that he had said in the burgh.   But said
he whatever he said, in sooth he it weened, that Arthur would
it forsake, and no whit take to (accept) the fight.   For if Frolle,
who was King in France, had it known, that Arthur would grant
him that he had yearned, he would not have done it for a
shipful of gold!   Nevertheless was Frolle to the fight exceeding
keen; tall knight and strong man, and moody in heart; and
said that he would hold the day, in the island that with water is
surrounded—the island standeth full truly in the burgh of Paris.
—" There I will with fight obtain my rights, with shield, and
with steel, and with knight's weed; now to-morrow is the day;
have it he that may it win! "

The tiding came to Arthur the king, that Frolle would with
fight win France! was he never so blithe ere in his life!   And
he gan to laugh, with loud voice; and said these words Arthur
the keen: " Now I know that Frolle will with me fight,
to-morrow in the day, as he himself determined, in the island
that with water is surrounded; for it becometh a king, that his
word should stand.   Let the trumpets blow, and bid my men, that
every good man watch to-night for that, and pray our Lord, that
all dooms wieldeth, that he preserve me from Frolle the fierce,
and with his right hand protect me from disgrace.   And if I
may obtain this kingdom to mine own hand, every poor man

the easier shall be, and work I will the great God's will! Now
aid me thereto that all things may well do; the high heavenly
king stand me in help; for him I will love (or praise), the while
that I live!"

There was all the long night songs and candle-light; loudly
sung clerks holy psalms of God. When it was day on the
morrow, people gan to stir. His weapons he took in hand,
Arthur the strong; he threw on his back a garment most
precious, a cheisil shirt, and a cloth kirtle; a burny exceeding
precious, embroidered of steel. He set on his head a good helm;
to his side he suspended his word Caliburn; his legs he covered
with hose of steel, and placed on his feet spurs most good. The
king with his weeds leapt on his steed; men reached to him a
good shield; it was all clean of elephant's bone (ivory). Men
gave him in hand a strong shaft; there was at the end a spear
most fair; it was made in Caermarthen by a smith that hight
Griffin; Uther it possessed, who was ere king here. When that
the stern man was weaponed, then gan he to advance; then
might he behold, who were there beside, the mighty king ride
boldly; since this world was made, was it nowhere told, that
ever any man so fair rode upon horse, as Arthur he was, son of
Uther! Bold chieftains rode after the king; in the foremost
flock forty hundred, noble warriors, clad in steel, bold Britons,
busy with weapon. After that marched fifty hundred, that
Walwain led, who was a bold champion. Afterwards there gan
out follow sixty thousand Britons most bold; that was the
rearward. There was the King Angel; there was Loth and
Urien; there was Urien's son, named Ywain; there was Kay
and Beduer, and commanded the host there; there was the
King Howel, noble man of Britanny; Cador there was eke, who
was keen in flock; there was from Ireland Gillomar the strong;
there was Gonwais the king, Orkney's darling; there was
Doldanim the keen, out of Gothland, and Rumaret the strong,
out of Winet-land; there was Æscil the king, Denmark's darling.
Folk there was on foot, so many thousand men, that was never
a man in this worlds-realm so wise, that might tell the thousands,
in ever any speech, unless he had with right wisdom of the Lord,
or unless he had with him what Merlin he had.

Arthur forth gan march, with innumerable folk; until he
came full surely unto the burgh of Paris; on the west side of
the water, with his mickle folk. On the east side was Frolle,
with his great force, ready to the fight, before all his knights.
Arthur took a good boat, and went therein, with shield and

with steed, and with all his weeds (armour); and he shoved the strong ship from the land, and stept upon the island, and led his steed in his hand; his men that brought him there, as the king commanded, let the boat drive forth with the waves.

Frolle went into ship; the king was uneasy that he ever thought with Arthur to fight. He proceeded to the island, with his good weapons; he stept upon the island, and drew his steed after him; the men that brought him there, as the king commanded them, let the boat drive forth with the waves; and the two kings alone there remained.

Then men might behold, that were there beside, the folk on the land, exceedingly afraid; they climbed upon halls, they climbed upon walls; they climbed upon bowers, they climbed upon towers, to behold the combat of the two kings. Arthur's men prayed with much humility to God the good, and the holy his mother, that their lord might have there victory; and the others eke prayed for their king. Arthur stept in steel saddle-bow, and leapt on his steed; and Frolle with his weeds leapt also on his steed; the one at his end, in the island, and the other at his end, in the island; they couched their shafts, the royal knights; they urged their steeds—good knights they were. Never was he found in ever any land, any man so wise, that should know it ere that time, whether (which) of the kings should lie overcome; for both they were keen knights, brave men and active, mickle men in might, and in force exceeding strong. They made ready their steeds; and together they gan ride; rushed fiercely, so that fire sprang after them! Arthur smote Frolle with might excessive strong, upon the high shield, so that it fell to the ground; and the steed that was good leapt out in the flood. Arthur out with his sword—mischief was on the point—and struck upon Frolle, where he was in the flood, ere their combat were come to the end. But Frolle with his hand grasped his long spear, and observed Arthur anon, as he came nigh, and smote the bold steed in the breast, so that the spear pierced through, and Arthur down drove. Then arose the multitudes' clamour, that the earth dinned again, the welkin resounded for shout of the folk. There would the Britons over the water pass, if Arthur had not started up very quickly, and grasped his good shield, adorned with gold, and against Frolle, with hostile glances cast before his breast his good broad shield. And Frolle to him rushed with his fierce assault, and up heaved his sword, and struck down right, and smote upon Arthur's shield, so that it fell on the field; the helm on his head, and his

mail gan to give way, in front of his head; and he received a
wound four inches long;—it seemed not to him sore, for it was
no more;—the blood ran down over all his breast. Arthur was
enraged greatly in his heart, and his sword Caliburne swung
with main, and smote Frolle upon the helm, so that it parted
in two; throughout the burnyshood, so that at his breast it
(the sword) stopt. Then fell Frolle to the ground; upon the
grass-bed his ghost he left. Then laughed the Britons, with
loud voice; and people gan to fly exceeding quickly.

Arthur the powerful went to land, and thus gan to call, noblest
of kings: "Where art thou, Walwain, dearest of men to me?
Command these Rome-men all with peace to depart hence;
each man enjoy his home, as God granteth it him; order each
man to hold peace, upon pain of limb and upon life; and I will
it order to-day a se'nnight; command this folk then to march
all together, and come to myself—the better it shall be for them.
They shall perform homage to me with honour, and I will hold
them in my sovereignty, and set laws most good among the
people. For now shall the Romanish laws fall to the ground,
that before stood here with Frolle, who lieth slain in the island,
and deprived of life-day. Hereafter full soon shall his kindred
of Rome hear tidings of Arthur the king, for I will speak with
them, and break down Rome walls, and remind them how King
Belin led the Britons in thither, and won to him all the lands
that stand unto Rome.

Arthur proceeded to the gate, before the burgh wise men
that took charge of the burgh, came, and let Arthur within,
with all his men; delivered to him the halls, delivered to
him the castles; delivered to him, full surely, all the burgh of
Paris—there was mickle bliss with the British folk! The day
came to burgh, that Arthur had set; came all the populace,
and his men became. Arthur took his folk, and divided
them in two; and the half part gave to Howel, and bade
him march soon, with the mickle host, with the British men
to conquer lands.

Howel did all thus as Arthur him bade; he conquered Berry,
and all the lands thereby; Anjou and Touraine, Alverne and
Gascony, and all the havens that belonged to the lands.
Guitard hight the duke, who possessed Poitou; he would not
submit to Howel, but held ever against him; he would ask no
peace, but Howel fought with him; oft he felled the folk, and
oft he made flight. Howel wasted all the land, and slew the
people. When Guitard saw, who was lord in Poitou, that all

his people went him to loss, with Howel he made peace, with all
his host, and became Arthur's man, the noble king. Arthur
became gracious to him, and loved him greatly, and bade him
enjoy his land, for (because) he bowed to his feet;—then had
Howel nobly succeeded!

Arthur had France, and freely it settled; he took then his
host, and marched over all the territory; to Burgundy he proceeded, and set it in his hand; and afterwards he gan fare into
Loraine, and all the lands set to himself in hand; all that
Arthur saw, all it submitted to him; and afterwards he went,
full truly, again home to Paris.

When Arthur had France established with good peace,
settled and composed, so that prosperity was among the folk,
then ordered he the old knights, that he had long retained, that
they should come to the king, and receive their reward; for
they many years had been his companions. To some he gave
land, some silver and gold; to some he gave castles, some he
gave clothes; bade them go in joy, and amend their sins;
forbade them to bear weapon, because age upon them went,
and bade them love God greatly in this life, that he at the end,
full surely, might give them his paradise, that they might enjoy
bliss with the angels. All the old knights proceeded to their land,
and the young remained with their dear king. All the nine
years Arthur dwelt there; nine years he held France freely in
hand, and afterwards no longer the land he governed.

But the while that the kingdom stood in Arthur's hand,
marvellous things came to the folk; many proud man Arthur
made mild, and many a high man he held at his feet! It was
on an Easter, that men had fasted, that Arthur on Easter-day
had his noble men together; all the highest persons that belonged
to France, and of all the lands that lay thither in; there he gave
his knights all their rights; to each one he gave possessions, as
he had earned. Thus quoth him Arthur, noblest of kings:
" Kay, look thee hitherward; thou art mine highest steward;
here I give thee Anjou, for thy good deeds, and all the rights
that thither in are set. Kneel to me, Beduer; thou art my
highest cup-bearer here; the while that I am alive, love thee
I will. Here I give thee Neustrie, nearest to my realm." Then
hight Neustrie the land that now hight Normandy. The same
two earls were Arthur's dear men, at counsel and at communing,
in every place. The yet said him Arthur, noblest of kings:
" Wend thee hither, Howeldin; thou art my man and my kin;
have thou Boulogne, and possess it in prosperity. Come near,

Borel; thou art knight wise and wary; here I deliver thee the Mans, with honour, and possess thou it in prosperity, for thy good deeds." Thus Arthur the king dealt his lordly lands, after their actions; for he thought them to be worthy. Then were blithe speeches in Arthur's halls; there was harping and song, there were blisses among!

When Easter was gone, and April went from town, and the grass was rife, and the water was calm, and men gan to say that May was in town, Arthur took his fair folk, and proceeded to the sea, and caused his ships to be assembled, well with the best; and sailed to this land, and came up at London; up he came at London, to the bliss of the people. All it was blithe that saw him with eyes; soon they gan to sing of Arthur the king, and of the great worship that he had won. There kissed father the son, and said to him welcome; daughter the mother, brother the other; sister kissed sister; the softer it was to them in heart. In many hundred places folk stood by the way, asking of things of many kind; and the knights told them of their conquests, and made their boast of mickle booty. Might no man say, were he man ever so skilled, of half the blisses that were with the Britons! Each fared at his need over this kingdom, from burgh to burgh, with great bliss; and thus it a time stood in the same wise—bliss was in Britain with the bold king.

When Easter was gone, and summer come to land, then took Arthur his counsel, with his noble men, that he would in Kaerleon bear on him his crown, and on Whitsunday his folk there assemble. In those days men gan deem, that no burgh so fair was in any land, nor so widely known as Kaerleon by Usk, unless it were the rich burgh that is named Rome. The yet many a man was with the king in land, that pronounced the burgh of Kaerleon richer than Rome, and that Usk were the best of all waters. Meadows there were broad, beside the burgh; there was fish, there was fowl, and fairness enow; there was wood and wild deer, wondrous many; there was all the mirth that any man might think of. But never since Arthur thither came, the burgh afterwards thrived, nor ever may, between this and dooms-day. Some books say certainly that the burgh was bewitched, and that is well seen, sooth that it be. In the burgh were two minsters exceeding noble; one minster was of Saint Aaron; therein was mickle relique; the other of the martyr Saint Julian, who is high with the Lord; therein were nuns good, many a high born woman.

The bishop's stool was at Saint Aaron; therein was many a
good man; canons there were, who known were wide; there was
many a good clerk, who well could (were well skilled) in learning.
Much they used the craft to look in the sky; to look in the
stars, nigh and far;—the craft is named Astronomy. Well
often they said of many things to the king; they made known
to him what should happen to him in the land. Such was the
burgh of Kaerleon; there was much wealth; there was much
bliss with the busy king.

The king took his messengers, and sent over his land; bade
come earls; bade come barons; bade come kings, and eke
chieftains; bade come bishops, bade come knights; bade all the
free men that ever were in the land; by their life he bade them
be at Kaerleon on Whitsunday. Knights gan to ride exceeding
wide, rode toward Kaerleon from lands of many kind. At the
Whitsunday there came the King Angel, King of Scotland, with
his fair folk; many was the fair man that followed the king.
Of Moray King Urien, and his fair son Ywain; Stater, King of
South Wales, and Cadwal, the King of North Wales; Cador,
Earl of Cornwall, whom the king loved; Morvith of Gloucester;
Maurin of Winchester; Gurguint, Earl of Hereford, and Beof,
Earl of Oxford; Cursal the bold, from Bath there came riding;
Urgent of Chester; Jonathas of Dorchester; Arnalf of Salis-
bury, and Kinmare of Canterbury; Balien of Silchester; Wigen
of Leicester; Argal, Earl of Warwick, with folk exceeding strange
(or numerous); Dunwale, son of Apries, and Kegein, son of
Elauth; Kineus, that was Coit's son, and Cradoc, Catel's son,
Ædlein, Cledauk's son; Grimarc, Kinmark's son; Run, Margoit,
and Netan; Clofard, Kincar, and Aican; Kerin, Neton, and
Peredur; Madoc, Trahern, and Elidur. These were Arthur's
noble earls, and the highest thanes brave of all this land, without (besides) the nobles of Arthur's board, that no man might
ken, nor all the folk name. Then were archbishops three in
this country; in London, and in York; and in Kaerleon, Saint
Dubrich—he was a man exceeding holy, through all things
excellent! At London lay the archbishop's stool, that to
Canterbury was subsequently removed, after that Englishmen
had won to them this land.

To tell the folk of Kaerleon, no man might it do! There
was Gillomar the king, of Irish men the darling; Malverus,
King of Iceland; Doldanet, King of Gutland; Kinkalin of
Frisland; and Æscil, King of Denmark. There was Loth the
keen, who was king by the North; and Gonwais, King of Orkney,

of outlaws the darling. Thither came the fierce man, the Earl
of Boulogne, who was named Læyer, and his people with him;
of Flanders the Earl Howeldin; of Chartres the Earl Geryn.
This man brought with him all the French men; twelve earls
most noble, who ruled over France. Guitard, Earl of Poitiers;
Kay, Earl of Angers; Bedver, Earl of Normandy — the land
then hight Neustrie;—of the Mans came the Earl Borel; of
Britanny the Earl Howel. Howel the earl was free man,
and fair were his weeds. And all the French folk were clothed
fair, all well weaponed, and horses they had fat. There were
besides fifteen bishops. Was there no knight nor any swain,
nor good man that were thane, from the ports of Spain to
the towns of Alemaine, that thither would not have come,
if he were (had been) invited; all for Arthur's dread, of noble
race. When all this folk was come; each king with his people,
there men might behold, who were there beside, many a strange
man, who was come to the burgh, and many kind of tidings
(novelties) with Arthur the king. There was many a marvellous
cloth (garment); there was many a wrath knight; there were
lodgings nobly prepared; there were the inns, built with
strength; there were on the fields many thousand tents; there
came lard and wheat, and oats without measure; may no
man say it in his tale, of the wine and of the ale; there came
hay, there came grass; there came all that was good!

When all this folk was assembled by the good king, when the
Whitsunday came, as the Lord it sent, then came all the bishops
before their king, and the archbishops three, before Arthur;
and took the crown, that was to him by right, and set upon his
head with great bliss; so they gan him lead, all with God's
counsel. Saint Dubrich went before—he was to Christ chosen;
—the Archbishop of London walked on his right hand, and by
his left side the same of York. Fifteen bishops went before,
of many lands chosen; they were all clothed with garments
most rich, that were all embroidered with burning gold. There
walked four kings before the kaiser; they bare in their hands
four swords of gold. Thus hight the one, who was a most
doughty man, that was Cador the king, Arthur's darling; the
second of Scotland, he bare sword in hand; and the King of
North Wales and the King of South Wales.

And thus they gan lead the king to church; the bishops gan
sing before the monarch; trumpets there blew; bells there
rung; knights gan ride, women forth glide. In certainty it is
said, and sooth it is found, that no man ever ere saw here with

earthly men half so great pomp, in ever any assembly, as was
with Arthur, of noble race.

Into church came Arthur the rich man; Dubrich the archbishop—the Lord was to him full good; of Rome he was legate,
and prelate of the people—he sang the holy mass before the
monarch. Came with the queen women fair; all wives of the
rich men that dwelt in the land, and daughters of the noble men
the queen had sought (or selected), all as the queen had ordered,
on pain of their paying full penalty. In the church, in the south
half, sate Arthur the king himself; by the north side Wenhaver
the queen. There came before her four chosen queens; each
bare in the left hand a jewel of red gold, and three snow-white
doves sate on their shoulders; who were the four queens, wives
of the kings who bare in their hands the four swords of gold
before Arthur, noblest of kings. There was many a maid-child
with the noble queen; there was many a rich garment on the
fair folk; there was mickle envy from land of many kind; for
each weened to be better than other. Many knights anon came
to the church; some for gain; some for the king; some to
behold the women that were noble. Songs there were merry,
that lasted very long; I ween if it had lasted seven years, the
yet they would more, that were thereat. When the mass was
sung, from church they thronged; the king with his folk went
to his meat, with his mickle folk—joy was among the people.
The queen on the other side sought her lodging; she had of
women wondrous many.

When the king was set, with his men to his meat, to the king
came the bishop Saint Dubrich, who was so good, and took
from his head his rich crown; on account of the mickle gold
the king would not it bear; and placed a less crown on the king's
head; and afterwards he gan do to the queen also (likewise).
In Troy this was the custom in their elders' days, of whom Brutus
came, who were excellent men; all the men at their meat sate
asunder by themselves; that to them seemed well done; and also
the women their station had.

When the king was set with all his people to his meat, earls
and barons, at the king's board, then came stepping the steward,
who was named Kay, highest knight in land under the king, of all
the assemblage of Arthur's folk. Kay had before him many a
noble man chosen; there were a thousand bold knights wondrous
well told, that served the king and his chiefs; each knight had
a cloth on, and adorned with gold, and all their fingers covered
with gold rings. These bare the things sent from the kitchen to

the king. On the other side was Beduer, the king's high cup-bearer; with him were earls' sons of noble race born, and the noble knights' sons, who were thither come; and seven kings' sons, that with him moved. Beduer went foremost, with golden bowl; after him a thousand pressed towards the folk, with drink of all the kinds that men could think of. And the queen at her end, women most fair attended; a thousand walked before her, rich and well choice, to serve the queen, and them that were with her.

Was he never born, of any man chosen, clerk nor layman, in ever any land, that could tell it in speech of any kind, of half the wealth that was in Kaerleon, of silver and of gold, and good weeds; of high born men that dwelt among the folk; of horses, and of hawks, of hounds for deer, and of rich weeds, that were among the people. And of all the folk that dwelt there in land, the folk of this land was accounted the fairest of people, and also the women, comely in hue, and most nobly clothed, and best of all educated. For they all had in declaration, by their quick lives, that they would have their clothes of one hue. Some had white, some had red; some had eke good green; and variegated cloth of each kind was to them wondrous odious; and each ill-usage they accounted unworthy.

Then had English land the best fame of all; and this country-folk eke was dearest to the king. The high born women that dwelt in this land had all declared in their sooth words, that none would take lord (husband) in this land, never any knight, were he nought (never) so well formed, unless he were thrice tried in combat, and his courage made known, and himself approved; then might he boldly ask him a bride. For that usage the knights were brave, the women excellent, and the better behaved; then were in Britain blisses enow.

When the king had eaten, and all his people, then proceeded out of the burgh the thanes most bold; all the kings, and their chieftains; all the bishops, and all the clerks; all the earls, and all the barons; all the thanes, and all the swains, fairly clad, spread over the fields. Some they gan to ride; some they gan to race; some they gan to leap, some they gan to shoot; some they wrestled, and contest made; some they in the field played under shield; some they drove balls wide over the fields. Games of many a kind there they gan to play; and whoso might win honour of his game, men lead him with song before the sovereign, and the king for his game gave him gifts good. All the queens, that there were come, and all the ladies, leaned over the walls, to behold the people, and the folk play. This lasted three days, such games and such plays.

Then on the fourth day, the king gan to speak, and gave his good knights all their rights; he gave silver, he gave gold; he gave horses, he gave land; castles eke and clothes; his men he pleased—there was many a bold Briton before Arthur. But now came to the king new tidings! Arthur the bold king sate at a board; before him sate kings, and many chieftains; bishops and clerks, and knights most brave.

There came into the hall marvellous tales!—there came twelve thanes bold, clad with pall; noble warriors, noble men with weapon; each had on hand a great ring of gold, and with a band of gold each had his head encircled. Ever two and two walked together; each with his hand held his companion; and glided over the floor, before Arthur, so long that they came before Arthur, the sovereign. They greeted Arthur anon with their noble words: "Hail be thou, Arthur king, darling of Britons; and hail be thy people, and all thy lordly folk! We are twelve knights come here forthright, rich and noble; we are from Rome. Hither we are come from our emperor, who is named Luces, who ruleth Rome-people. He commanded us to proceed hither, to Arthur the king, and bade thee to be greeted with his grim words, and saith that he is astonished, wondrously much, where thou tookest the mood in this middle-earth, that thou darest of Rome oppose any doom (will), or heave up thine eyes against our ancestors; and who dared it thee to counsel, that thou art so doughty become, that thou darest threaten the lord of dooms, Luces, the emperor, highest of men alive! Thou holdest all thy kingdom in thine own hand, and wilt not serve the emperor of the land; of the same land that Julius had in hand, who in former days won it with fight; and thou it hast retained in thy power; and with thy bold knights deprivest us of our rights. But say us, Arthur, soon, and send word to Rome; we shall thine errand bear to Luces our emperor, if thou wilt acknowledge that he is king over thee, and if thou wilt his man become, and acknowledge him for lord, and do right to the emperor on account of Frolle the king, whom thou slewest with wrong at Paris, and now holdest all his land with un-right in thy hand. If thou within these twelve weeks turn to the right, and if thou wilt of Rome any doom suffer, then mightest thou live, among thy people. And if thou wilt not do so, thou shalt receive worse, for the emperor will come here, as king shall to his own, king most keen; and take thee with strength, lead thee bound before Rome-folk;—then must thou suffer what thou erst despisedest!"

At these words the Britons leapt from the board; there was Arthur's court exceedingly enraged; and swore mickle oath, upon our mighty Lord, that they all were (should be) dead, who this errand bare; with horses drawn in pieces, death they should suffer. There leapt towards them the Britons exceeding wrath; tore them by the hair, and laid them to the ground. There were (would have been) the Romanish men pitifully treated, if Arthur had not leapt to them, as if it were a lion; and said these words —wisest of all Britons!—" Leave ye, leave quickly these knights alive! They shall not in my court suffer any harm; they are hither ridden out of Rome, as their lord commanded them, who is named Luces. Each man must go where his lord biddeth him go; no man ought to sentence a messenger to death, unless he were so evilly behaved, that he were traitor of his lord. But sit ye down still, knights in hall; and I will me counsel of such need, what word they shall bear to Luces the emperor.

Then sate all down, the folk on their benches, and the clamour ceased before the monarch. Then stood him up Arthur, noblest of kings, and he called to him seven sons of kings, earls and barons, and those that were boldest, and all the wisest men that dwelt in the folk, and went into a house that was fast inclosed, of old stone work—strong men it wrought—therein they gan to commune, his wise councillors, what answer he would give to Luces the emperor. When all the nobles were come to bench then was it all still that dwelt in the hall; there was great awe with the mighty king; durst there no man speak, least the king would it punish.

Then stood there up Cador, the earl most rich here, and said these words before the rich king: " I thank my Lord, who formed the daylight, to abide (have abode) this day, that is arrived to the folk, and this tiding that is come to our king; so that we need no more lie here inert! For idleness is evil in each land; for idleness maketh man lose his manhood; idleness maketh knight lose his rights; idleness causeth many wicked crafts; idleness destroyeth many thousand men; through idle deeds little men well-speed. For long we have lain still; our honour is the less! But now I thank the Lord, who formed the daylight, that the Romanish folk are so fierce, and make their threat to come to our burghs, our king to bind, and to Rome him bring. But if it is sooth that men say, as people it tell, that the Romanish people are so fierce, and are so bold, and so mischievous, that they will now come into our land, we shall prepare for them rueful tales; their fierceness shall turn to themselves to sorrow. For never loved I long peace in my land; for through peace we are bound, and well nigh all in swoon."

That heard Walwain, who was Arthur's relative, and angered him much with Cador, who said these words; and thus answered Walwain the good: "Cador, thou art a powerful man; thy counsels are not good; for good is peace and good is amity, whoso freely therewith holdeth, and God himself it made, through his divinity; for peace maketh a good man work good works, for all men are the better, and the land is the merrier."

Then heard Arthur the dispute of these knights; and thus spake the mighty man with his fierce folk: "Sit ye down quickly, my knights all, and each by his life listen my words!" All it was still that dwelt in the hall. Then spake the bold king to his noble folk: "My earls, my barons, my bold thanes, my doughty men, my dear friends; through you I have conquered under the sun, so that I am man most powerful, and fierce against my enemies; gold I have and treasure; of men I am ruler. I won it not alone, but we did, all clean. To many a fight I have led you, and ever ye were well skilled, so that many kingdoms stand in my hand. Ye are good knights, brave men and active; that I have proved in well many lands." The yet spake him Arthur, noblest of kings: "But now ye have heard, my noble thanes, what the Romanish men counsel them between, and what words they send us here, into our land, with writ and with words, and with great wrath. Now we must bethink how we may with right defend our country and our great honour, against this powerful folk, against this Rome-people, and send them answer with our good words; with much wisdom send our writ to Rome, and learn at the emperor, for what thing he us hateth; for what thing he greets us with threat and with scorn. Exceeding sorely it incenseth me, and immoderately it shameth, that he reproaches us our loss that we before have lost. They say that Julius Cæsar won it (Britain) with combat in fight. With strength and with fight men do many wrongs; for Cæsar sought Britain with bold strength. The Britons might not against him defend their land, but with strength they went in hand, and delivered him all their land; and thereafter soon all became his men. Some of our kin they had slain, and some with horses drawn to pieces; some they led bound out of this land; and thus this land won with wrong and with sin, and now

asketh by right tribute of this land! All so we may do, if we it
do will; through right of Belin king, and of Brenne, his brother,
the Duke of Burgundy. These were our ancestors, of whom
we are come; these belay Rome, and the realm all conquered,
and before Rome the strong their hostages up-hung; and afterwards they took all the land, and set it in their own hand; and
thou ought we with right to besiege Rome. Now will I let
remain Belin and Brenne, and speak of the caiser, Constantine
the strong; he was Helen's son, all of Britons come (descended);
he won Rome, and possessed the realm. Let (leave) we now of
Constantine, who won Rome all to him, and speak of Maximian,
who was a man most strong; he was King of Britain, he conquered France. Maximian the strong he took Rome in hand, and
Alemaine (Germany) he won eke, with wondrous great strength,
and all from Rome into Normandy. And all these were my
ancestors, my noble progenitors; and possessed all the lands
that unto Rome lay; and through such authority I ought to
obtain Rome. They yearn of me in hand tribute of my land;
all so will I of Rome, if I have counsel. I desire in my thoughts
to possess all Rome; and he desireth in Britain to bind me
most fast, and slay my Britons, with his evil attacks. But if
my Lord grant it, who formed day and night, he shall sorely
pay for his bold threat, and his Rome-people shall therefore
perish; and I will be bold, wherein he now ruleth! Dwell ye
now all still, I will say my will; no man shall do it otherwise,
but it shall stand thereon. He desireth all, and I desire all that
we both possess; have it now and ever who may it easier win,
for now we shall prove to whom God will grant it!"

Thus spake the bold king, that had Britain under his rule,
that was Arthur the king, Britain's darling! His warriors sate,
and to his words listened; some they sate still, a great while;
some they made much communing between them; some it
seemed to them good; some it disturbed their mood.

When they had long listened to the king, then spake Howel
the fair, noble man of Britanny, and said these words before the
fierce king: "Lord king, hearken to me, as I ere did to thee.
Thou hast said sooth words—may fortune be given to thee!—
For it was of old said, what we now shall learn, in the years before
what is now here found. Sibeli it said; her words were sooth;
and set it in book, for example to folk, that three kings should
go out of Britain, who should conquer Rome, and all the realm,
and all the lands that thereto lie. The first was Belin, who
was a British king; the other was Constantine, who was king

in Britain; thou shalt be the third, that Rome shalt have. And if thou wilt it begin, thou shalt it win, and I will thereto help, with great strength; I will send over sea, to my good thanes, to my bold Britons—the better we shall proceed;—I will command all, the nobles of Britain, by their limbs and by their lives, over all my lands, that they be ready soon with thee to march to Rome. My land I will set in pledge for silver, and all the possessions of my land for silver and for gold; and so we shall proceed to Rome, and slay Luces the emperor; and for to win thy rights, I will lead to thee ten thousand knights." Thus spake Howel, noblest of Britanny.

When that Howel had said what seemed good to him, then spake Angel the king, Scotland's darling, and stood upon a bench, and both his brothers, that was, Loth and Urien, two most noble men. Thus said Angel the king to Arthur the keen: "Lord Arthur, I say to thee through my sooth words; the same that Howel hath spoken, no man shall it avoid, but we shall perform it by our quick lives! And, lord Arthur the noble, listen to me a while; call to thee to counsel thy earls rich, and all the highest that are in thy folk, and bid them say to thee with their sooth words, in what they will help thee thy foes to destroy. I will lead to thee knights of my land, three thousand champions brave, all chosen; ten thousand men on foot, to fight most good; and go we to Rome, and conquer the realm. Full greatly it may shame us, and full greatly it may us anger, that they should send messengers after tribute to our land. But so help us the Lord that formed the daylight, they shall pay for it with their bare life! For when we have Rome, and all the realm, we shall seize the lands that thereto lie; Poille (Apulia?) and Alemaine, Lumbardy and Britanny, France and Normandy—then it hight Neustrie—and so we shall tame their immoderate mood (pride)." When the king had said then answered all: "Disgraced be that man that will not help thereto, with goods and with weapons, and with all his might!"

Then was Arthur's folk sternly incensed; knights were so enraged, that all they gan to be agitated. When Arthur had heard the clamour of his folk, then gan he call—the king was angry—"Sit ye down still, knights in hall, and I will you tell what I will do. My writs I will make, that shall be well indited, and send to the emperor mind's sorrow and mickle care; and I will full soon fare into Rome. I will not thither any tribute bring, but the emperor I will bind, and afterwards I will him hang; and all the land I will destroy, and all the knights put to death, that stand against me in fight!"

Arthur took his writ in hand, with hostile words, and delivered it to the men, that had brought the errand; and afterwards he caused them to be clothed with each pomp, with the noblest garments that he had in bower, and bade them fare soon to Luces of Rome, and he would come after them as quickly as he might.

These twelve went their way toward their land; were in no land knights so bedecked with silver and with gold, nor through all things so well arrayed as these were by Arthur the king. Thus Arthur them treated, all for their words! These twelve knights proceeded until they came to Rome; they greeted their emperor, their sovereign: " Hail be thou, Luces, thou art highest over us! We were with the fierce man, with Arthur the king; we have brought thee writs, words exceeding great Arthur is the keenest man that we ever looked on, and he is wondrous powerful, and his thanes are bold; there is every knave as if he were knight, there is every swain as if he were rich thane; there are the knights as if it were kings; meat there is most abundant, and men most bold, and the fairest women that dwell alive; and Arthur the bold himself fairest over all! By us he sendeth word to thee, that he will come to this land; no tribute he will bring, but thyself he will bind; and afterwards he will thee hang, and this land all destroy, and take Alemaine and Lumbardy, Burgundy, France, and Normandy. And Frolle he slew, his foe, so he will to us all do; and possess himself alone the land that we own all clean; hereto he will lead kings, earls, and chieftains. And here we have in hand the writs that he thee sendeth that telleth thee what he will do, when he cometh in hither."

When the errand was said, the emperor was a full sorrowful man, and all the Rome-folk were stirred with strong wrath. Oft they went to counsel, oft they went to communing, ere to them might be determined what they would do. Nevertheless at the end a counsel they found, that was through the senator, who held the senate; the emperor they counselled that he should write letters, and send his messengers over many kingdoms, and bid them all come soon to Rome, from every land, who loved them aught, and all that willeth with fight obtain land or goods. Folk there came soon to the burgh of Rome; so mickle as there never ere any man assembled! They said that they would march over Muntgiu, and fight with Arthur, wheresoever they him found, and Arthur slay or hang, and his host all destroy, and possess for the emperor Arthur's realm.

The first king that there came, he was a man exceeding keen, Epistrod, king of Greece; Ethion, Duke of Bœotia, came with a great force; Irtac, King of Turkey; Pandras, King of Egypt; of Crete the King Ypolite; of Syria the King Evander; of Phrygia the Duke Teucer; of Babylon, Maptisas; of Spain the Caiser Meodras; of Media the King Boccus; of Libia the King Sextorius; of Bitunia, Pollidices; of Ituria the King Xerxes; Ofustesar, King of Africa; was there no king his like; with him came many an African; of Ethiopia he brought the black-men. The Rome-people themselves marched them together, that were at nearest, of Rome the noblest; Marcus, Lucas, and Catel, Cocta, Gaius, and Metel; these were the six, who the Senate all ruled.

When this folk was assembled, from lands of many kind, then caused the emperor all the host to be numbered. Then were there told right, to fight most bold, four hundred thousand knights in the heap (assemblage), with weapons and with horses, as behoveth to knights. Never was he born, in every any burgh, that might tell the folk, that there went on foot! Before harvest-day forth they gan to march, ever right the way that toward Muntgiu lay.

Let us now leave this host a while, and speak we of Arthur, noblest of kings, when that he had besought his good thanes, and each had gone home where he had land. And soon again came the knights in assemblage, with weapons well provided, through all their might, of Scotland, of Ireland, of Gutland, of Iceland, of Norway, of Denmark, of Orkney, of Man; of these same lands are a hundred thousand brave thanes, all well weaponed in their country's wise. They were not all knights, nor in this wise arrayed, but they were the keenest men that any man knew, with great battle-axes, and with long sæxes. Of Normandy, of Anjou, of Britain, of Poitou, of Flanders, of Boulogne, of Lorraine, of Lovaine, came a hundred thousand to the king's host, knights with the best, completely provided with weapons. There came the twelve companions that France should obey; twelve thousand knights they brought forth-right; and of this land Arthur took in hand fifty thousand knights, keen and brave men in battle. Howel of Brittany led ten thousand of his land-folk, knights with the best. Of foot-men; when they forth marched, through no kind of speech could any man them number!

Arthur then ordered, noblest of kings, the folk to be assembled at a set time, by their bare life, at Barbefleote; and there he would gather his good people. This land he delivered to a famous knight; he was Walwain's brother, there was no other; he was named Modred, wickedest of men; truth he had none to ever any man; he was Arthur's relation, of his noble race; but knight he was wondrous good, and he had very much pride; he was Arthur's sister's son; to the queen was his resort—that was evilly done—to his uncle he did treachery. But it was all secret, in host and in hall, for no man it weened, that it should be, but men in sooth weened him, because Walwain was his brother, the truest man of all that came to the folk; through Walwain was Modred by men the more beloved, and Arthur the keen full well was pleased with him. He took all his kingdom, and set it to Modred in hand, and Wenhaver, his queen, worthiest of women, that then in this nation dwelt in land. Arthur gave to them all that he possessed, to Modred and the queen—that to them was pleasing. That was evilly done, that they were (should have been) born; this land they destroyed with numerous sorrows; and themselves at the end the Worse gan disgrace (or destroy), so that they there lost their lives and their souls, and ever afterwards became odious in every land, so that never any man would offer a good prayer for their souls, on account of the treachery that he did to Arthur, his uncle. All that Arthur possessed he gave to Modred, his land and his people, and his dear queen; and afterwards he took his army of folk most fair, and marched full soon toward Southampton.

There came numerous ships soon sailing over the wide sea, to the king's folk; the king distributed the folk over the long ships; by thousands and by thousands to the ships they thronged; the father wept on the son, sister on the brother; mother on the daughter, when the host departed. The weather stood at will, the wind waxed in hand; anchors they up drew, joy was among the folk. The thanes wondrous blithe wound their way into the wide sea, the ships thereforth pressed, the glee-men there sung; sails there they hoist, ropes there they right; weather they had softest of all, and the sea slept. For the softness (calm) Arthur gan to sleep; as the king slept a dream he dreamt; marvellous was the dream, the king it alarmed!

When the king him awoke, greatly he was frightened, and he gan to groan with loud voice. Was there none so bold knight under

Christ, who durst ask the king of his welfare, ere the king himself spake, and discoursed with his barons there; and thus Arthur him said, when he awoke from his sleep: "Lord governor Christ, ruler of dooms, protector of middle-earth, comforter of men through thy merciful will, ruler of angels; let thou my dream turn to good!" Then spake Angel the king, Scotland's darling: "Lord, say us thy dream, for prosperity is given to us." "Blithely," quoth the king, "to bliss may it turn! Where I lay in slumber, and I gan for to sleep, methought that in the welkin came a marvellous beast, eastward in the sky, and loathsome to the sight; with lightning and with storm sternly he advanced; there is in no land any bear so loathly. Then came there westward, winding with the clouds, a burning dragon; burghs he swallowed; with his fire he lighted all this land's realm; methought in my sight that the sea gan to burn of light and of fire, that the dragon carried. This dragon and the bear, both together, quickly soon together they came; they smote them together with fierce assaults; flames flew from their eyes as firebrands! Oft was the dragon above, and eftsoons beneath; nevertheless at the end high he gan rise, and he flew down right with fierce assault, and the bear he smote, so that he fell to the earth; and he there the bear slew, and limbmeal him tore. When the fight was done, the dragon back went. This dream I dreamt, where I lay and slept."

The bishops heard this, and book-learned men; this heard earls, this heard barons; each by his wit said wisdom, and this dream they interpreted, as to them best seemed. There durst no knight to evil expound no whit, lest he should lose his limbs that were dear to him. Forth they gan to voyage exceeding quickly; the wind stood to them at will, weather best of all; they had all that to them was need; to land they came at Barbefleot. To Barbefleot, at Constantin, therein came a mickle multitude, from all the lands that Arthur had in hand. So soon as they might, out of ship they moved; the king ordered his folk to seek lodging, and the king would rest, until his folk came.

He was not there but one night, that a fair knight came to him; he told tiding to Arthur the king; he said that there was arrived a monster, westward from Spain; a fiend well loathsome; and in Britanny was busy to harm. By the seaside the land he wasted wide—now it hight Mount Saint Michel—the land he possesseth every part.—"Lord king," quoth the knight, "in sooth I make known to thee right here, he hath taken away thy relative, with great strength, a nobly born woman, Howel's daughter choice, who was named Helen, noblest of maidens. To the mount he carried her, noblest of maidens; now full a fortnight the fiend hath holden her there right; we know not in life whether he have her not to wife. All the men that he seizeth, he maketh to him for meat, cattle, horses, and the sheep; goats, and the swine eke; all this land he will destroy, unless thou allay our care, the land and this people; in thee is our need." Yet said the knight to the monarch: "Seest thou, lord, the mount, and the great wood, wherein the fiend dwelleth that destroyeth this people? We have fought with him well many times; by sea and by land this folk he destroyed; our ships he sank, the folk he all drowned; those that fought on the land, those he down laid. We have driven (suffered) that so long, that we let him alone, to act how so he will, after his will; the knights of this land dare not with him any more fight."

Arthur heard this, noblest of all kings; he called to him the Earl Kay, who was his steward and his relative; Beduer eke to him he called, he who was the king's cup-bearer. He bade them forth-right be all ready at midnight, with all their weapons, to go with the king, so that no man under Christ should know of their journey, except Arthur the king, and the two knights with him, and their six swains, brave men and active; and the knight that counselled it to the king should lead them. At the midnight, when men were asleep, Arthur forth him went, noblest of all kings. Before rode their guide, until it was daylight; they alighted from their steeds, and righted their weeds. Then saw they not far a great fire smoke, upon a hill, surrounded by the sea-flood; and another hill there was most high; the sea by it flowed full nigh; thereupon they saw a fire that was mickle and most strong. The knights then doubted, to whether of the two they might go, that the giant were not aware of the king's movement. Then Arthur the bold took him to counsel, that they should go together near the one fire; and if they there him found, kill him to death. Forth went the king, so that he came near; nought he there found but a mickle fire there burning. Arthur went about, and his knights by his side; nought they found alive upon earth but the great fire, and bones innumerable; by estimation it seemed to them thirty fother. Arthur then knew not any good counsel, and began him to speak to Beduer, his earl:—"Beduer, go quickly down from this hill, and pass thee over the deep water, with all thy weeds; and with wisdom advance to the fire; and go thou aside, and behold diligently, if thou mayest find ought of the fiend. And if thou mayest him perceive, in wise of any kind, go down still, until thou come to the water, and say me there soon what thou hast seen. And if it so befalleth, that thou come to the fire, and the fiend thee perceive, and proceed toward thee, have my good horn, that all with gold is adorned, and blow it with strength, as man shall for need. And advance thee to the fiend, and begin to fight, and we shall come to thee, as most quickly we may do it. And if thou findest him near the fire and thou all unperceived back mayest go; then forbid I thee, by thy bare life, that thou ever with the monster begin fight."

Beduer heard what his lord said to him; his weapons he put him on, and forth he went, and ascended up the mount that was immense. He bare in his hand a spear exceeding strong; a shield on his back, ornamented all with gold; a helm on his head, high, of steel; his body was covered with a fair burny; he had by his side a brand all of steel; and forth he gan step, the powerfully strong earl, until he arrived near the fire; and he under a tree gan him tarry. Then heard he one weep, wondrously much, weep and whine with piteous cries. Then the knight weened that it were the giant, and he became incensed as if it were a wild boar, and soon forgot what his lord said to him. His shield he drew on his breast, his spear he grasped fast, and near gan wend toward the fire; he thought to find the stern fiend, that he might fight, and prove himself. Then found he there a woman shaking with her head, a hoary-locked wife, who wept for her wretchedness; she cursed her lot that she was alive; that sate by the fire, with piteous cries, and sat and ever she beheld a grave, and said her words with plaintive voice: "Alas! Helen; alas! dear maid; alas! that I thee fed, that I thee fostered; alas! that the monster hath thee here thus destroyed; alas! that I was born; my limbs he hath broken in pieces!"

Then looked the woman about, where the giant should arrive; and looked on the Earl Beduer, who was come there. Then said the woman hoar, where she sate by the fire: "What are thou, fair wight? art thou angel, art thou knight? are thy wings hung with gold? If thou art from heaven, thou mayest in safety go hence, and if thou art earthly knight, harm thou wilt have forth-right. For now anon cometh the monster that all thy limbs will draw in pieces; though thou wert all steel, he would thee destroy, every bit. He went to Britany, to the best of all mansions, to Howel's castle, noble man in Britanny;

accounted on earth; and from what land thou art hither arrived; and why thou hast destroyed with murder my relative?" Then answered the fiend, where he lay and beheld: "All this I will do, and thy troth receive, on condition that thou let me live, and heal my limbs." Arthur him wrathed, wondrously much; and he called Beduer, his bold champion: "Go near, Beduer, and take off from him here the head; and carry it forth with thee, down from this mount." Beduer came near, and deprived him of his head; and so they proceeded thence down to their companions. Then sate the king down, and gan him rest; and said these words Arthur the good: "Never fought I any such fight, upon this land, but when I slew the King Riun, upon the mount of Ravin!"

Afterwards they forth went, and came to the host; when that they the head saw, wondrous it seemed to them, wherever under heaven were such head begotten! Howel of Britanny came to the king, and the king said to him all of the maiden. Then was Howel sorry, and sorrowful therefore in heart; and took all his companions, and fared to the mount where the British maid lay buried in earth. He caused there to be areared soon a church most fair, in Saint Mary's name, the Lord's mother; and afterwards he gave a name to the hill, ere he thence departed, and named it Helen's Tomb,—now it hight Mount Saint Michel.

Then was Arthur's host numerously collected; from Ireland, from Scotland, thither were they come. Then caused the king the trumpets to be blown in the host, and marched from Britain, busy men and keen, throughout Normandy, that then hight Neustrie. They proceeded throughout France, and the folk marched after them; they went out of France into Burgundy. His spies there came, and held his companions; and made known to the king, there in the country, that Luces the emperor, and all his Romanish host, thitherward they came, out of their land; and so they would march in toward France; and all the land conquer; and afterwards proceed hither, and kill all the Britons, quick that they found, and Arthur the keen led bound to France. Then was enraged the boldest of all kings, and ordered all his tents to be pitched in the fields; and there he would abide until he the sooth knew, where he might the emperor certainly intercept (or hostilely engage). The water hight Albe, where the bold king lay. A wise knight there came riding to the king's host, who was all wounded, and his folk greatly felled; the Romanish men had bereaved him of all his land. He told to the king new tiding, where the emperor lay, and all his Romanish army, and where he might him find, if he him would with him fight, or make peace with the Romanish men. " But, lord Arthur," quoth the knight, " I will shew to thee here right, that better for thee is it to have friendship, than for to fight; for against thy two they have twelve; so many kings, so many chieftains! He is in no land who may it make known to thee, for all the folk, that followeth the emperor, without (besides) the Rome-people, of his own territory, and without the folk that yearn the king's favour."

When the tales were all told, and Arthur had them understood, then called the king forth-right his dearest knights; and they counselled them between a castle to arear, beside the water that Albe was named. On a spot exceeding fair it was built full soon; there helped many a hand; in haste was it done; for if Arthur mis-fared, when he came to the fight, or his folk fell, or set to flight, then thought he to remain in the strong castle. Then called he earls twain, noble men and wise; high men born, to the king exceeding dear; the one was of Chartres, and hight Gerin—much wisdom dwelt with him; the other hight Beof of Oxford—well wide sprang the earl's fame. The yet the king called Walwain, who was his dearest relative; for Walwain understood Romanish; Walwain understood British; he was nurtured in Rome well many winters. The king took these three knights fair, and to the emperor them sent, and bade him with his army go back to Rome, and that he never into France his host should lead. " And if thou thither marchest, and leadest thine host, thou shalt be received to thy destruction! For France is mine own land, and I won it with fight; and if thou wilt not relinquish, that thou wilt not hither come, go we two to the fight, and fall the worst; and let we the poor folk dwell in quiet. For whilom the Rome-people conquered all the land, and afterwards they losed the land with fight; and I with fight it won, and with fight will hold."

Forth the knights went, goodly champions; that was, Gerin, and Beof the fair, and Walwain the bold, cuirassed and helmeted on their noble steeds; and each carried on his shoulder a shield exceeding good; they bare in their hands spears most strong. Forth they gan ride, noble men, from the host; much of the folk that with Arthur dwelt, with Walwain went, and earnestly prayed him, that he should raise some dispute with the Rome-folk:—" That we may with fight prove ourselves; for it is many years that (since) their threats came here; and their menace they make, that they will us behead. Now is it much

folk-shame, if it thus shall allay, unless there be some strife ere
we become reconciled; shafts broken in pieces, burnies torn,
shields shivered, warriors hewed, and swords bathed in the red
blood." Forth the earls proceeded through a great wood, and
marked a way that over a mount lay, so that they came soon
to the folk of Rome; worthily weaponed they rode on their
horses. There men might behold, the man who were beside,
many thousands throng out of the tents, all to behold these
three bold knights; and beheld their steeds, and beheld their
weeds, and hearkened tidings from Arthur the king. And next
forthright questioned the knights, and if the king had sent them
to the emperor, for to speak with the emperor, and to yearn his
peace. But for never any speech these three noble earls would
abide, ere they came riding before the tent's door, wherein was
the emperor. Down they gan alight, and delivered their steeds;
and so they weaponed with all advanced into the tent, before
the emperor that Luces was named. Where he sate on his bed
their errand they to him made known; each said his say as to
him seemed best, and bade him go back to his land, so that he
never more with hostility should seek France. The while that
these three earls said their errand, the emperor sate as if he were
dumb, and answer never any gave to these earls; but he listened
eagerly, wicked in his thought. Then Walwain became angry,
as a thane enraged; and said these words Walwain the keen:
" Luces the mighty, thou art emperor of Rome! We are
Arthur's men, noblest of Britons. He sendeth to thee his
messengers, without greeting; he bids thee march to Rome,
that is thine own realm, and let him hold France, that he
won with fight; and hold thou thy realm, and thy Rome-folk.
Whilom thy ancestors invaded France; with fight they there
won immense possessions; so awhile they there lived, and
afterwards they it lost. With fight Arthur it won, and he it
will possess. He is our lord, we are his warriors; he ordered us
to say sooth to thyself, if thou wilt not back march, thy bane
he will be. And if thou wilt not back turn, but execute thy will,
and thou wilt win the kingdom to thine own hand, now to-morrow
is the day, have it if thou it may obtain! "
　　Then answered the emperor, with great wrath: " I will not
back march, but France I will win; my ancestors it held, and
I will it have. But if he would become my man, and acknowledge me for lord, and truely serve me, and hold me for master,
I will make peace with him, and all his men; and let him hold
Britain, that Julius had awhile in his hand, and many other lands,

that Julius had in hand, that he hath no right to, though he possess the realm, that he shall all lose, unless he make peace."

Then answered Walwain, who was Arthur's relative: " Belin and Brenne, both the brothers, Britain they possessed, and France they conquered; and afterwards they marched soon, and won Rome, and there they dwelt afterwards well many years. When this was all done, then was Brenne emperor, and ruled Rome, and all the people. And thus is Rome our right, that thou holdest in hand; and if we may live, we will it have, unless thou wilt acknowledge that Arthur is king over thee, and each year send him tribute of thy land; and if thou goest to him in amity, thou mayest live the quieter! "

Then sate by the emperor a knight of his kin, named Quencelin; noble man in Rome. This knight answered before the emperor, and thus him said—the knight was wicked:—" Knights, return you back, and make known to your king, that the Britons are bold, but they are accounted worthless; for ever they make boast—their honour is little! " More he thought to say, when Walwain drew his sword, and smote him upon the head, so that it fell in two; and he hastily anon ran to his horse; and they up leapt with grim countenance; and these words said Walwain the good: " So help me the same Lord, that formed the daylight, if ever any of your men is so keen, that after us he pursue, I will him kill; he shall be cut in pieces with my broad sword! " Even with the same speech then called the emperor: " Hold them! hold! They all shall hang upon high trees, or with horses be drawn in pieces! " Even with this saying that the emperor said, the earls gan to ride, and spurred their steeds; they shook in their hands spears exceeding long; bare their broad shields before breast. Soon gan to ride the bold earls, and ever the emperor loud gan to call: " Seize them! slay them! They have us disgraced! " There men might hear, who were there beside, thousands of the people call: " Hither, hither, weapons! Go we after them! Hither our shields; the men will escape! " Soon after them went weaponed warriors; there six, there seven, there eight, there nine. And ever the earls rode quickly, and ever awhile looked behind them; and ever the knights of Rome quick after came.

And there came near a knight, riding swiftest of all, and ever he called most keenly: " Turn again, knights, and defend you with fight! It is to you much shame, that ye will fly." Walwain knew the shout of the Romanish men; he turned his steed, and

to him gan ride; and smote him through with the spear, as if
he were spitted, and drew to him the spear—the man died soon—
and these words said Walwain the keen: " Knight, thou rodest
too fast; better were it to thee (haddest thou been) at Rome! "
Marcel hight the knight, of noble lineage.   When Walwain saw
that he fell to ground, soon his sword he out drew, and smote
from Marcel the head; and these words said Walwain the good:
" Marcel, go to hell, and there tell them tales, and dwell there
for ever, with Quencelin, thy companion; and hold there your
communing,—better it were to you in Rome; for thus we shall
teach you our British speech! "

Gerin saw how it fared, how that the Romanish lay there
down; and spurred his horse, and met another, and smote him
throughout with his spear; and these words spake: " Ride now
so, Roman, and sink thee to hell; and thus we shall sink you,
if God will us help! Threat is worth nought, unless there be
deeds eke! " Beof saw, the brave man, how his comrades had
done; and turned his horse wondrously quick, and with all his
might advanced to a knight, and smote him above the shield,
so that his good burny burst, and throughout the neck the spear
drove full soon. And thus the earl gan to call keenly to his
companions: " The Britons will us destroy, if we hence go,
unless we the better begin ere we hence depart! " Even with
the speech that the earl said, they turned them soon, wondrously
prompt; and each drew his sword quickly, and each slew his
Roman; and afterwards their horses they turned, and held their
way. And the Romanish men rode ever after them; oft they
smote on them, oft they them reproached; oft they said to
them: " Ye shall pay for the deed! " but they might not
through anything any of them down bring, nor any harm there
do to them in the conflicts. But ever awhile the earls back
turned, and ere they separated, the worse was to the Rome-folk.

Thus they proceeded fifteen miles, until they came to a place
under a fair wood, hard by the castle where Arthur lay fast.
Three miles therefrom to the wood thronged nine thousand bold
Britons, whom Arthur thither sent, who best knew the land;
they would learn the sooth, of Walwain the keen, and of his
companions, how they had fared; whether they were alive, or
they lay by the way. These knights proceeded through the
wood wondrously still, upon a hill, and eagerly beheld. They
caused all the horsemen to alight in the wood, and get ready
their weapons, and all their weeds (garments), except an hundred
men, that there should look out, if they might descry through

thing of any kind. Then saw they afar, in a great plain, three
knights ride with all their main. After the three knights there
came thirty; after the thirty they saw three thousand; thereafter came thronging thirty thousand anon, of Romanish folk,
clad in armour. And ever the earls before them quickly rode,
ever the right way that toward the wood lay, where their comrades were well hid. The earls rode to the wood; the Romanish
men rode after; the Britons attacked them on their rested
steeds, and smote in front, and felled an hundred anon. Then
weened the Rome-folk that Arthur came riding, and were very
greatly afraid; and the Britons pursued after them, and slew
of the folk fifteen hundred. Then came them to help sixteen
thousand of their own folk, whom Arthur had thither sent, bold
Britons, with burnies clad.

Then came there riding one that was a rich earl, named
Petreius, a noble man of Rome, with six thousand warriors, to
help the Romanish forces; and with great strength they leapt
to the Britons, and few there they captured, but many they
slew. The Britons fled to the wood; the others pursued after
them; and the Britons on foot firmly against them stood, and
the Romanish men fought riding; and the Britons advanced
to them, and slew their horses, and many there took, and into
the wood drew. Then was Petreius wrath, that his force was
there the worse; and he with his host retreated from the wood;
and the Britons followed them, and slew them behind. When
the Britons were out of the wood, come out in the field, then
withstood the Rome-folk with fierce strength. Then began the
mickle fight!—there fell earls and many a good knight; there
fell in that day fifteen thousand of noble men, ere it were
even. There might he find, whoso would prove his strength, hand
against hand, the strong against the strong, shield against shield,
knights there fell! The paths ran with bloody streams; gold-
coloured shields lay over the fields; all the day long they held
the strong fight. Petreius on his side his folk held together;
then it soon happened that the Britons had the worse. The
noble Earl of Oxford, who was named Beof, a noble British man,
saw that, that in no wise might it be, that the Britons should not
fall, unless they had counsel. The earl then called to him noble
knights, of the best of all, the Britons, and of the keenest of all,
that there were alive, and drew him in the field, near the host;
and thus him said—in heart to him was uneasiness: "Knights,
hearken now to me; the Lord us help! We are hither come,
and have undertaken this fight, without Arthur's counsel who

is our chief. If to us good befalleth, we shall please him the better, and if to us befalleth evil, he will hate us. But if ye will do my counsel, then shall we ride all merry. We are three hundred knights, helmed thanes, brave men and keen, nobly born; shew ye your courage—we are of one kith—ride ye when I ride, and follow my counsel. Advance ye all to him, to the knight that I do; take ye no steed, nor any knight's weed, but every good knight slay ever downright!"

Even with the words that the knight of Oxford said to his companions beside, then gan he to ride, even all they rode then as swift as hound driveth the hart, and his comrades after, with all their might, throughout the mickle fight, all the troop; they flew on their steeds; the folk they there killed. Woe was to them born, that were in the way before them, for all they it trod down, with horses and with steeds; and so they came near, and Petreius they captured. Beof rode to him, and with arms him clasped, and drew him off his steed, and on earth him stretched; he knew beside him were his bold knights. The Britons down smote; Petreius they drew along; and the Rome-folk fought boldly; and at the last man might not know who smote other; there was much blood shed, mischief was in the conflict! Then saw Walwain truly, where he was beside; with seven hundred knights he gan thither move, and what he found in his way, all he it destroyed. And riding he took Petreius, on his good steed; and led forth Petreius, loath though it were to him, until they came to the wood, where he well knew surely to hold the noble man of Rome; and eft out in the field proceeded, and began to fight. There men might see sorrow enough! shields break; knights fall; helms dropping; noble men dying; bloody fields; paled faces! The Britons rushed towards them; then the Rome-folk fled; and the Britons them slew, and many they took alive; and when the day ended woe was to the Rome-folk, woe! Then bound men fast the Romanish knights, and led them to the wood, before Walwain; twenty hundred knights watched them in the night.

When it was day on the morrow, the folk gan to stir; forth they gan march to their sovereign, and brought him such offering, that was lief to him to have. Then spake him Arthur thus: "Welcome, Petreius! Now is one here that will teach thee British speech. Thou boasted before the emperor, that thou wouldest me kill; take all my castles, and my kingdom; and much good should be to thee of that thou desiredest to have. I will give thee, full truly, my castle in Paris; and there

thou shalt dwell, as to thee will be most loathsome of all; shalt
thou nevermore thy life thence lead!" Arthur took the knights
that there were captured; three hundred riders he took eke
anon, who all were comrades, knights most brave, and keen men
in fight; and bade them on the morrow manly arise, bind the
Romanish men with strong chains, and lead Petreius to the
burgh of Paris. Four earls he commanded to bring them forth;
Cador, Borel, Beduer, and Richer; he ordered them to be companions, so that they were secure, and to come again soon to
their sovereign.

This was all thus spoken, but it was soon known. Spies went
over the king's host, and heard say sooth words, whither Arthur
would send the knights that he had in bonds; and the spies
forthright proceeded forth by night, until they came soon to the
emperor of Rome, and told all their tale, how these four earls
should march, and lead forth Petreius to the burgh of Paris;
and all they told the way that in to Paris lay, and where men
might them intercept in a deep valley, and take from them
Petreius the noble man, and the four earls conquer, and fast them
bind. Luces heard this, the emperor of Rome, and he leapt to
weapon as it were a lion; and ordered ten thousand chosen
knights to horse and to arms, quickly forwards to march. He
called Sextorius, of Lybia he was king, of Turkey duke; he
sent after Evander, who from Babylon was come there; he
called to the senators Bal, Catel, and Carrius,—these were all
of royal birth, and these were all chosen,—promptly to ride,
and to liberate Petreius.

Anon as it was even forth they marched; twelve knights
them led of the people that were exceeding wary, and knew the
ways. When the Rome-folk rode, resounded burnies; they set
on their heads high helms; shields on their backs—the valiant
Rome-folk. They marched all night, exceedingly fast, until they
came in the way that into Paris lay; then were they before,
and the Britons behind. But alas! that Cador the keen knew
it not, that the Rome-folk had before rode them! They came
in a wood, in a spot exceeding fair, in a deep dale, dark on the
sides; they swore between them, that there they would engage.
There they lay still a little while; and it gan to dawn, and the
beasts gan to stir. Then came Arthur's men advancing by
way, right the same way where the other host lay; they rode
singing—the men were blithe! Nevertheless Cador was there,
most wise and most wary; he and Borel the earl rich, advanced
them together, and took between them five hundred knights,

and marched before, weaponed champions. Richer and Beduer
came behind them there, and led the knights, whom they had
captured, Petreius and his companions, who were taken. Then
came they riding upon the Rome-folk; and the Rome-folk
rushed towards them with fierce strength, and smote on the
Britons with exceeding bitter blows; brake the Britons' ranks—
mischief was among the folk—the wood gan resound, warriors
there fell! The Britons withstood them, and strongly defended
themselves. Richer heard that, and the earl Beduer, how their
comrades before them fought. Petreius they took, and all their
prisoners, and with three hundred swains sent them into the
wood. And they themselves advanced toward their comrades,
and smote on the Rome-folk with fierce strength; there was
many a blow given, and many a man there was slain. Then
perceived Evander, who was a heathen king most wary, that
their folk gan wax, and the Britons gan wane; and his best
knights approached them together, and advanced upon the
Britons, as if they would them bite. The Britons then were
weakened, and theirs was the worse; they (the Romans) slew,
they took all that they came nigh.

Woe was there to the Britons without Arthur! Their remedy
was too little there, at their great need. There was Borel slain,
and deprived of life-day. Evander the king him killed with his
wicked craft, and three Britons eke, high men born. There
were slain three hundred of their companions; and many they
took alive, and fast them bound;—then knew they not any good
counsel, for they all weened to be dead; nevertheless they
fought as bravely as they might.

Then had out marched from Arthur's host the king of
Poitou, hardy man renowned; Guitard he hight; Gascony he
possessed; he had for companions five hundred riders, three
hundred archers, keen men to fight, and seven hundred on
foot that were prompt for harm. They were gone in to the
land to obtain fodder, both fodder and meat, to carry to their
host. The clamour they heard of the Rome-folk; their deeds
they relinquished, and thitherward gan ride the strong-mooded
men and swift, of sloth devoid, until they came soon near to the
fight. Guitard and his knights there right forthright grasped
their shields, knights most bold; and all the archers pressed
them beside; and the men on foot gan advance; and all together
they on smote, with their smart blows. At the first onset the
Romanish men fell; fifteen hundred to the ground; there was
slain Evander, who was ere king full stern; Catellus of Rome

forgot there his decrees! Then made they there flight, who ere
held conflict; the Rome-folk turned the backs, and fled. The
Britons pursued after them, and greeted them with mischief;
and so many there they took, and so many there they slew, that
the Britons' host might not fell any more! And the Romanish
men, that there might escape, rode full soon to the emperor,
and told him tiding of Arthur the king;—for they weened in
sooth that Arthur thither were come; then was the emperor
and his host greatly afraid, whom the Britons had slain—that
to them seemed good. Backward they (the Britons) then went,
with bold booty, and came again to the place where the fight
had been, and buried the dead, and the alive they gan forth
lead. And they sent after Petreius, whom they previously
captured, and after his companions, that were previously taken,
and sent them all full truly in to the burgh of Paris; and filled
three castles, and fast them inclosed, after Arthur's command,
noblest of all kings. All the Britons loved Arthur; to all of
them stood dread of him that dwelt in the land; so did it to the
emperor, of Arthur he had mickle care; and all the Rome-folk
of Arthur were afraid.

Then was it in sooth found, what Merlin whilom said, that
Rome should for Arthur fall in fire, and the walls of stone
quake and fall. This same token should be of Luces the
emperor, and of the senators, who with him came from Rome;
and in the same wise, they there gan fall; what Merlin in fore-
days said, all they it found there, as they did ere, and subsequently well everywhere; ere Arthur were born, Merlin it all
predicted.

The emperor heard say sooth words, how his men were taken,
and how his folk was eke slain. Then were in his army manifold
sorrows; some lamented their friends; some threatened their
enemies; some got ready their weapons—mischief was given to
them! Then saw Luces, that evil was befallen to him, for each
day he lost of his people; but he the harm felt, his noble men he
lost. He became then afraid wondrously much, and betook him
to counsel and to some communing, that he would march to
Aust, with all his host; forth by Lengres he would proceed,—of
Arthur he had mickle care!

Arthur had his spies in the army of the emperor, and they
soon caused him to know whither he (the emperor) would go.
Arthur caused soon his host to be assembled, stilly by night his
best knights; and forth the king marched with his good folk.
On his right hand he let Lengres stand, and proceeded forward

in the way that Luces would pass. When he came in a dale, under a down, there he gan halt, keenest of all kings;—the dale is in sooth named Sosie. Arthur there alighted down, and ordered all his people that they in haste should get ready their weapons, and prepare them to fight, as brave knights should; so that when the Rome-folk there should come riding, that they should attack them, as brave knights should do. All the swains, and the impotent thanes, and of the small (base) folk many thousands, the king set them on a hill, with many standards;—that he did for stratagem; thereof he thought to boast, as it afterwards happened, thereafter full soon. Arthur took ten thousand of his noble knights, and sent on the right hand, clad in armour; he caused other ten thousand to march on his left hand; ten thousand before; ten thousand behind; with himself he held sixteen thousand; aside he sent into a fair wood seventeen thousand good knights, well weaponed men, the wood to guard, so that they might fare thither, if to him were need. Then was of Gloucester an earl with the best, Moruith he was named, a man exceeding keen; to him he committed the wood and the host. "And if it befalleth, as the living God will, that they be overcome, and begin to flee; pursue ye after them, with all your might, and all that ye may overtake deprive it of life-day; the fat and the lean, the rich and the poor. For in never any land, nor in any nation are knights all so good as are with myself; knights all so brave, knights all so powerful, knights all so strong, in ever any land! Ye are under Christ knights keenest of all; and I am mightiest of all kings under God himself. Do we well this deed; God us well speed!" The knights then answered, stilly under heaven: "All we shall well do, and all we shall undertake; nithing be the knight, that sheweth not his might here right!" Then sent they on both sides, all the men on foot; then caused he the Dragon to be set up, the matchless standard; delivered it to a king who well could it hold. Angel, King of Scotland, held in hand (commanded) the foremost troop; Cador, the Earl of Cornwall, held the troop behind; Beof had one, the Earl of Oxford; the Earl of Chester, Gerin, the fourth troop held with him. The force upon the down held Æscil, King of Denmark. Lot held the one, who was dear to the king; Howel of Britanny held another. Walwain the keen was by the king. Kay commanded one, who was steward of the king; Beduer another, who was the king's cup-bearer. The Earl of Flanders, Howeldin, had a troop with him. A mickle troop had Gwitard, the King of

Gascony land. Wigein, Earl of Leicester, and Jonathas, Earl of
Dorchester, they commanded the two troops that there were
on foot. The Earl of Chester, Cursaleyn, and the Earl of Bath,
who hight Urgein, they commanded both the troops that were
there beside; these should on two sides advance to the fight, with
these two earls, that brave knights were;—Arthur had troth
the earls were true. When all the troops were set as Arthur
thought good, then called to him the King of Britain all his
councillors, that were skilfullest in judgment; and thus said
Arthur anon to his noble men: " Hearken now towards me, my
dear friends; ye have twice attacked the Romanish men, and
twice they are overcome, and slain, and captured, because they
all with wrong covet our land. And my heart saith to me,
through our high Lord, that yet they shall be overcome, both
slain and captured. Ye have overcome Norwegians; ye have
overcome Danes; Scotland and Ireland ye have all won to your
hand; Normandy and France ye have conquered with fight.
Three and thirty kingdoms I hold in mine own hand, that ye
have won for me under the sun! And these are the worst men
of all men alive; heathen people! To God they are loathsome;
our Lord they desert, and to Mahoun they draw. And Luces,
the emperor, of God's self hath no care, who hath for companions
heathen hounds, God's enemies; we shall them destroy, and lay
them to ground, and ourselves be safe, with the Lord's will,
that ruleth all deeds! " Then answered the earls there: " All
we are ready, to live and to lie with our dear king! "

When this army was all prepared, then was it daylight; and
Luces at Langres moved, and all his Rome-folk; he commanded
his men to blow his golden trumpets, get ready his host, for
forth he would march from Lengres to Aust, as his way right
lay. And forth gan ride the Romanish people, until they came
a mile near to Arthur.

Then heard the Rome-folk hard tidings; they saw all the
dales, and all the downs, and all the hills covered with helms;
high standards, warriors them held, sixty thousand waving with
the wind; shields glitter, burnies shine; gold-coloured vests,
men most stern; steeds leap—the earth stirred! The emperor
saw the king fare, where he was by the wood-shaw; then said
he Luces, the lord of Rome, and spake with his men with loud
voice: " What are these outlaws, that have preceded us in this
way? Take we our weapons, and march we to them; they shall
be slain, and some alive flayed; they all shall be dead, with
torment destroyed! " Even with the words they seized their

weapons. When they were arrayed with their good weapons, then spake soon Luces, the lord of Rome: " Quickly advance we to them; we all shall do well! " There were come with him five and twenty kings, heathen folk all, that held of Rome, earls and eke dukes, of the eastern world. " Lordings," quoth Luces then, " Mahoun be gracious to you! Ye are powerful kings, and obey unto Rome. Rome is my right, richest of all burghs; and I ought to be highest of all men alive. Ye see here on the field those who are our foes; they think to rule highly over our realm; hold us for base, and themselves become rich. But we shall oppose them with bold strength; for our race was highest of all men alive, and won all the lands that they looked on; and Julius the strong marched into Britain, and won to his hands many kingdoms. Now would our underlings be kings over us, but they shall buy it with their bare backs; never again shall they return to Britain! "

Even with the words then moved the army; by thousands and by thousands they thronged together; each king prepared host of his folk. When it was all formed, and the army appointed, then were there right told full fifteen hosts; two kings there were ever comrades; four earls and a duke disposed them together; and the emperor by himself, with ten thousand champions. When the folk gan to stir, the earth gan to din; trumpets there blew; hosts were arrayed; horns there resounded with loud voice, sixty thousand blew together. More there sounded of Arthur's companions than sixty thousand men with horns; the welkin gan to din, the earth gan to tremble! Together they charged as if heaven would fall! First they let fly, exceedingly quick darts all as thick as the snow down falleth; stones they let afterwards sternly wind through the air. Then cracked spears; shivered spears;—helms rolled; noble men fell; —burnies brake in pieces, blood outflowed;—the fields were discoloured; standards fell! Wounded knights over all wandered over the weald; and sixty hundred there were trodden to death by horses! Knights there perished; blood out ran;—flowed by paths bloody streams;—woe was among the folk,—the harm was without bounds! So all as say the writings that skilful men made, that was the third greatest battle that ever here was fought, so that at the last no warrior knew on whom he should smite, and whom he should spare; for no man knew other there, for the quantity of blood!

Then removed the fight from the place where they ere fought, and they began widely to rush together; and a new conflict

began, narrowly contested;—there were the Rome-people grievously treated! Then came there three kings, of heathen land;
of Ethiopia was the one; the second was an African; the third
was of Lybia, of heathen land. They came to the host at the
east end, and brake the body-of-troops that the Britons there
held, and anon felled fifteen hundred bold thanes of Arthur's
folk; then the Britons turned the backs soon. But then came
there riding two keen earls, that was, Beduer and Kay, Arthur's
cup-bearer and his relative; their Britons they saw hewed in
pieces with swords. There became enraged the earls most bold,
and with ten thousand knights pressed to the fight, amid the
throng, where they were thickest, and slew the Rome-folk very
grievously; and went over the fight, after their will. Then
were they too daring, and ruled them too evilly; alas! alas!
that they were not then wary; that they could not guard themselves against their enemies! For they were too keen, and too
presumptuous, and fought too rashly, and too far advanced, and
spread too widely over the broad conflict. Then came the King
of Media, the mickle and the broad; a heathen chief,—there he
harm wrought; he led for companions twenty thousand riders;
he held in his hand a spear exceeding strong. The spear he
forth thrust with his strong might, and smote the Earl Beduer
before in the breast, so that the burny soon burst, before and
behind, and his breast was opened; the blood came forth luke-
warm. There fell Beduer anon, dead upon the ground; there
was misery and sorrow enow! There Kay found Beduer lie him
dead there, and Kay would carry away the body with himself;
with twenty hundred knights he approached thereabout, and
strongly fought, and felled the Rome-folk, and slew there many
thousand men of Media; the fight was exceeding strong, and
they were thereat long. Then arrived there a king most hateful,
with sixty thousand good men of his land; Setor the keen, who
came him from Lybia. There the strong king gan him fight
with Kay, and wounded Kay sorely in the strong fight, to the
bare death—grievous was the deed!

His knights there right carried him from the fight, with mickle
strength through the fight they pierced. Woe was to Arthur
the king for the tiding! That saw the rich thane, who was
named Ridwathlan, Beduer's sister's son, of noble Britons he
was descended, that Boccus with his strong spear had slain
Beduer. Woe was to him alive, when his uncle was dead; for
he of all men most him loved. He called knights most good of
his kindred, and of the dearest of all that he knew alive; five

hundred by tale advanced together. Then said Ridwathlan, noble man of Britain: " Knights, ye are of my kindred, come ye here to me, and avenge we Beduer, mine uncle, who was best of our race, whom Boccus hath slain with his strong spear. Go we all together, and fell our foes! "

Even with the words he forth pushed, and all his noble companions with him anon; and Boccus the king they knew, where he was in the combat; with his spear and with his shield many a knight he killed. Ridwathlan drew out his sword soon, and struck at him, and smote the king on the head, so that it severed in two, and eke the burny-hood, so that it (the sword) stopt at the teeth; and the heathen king fell to the ground, and his foul soul sank into hell! Ridwathlan then said—cruel he was in mood—" Boccus, now thou hast bought dear that Beduer thou slew; and thy soul shall now be companion of the Worse! " Even with the words, as if it were the wind, he pressed to the fight; as a whirlwind doth in the field, when it heaveth the dust high from the earth, all so Ridwathlan rushed on his enemies. All they it slew that they came nigh, the while that they might wield their noble weapons; in all the fight were no knights better, the while that the life lasted them in their breasts. Boccus the king they slew, and a thousand of his knights; then was Beduer avenged well with the best!

There was a brave earl, of noble race, who was named Leir, lord of Boulogne; he beheld in the fight an enemy advance, that was an admiral, of Babylon he was prince; much folk he felled down to the ground. And the earl that perceived; in heart was to him uneasiness; he drew to his breast a broad shield, and he grasped in his hand a spear that was most strong, and spurred his horse with all his main, and hit the admiral with a smart blow under the breast, that the burny gan to burst, so that the spear pierced through there behind him full a fathom; the wretch fell to the ground! That saw soon the admiral's son, who is named Gecron; and grasped his spear anon, and smote Leir the earl sore on the left side, throughout the heart,—the earl down fell. Walwain perceived that, where he was in the fight; and he wrathed him wondrously much; that saw Howel, noble man of Brittany, and he thither advanced, with fifteen hundred men; hardy warriors with Howel went; and Walwain before them man most stern of mood; he had for comrades five and twenty hundred bold Britons,—then began they to fight!

There were the Rome-folk grievously treated; Howel them

attacked, Walwain them met; there was wondrous cry, the
welkin resounded; the earth gan to tremble, the stones there
shivered! Streams of blood ran from the wretched folk, the
slaughter was immense, then were the Britons weary! Kinard,
the Earl of Striguil, left the King Howel, and took with him
Labius, Rimarc, and Boclovius. These were the keenest men
that any king had; these were among men earls mighty strong!
They would not, for their mickle mood (pride), follow Howel
the good, but by themselves they slew all that they came nigh.
That saw a powerful man of the Rome-people, how Kinard the
keen killed there their folk; and the knight gan him alight from
his dear steed, and took him in his hand a spear made of steel,
and bathed it in blood; and he aside went, until he came to
the spot where Kinard the strong fought. Kinard's burny he
up raised, and he the earl there slew. Then shouted loud all the
Rome-folk, and turned to the Britons, and brake their troops;
and felled the standards, the folk down sank; shields there
shivered, warriors there fell; there fell to ground fifteen thousand
bold Britons—mischief there was rife! So lasted long the fight
exceeding strong.

Walwain gan pass over the mickle slaughter, and assembled
all his knights, where he found them in the fight. There near
came riding Howel the mighty; they assembled their fair folk
anon, and forth they gan wend, and rode to the Rome-folk
with strong wrath, and quickly approached them, and brake
their French ranks. And Walwain forth right, there he found
Luces the emperor live under shield; and Walwain struck at
him with the steel sword, and the emperor struck at him, who
was man exceeding stern; shield against shield, the pieces
there flew; sword against sword clashed well often, fire flew
from the steel; the adversaries were enraged! There was
fight most strong—all the host was stirred! The emperor
weened to destroy Walwain, that he might in after days boast
for the deed. But the Britons thronged towards them, most
angrily, and the Romanish men liberated their emperor; and
they charged together as if heaven would fall! All the daylight
they held afterwards the fight, a little while ere the sun went
to ground. Arthur then called—noblest of all kings: "Now
go we all to them, my brave knights! And God himself aid
us our enemies to fell!"

Even with the words then blew men the trumpets; fifteen
thousand anon thronged together to blow horns and trumps;
the earth gan to tremble for the great blast, for the mickle

clamour! The Rome-folk turned backs to the fight; standards fell,—noble men perished,—those fled who might,—the fated there fell! Much man-slaughter was there; might it no man tell, how many hundred men were there hewed in pieces in the mickle throng, in the man-slaughter! The emperor was slain in strange manner, so that no man of ever any country afterwards ever knew it to say, who killed the emperor. But when the fight was all done, and the folk was all in joy, then found men the emperor pierced through with a spear.

Word came to Arthur, where he was in his tent, that the emperor was slain, and deprived of life-day. Arthur caused a tent to be pitched, amidst a broad field, and thither caused to be borne Luces the emperor, and caused him to be covered with gold-coloured clothes; and caused him there to be watched three full days, the while he caused to be made a work exceeding rich, a long chest; and it to be covered all with gold. And he caused to be laid therein Luces of Rome, who was a most doughty man, the while his days lasted. The yet did Arthur more, noblest of all Britons; Arthur caused to be sought all the powerful men, kings and earls, and the richest barons, who in the fight were slain, and deprived of life-day; he caused them to be buried with great pomp. But he caused three kings to bear Luces the emperor, and caused a bier to be made, rich and exceeding lofty; and caused them soon to be sent to Rome. And greeted all the Rome-people with a great taunt, and said that he sent them the tribute of his land, and eft would also send them more greeting, if they would yearn of Arthur's gold; and thereafter full soon ride into Rome, and tell them tidings of the King of Britain, and Rome-walls repair, that were of yore fallen down;—" And so will I rule the fierce Rome-folk!" All this boast was idly done, for otherwise it fared, all otherwise it happened: the people he left, through wicked tiding, all through Modred his relative, wickedest of all men!

In the mickle fight Arthur lost of his knights, five and twenty thousand, hewed in pieces on the ground, of Britons most bold, bereaved of life. Kay was wounded sore, wondrously much; to Kinun he was carried, and soon thereafter he was dead. He was buried there beside the castle, among hermits, who was the noble man. Kay hight the earl, Kinun the castle; Arthur gave him the town, and he thereat was entombed, and set there the name after himself; for Kay's death he named it Kain (Caen); now and evermore so it hight there. After Beduer was slain, and deprived of life-day, Arthur caused him to be borne to his

castle Bæios (Bayeux), and there he was buried, in the burgh;
without the south gate in earth men him laid. Howeldin was
floated forth into Flanders; and all his best knights there
floated forth-right into the earldoms whence they there came.
And all the dead in earth men them laid; in Terouane they lie
all clean.

Leir, the earl, men carried into Boulogne; and Arthur then
thereafter dwelt in a land in Burgundy, that to him seemed best;
the land he all ruled, and all the castles appointed; and said
that he would himself hold the land. And afterwards he made
his threat, that he would in summer march into Rome, and
acquire all the realm, and himself be emperor where Luces ere
dwelt. And many of the Rome-folk would that it so should be,
for they were adread to their bare death, so that many away
there fled, and their castles abandoned; and many sent messengers to Arthur the strong; and many spake with him, and
yearned Arthur's peace; and some they would against Arthur
hold, and hold Rome against him, and defend the realm. And
nevertheless they were afraid for their destruction, so that they
knew not under Christ any good counsel. Then was it there
come to pass, what Merlin said erewhile, that Rome-walls should
fall down before Arthur; that was fulfilled there by the emperor,
who fell there in the fight, with fifty thousand men; there sank to
the ground the rich Rome-people! Then Arthur weened in sooth
to win all Rome, and dwelt in Burgundy, noblest of all kings.

Then came there on a time a brave man riding, and brought
tiding to Arthur the king, from Modred, his sister's son; to
Arthur he was welcome, for he weened that he brought news
most good. Arthur lay all the night long, and spake with the
young knight; so never would he say to him sooth how it fared.
When it was day on the morrow, and people gan to stir, Arthur
then up arose, and stretched his arms; he arose up, and sate
down, as if he were exceeding sick. Then asked him a fair
knight: " Lord, how hast thou fared to-night? " Arthur then
answered—in mind he was uneasy: " To-night in my sleep,
where I lay in chamber, I dreamt a dream—therefore I am full
sorry. I dreamt that men raised me upon a hall; the hall I
gan bestride, as if I would ride; all the lands that I possessed,
all I there overlooked. And Walwain sate before me; my
sword he bare in hand. Then approached Modred there, with
innumerable folk; he bare in his hand a battle-axe strong; he
began to hew exceeding hardily; and the posts all hewed in
pieces, that held up the hall. There I saw Wenhaver eke,

dearest of women to me; all the mickle hall roof with her hand she drew down; the hall gan to tumble, and I tumbled to the ground, so that my right arm brake in pieces,—then said Modred, 'Have that!' Down fell the hall; and Walwain gan to fall, and fell on the earth; his arms both brake. And I grasped my dear sword with my left hand, and smote off Modred his head, so that it rolled on the field. And the queen I cut all in pieces with my dear sword, and afterwards I set her down in a black pit. And all my good people set to flight, so that I knew not under Christ, where they were gone. But myself I gan stand upon a weald, and I there gan to wander wide over the moors; there I saw gripes, and grisly fowls! Then approached a golden lion over the down;—a beast most fair, that our Lord made;—the lion ran towards me, and took me by the middle, and forth gan her move, and to the sea went. And I saw the waves drive in the sea; and the lion in the flood went with myself. When we came in the sea, the waves took her from me; but there approached a fish, and brought me to land;—then was I all wet, and weary from sorrow, and sick. When I gan to wake, greatly gan I to quake; then gan I to tremble as if I all burnt with fire. And so I have all night of my dream much thought; for I wot with certainty, gone is all my bliss, for ever in my life sorrow I must endure! Alas! that I have not here Wenhaver, my queen!"

Then answered the knight: "Lord, thou hast wrong; men should never a dream with sorrow interpret. Thou art the mightiest man, that reigneth in land, and the wisest of all that dwelleth under heaven. If it were befallen—as will it not our Lord!—that Modred, thy sister's son, had taken thy queen, and set all thy royal land in his own hand, that thou to him committedest, when thou thoughtest to go to Rome; and had he done all this with his treachery, the yet thou mightest thee avenge with weapon worthily, and eft thy land hold, and govern thy people, and thine enemies fell, who did evil to thee, and slay them all clean, that there remain not one."

Arthur then answered, noblest of all kings: "So long as is ever, weened I that never, that ever Modred, my relative, who is man dearest to me, would betray me, for all my realm, nor Wenhaver, my queen, weaken in thought; would it not begin, for any worldly man!"

Even with the words forth-right then answered the knight: "I say thee sooth, dear king, for I am thy underling. Thus hath Modred done; thy queen he hath taken, and thy fair land

set in his own hand. He is king, and she is queen; of thy coming
is there no expectation, for they ween not ever in sooth, that
thou shalt come back from Rome. I am thine own man, and
saw this treason; and I am come to thyself, to say thee sooth.
My head be in pledge, that I have said thee sooth, without
leasing, of thy loved queen, and of Modred, thy sister's son,
how he hath taken Britain from thee."

Then sate it all still in Arthur's hall; then was there sorrow
with the good king; then were the British men therefore
exceedingly dispirited. Then after a while voices there stirred;
wide men might hear the Britons' clamour, and gan to tell in
speeches of many kind, how they would destroy Modred and
the queen, and slay all the people that held with Modred.

Arthur then called, fairest of all Britons: " Sit ye down still,
knights in hall, and I will you tell strange discourse. Now
to-morrow, when it is day, and the Lord it sendeth, forth I will
march in toward Britain; and Modred I will slay, and burn the
queen; and all I will destroy, that approved the treachery.
And here I will leave the dearest of men to me, Howel, my loved
relative, noblest of my kin; and half my army I will leave in this
land, to maintain all this kingdom, that I have in my hand.
And when these things are all done, back I will come to Rome,
and deliver my fair land to Walwain my relation; and afterwards perform my threat, by my bare life; all my enemies shall
be destroyed!"

Then stood him up Walwain, who was Arthur's relative, and
said these words,—the earl was incensed: " Almighty God!
ruler of dooms, guardian of all middle-earth! Why is it befallen,
that my brother Modred this sin has wrought? But to-day I
forsake him here, before this assembly; and I will him destroy
with the Lord's will; myself I will him hang, highest of all
wretches; the queen I will, with God's law, draw all in pieces
with horses. For may I never be blithe, the while I am alive,
until I have avenged mine uncle with the best!"

Then answered the Britons with bold voice: " All our weapons
are ready; now to-morrow we shall march!" On the morrow
when it was day, and the Lord it sent, Arthur forth him moved,
with his good folk; half he it left, and half it forth led. Forth
he marched through the land until he came to Whitsand; ships
he had soon, many and excellent; but full a fortnight there lay
the host, abiding the weather, deprived of wind (becalmed).

Now was there some wicked knight in Arthur's army, anon
as he heard it determined of Modred's death, he took his swain

quickly, and sent to this land; and sent word to Wenhaver, how it had happened, and how Arthur was on his march, with a great host; and how he would take on, and all how he would do. The queen came to Modred, who was to her dearest of men, and told him tiding of Arthur the king, how he would take on, and all how he would do.

Modred took his messengers, and sent to Saxland, after Childrich, who was king most powerful; and bade him come to Britain—thereof he should have possession. Modred bade Childrich, the strong and the rich, to send messengers wide, on the four sides of Saxland, and bid all the knights that they might get, that they should come soon to this kingdom; and he would to Childrich give part of his realm, all beyond the Humber; because he should him help to fight against his uncle King Arthur. Childrich proceeded soon into Britain. When Modred had assembled his host of men, then were there told sixty thousand hardy warriors of heathen folk, when they were come hither, for Arthur's harm, and to help Modred, wickedest of men! When the army was gathered of each people, then were they there in a heap an hundred thousand, heathens and christians, with Modred the king.

Arthur lay at Whitsand; a fortnight seemed to him too long; and Modred knew all what Arthur there would; each day came messengers to him from the king's army. Then befell it on a time, much rain it gan to rain, and the wind it gan to turn, and stood from the east end. And Arthur proceeded to ship with all his host, and ordered that his shipmen should bring him to Romney, where he thought to come up into this land. When he came to the haven, Modred was opposite to him; as the day gan light, they began to fight, all the day long; many a man dead there lay! Some they fought on land, some by the strand; some they let fly sharp spears out of the ships. Walwain went before, and cleared the way; and slew there soon eleven thanes; he slew Childrich's son, who was come there with his father. To rest went the sun; woe was then to the men! There was Walwain slain, and deprived of life-day, through a Saxish earl—sorry be his soul! Then was Arthur sorry, and sorrowful therefore in heart; and these words said, mightiest of all Britons: " Now I have lost my loved swains! I knew by my dream, what sorrow were given to me! Slain is Angel the king, who was mine own darling, and Walwain, my sister's son—woe is me that I was born man! Up now from ship, quickly, my brave knights!"

Even with the words sixty thousand good warriors pressed anon to the fight, and brake Modred's ranks, and well nigh himself was taken. Modred began to flee, and his folk to follow after; they fled exceedingly, the fields eke trembled; the stones jar with the blood-streams! There would have been all the fight ended, but the night came too soon; if the night had not been, they all would have been slain!

The night separated them over slades and over downs; and Modred came so far forth, that he was at London. The burgh-men heard how it had all fared, and denied him entry, and all his folk. Modred thence went toward Winchester; and they him received, with all his men. And Arthur pursued after, with all his might, until he came to Winchester, with a mickle host, and the burgh all besieged; and Modred therein abode. When Modred saw that Arthur was so nigh to him, oft he bethought him what he might do. Then on the same night, he ordered all his knights, with all their weapons, to march out of the burgh; and said that he would with fight there make a stand. He promised the burghmen free law evermore, on condition that they should help him at his great need.

When it was daylight, then ready was their fight. Arthur that perceived—the king was enraged; he caused trumpets to be blown, and men to be assembled to battle; he commanded all his thanes, and his noble knights, together to take the fight, and fell his enemies, and the burgh all to destroy, and hang the burgh-folk. They stept together, and sternly fought. Modred then thought what he might do; and he did there as he did elsewhere, treachery with the most! For ever he did wickedly; he betrayed his comrades before Winchester, and caused his dearest knights to be called to him anon, and his dearest friends all, of all his folk; and stole away from the fight—the fiend him have!—and let the good folk all there perish. They fought all day; they weened that their lord there lay, and were near them at their great need. Then bent he the way that toward Hampton lay; and bent toward the haven—wickedest of men—and took all the ships that there good were, and all the steersmen, to the need of the ships; and proceeded into Cornwall—wickedest of kings in those days! And Arthur besieged well firmly Winchester the burgh; and slew all the people—there was sorrow enow—the young and the old, all he killed. When the folk was all dead, and the burgh all burnt, then caused he withal all the walls to be broken in pieces.

Then was it there come to pass, that Merlin whilom said:

" Wretched shalt thou be, Winchester! the earth shall thee swallow!" So Merlin said, who was a great prophet.

The queen lay in York; never was she so sorrowful; that was Wenhaver the queen, most miserable of women! She heard say sooth words, how often Modred fled, and how Arthur him pursued; woe was to her the while, that she was alive! Out of York she went by night, and toward Kaerleon drew, as quickly as she might; thither she brought by night two of her knights; and men covered her head with a holy veil, and she was there a nun; woman most wretched! Then men knew not of the queen, where she were gone, nor many years afterwards man knew it in sooth, whether she were dead, or whether she herself were sunk in the water.

Modred was in Cornwall, and gathered many knights; to Ireland he sent his messengers quickly; to Saxland he sent his messengers quickly; to Scotland he sent his messengers quickly; he ordered them all to come anon, that would have land, or silver, or gold, or possessions, or land; in each wise he warned himself each man;—so doth each prudent man upon whom cometh need.

Arthur that heard, wrathest of kings, that Modred was in Cornwall with a mickle army, and there would abide until Arthur approached. Arthur sent messengers over all his kingdom, and bade all to come that was alive in land, that to fight were good, weapons to bear; and whoso it neglected, that the king commanded, the king would him all consume alive in the land. Innumerable folk it came toward the host, riding and on foot, as the rain down falleth!

Arthur marched to Cornwall, with an immense army. Modred heard that, and advanced against him with innumerable folk—there were many fated! Upon the Tambre they came together; the place hight Camelford, evermore lasted the same word. And at Camelford was assembled sixty thousand men, and more thousands thereto; Modred was their chief. Then thitherward gan ride Arthur the mighty, with innumerable folk—fated though it were! Upon the Tambre they encountered together; elevated their standards; advanced together; drew their long swords, and smote on the helms; fire out sprang; spears splintered; shields gan shiver; shafts brake in pieces! There fought all together innumerable folk! Tambre was in flood with blood to excess; there might no man in the fight know any warrior, nor who did worse, nor who did better, so was the conflict mingled! For each slew downright, were he swain, were he knight. There was Modred slain, and deprived of life-day, and all his knights slain in the fight. There were slain all the brave, Arthur's warriors, high and low, and all the Britons of Arthur's board, and all his dependants, of many kingdoms. And Arthur himself wounded with a broad slaughter-spear; fifteen dreadful wounds he had; in the least one might thrust two gloves! Then was there no more remained in the fight, of two hundred thousand men that there lay hewed in pieces, except Arthur the king alone, and two of his knights.

Arthur was wounded wondrously much. There came to him a lad, who was of his kindred; he was Cador's son, the Earl of Cornwall; Constantine the lad hight, he was dear to the king. Arthur looked on him, where he lay on the ground, and said these words, with sorrowful heart: "Constantine, thou art welcome; thou wert Cador's son. I give thee here my kingdom, and defend thou my Britons ever in thy life, and maintain them all the laws that have stood in my days, and all the good laws that in Uther's days stood. And I will fare to Avalun, to the fairest of all maidens, to Argante the queen, an elf most fair, and she shall make my wounds all sound; make me all whole with healing draughts. And afterwards I will come again to my kingdom, and dwell with the Britons with mickle joy."

Even with the words there approached from the sea that was a short boat, floating with the waves; and two women therein, wondrously formed; and they took Arthur anon, and bare him quickly, and laid him softly down, and forth they gan depart.

Then was it accomplished that Merlin whilom said, that mickle care should be of Arthur's departure. The Britons believe yet that he is alive, and dwelleth in Avalun with the fairest of all elves; and the Britons ever yet expect when Arthur shall return. Was never the man born, of ever any lady chosen, that knoweth of the sooth, to say more of Arthur. But whilom was a sage hight Merlin; he said with words—his sayings were sooth—that an Arthur should yet come to help the English.

Everyman
A selection of titles

ESSAYS AND CRITICISM

Arnold, Matthew. *On the Study of Celtic Literature*
*Bacon, Francis. *Essays*
Coleridge, Samuel Taylor
 Biographia Literaria
 Shakespearean Criticism (2 vols)
*Emerson, Ralph. *Essays*
*Milton, John. *Prose Writings*
Montaigne, Michael Eyquem de. *Essays* (3 vols)
Paine, Thomas. *The Rights of Man*
Spencer, Herbert. *Essays on Education and Kindred Subjects*
*Swift, Jonathan. *Tale of a Tub and other satires*

HISTORY

*The Anglo-Saxon Chronicle
Burnet, Gilbert. *History of His Own Time*
*Crèvecoeur. *Letters from an American Farmer*
Gibbon, Edward. *The Decline and Fall of the Roman Empire* (6 vols)
Green, John. *A Short History of the English People* (2 vols)
Prescott, W.H. *History of the Conquest of Mexico*

LEGENDS AND SAGAS

*Beowulf and Its Analogues
*Chrétien de Troyes. *Arthurian Romances*
*Egils saga
 Holinshed, Raphael. *Chronicle*
*Layamon and Wace. *Arthurian Chronicles*
*The Mabinogion
*The Saga of Gisli
*The Saga of Grettir the Strong
 Snorri Sturluson. *Heimskringla* (3 vols)
*The Story of Burnt Njal

POETRY AND DRAMA

*Anglo-Saxon Poetry
*American Verse of the Nineteenth Century
*Arnold, Matthew. *Selected Poems and Prose*
*Blake, William. *Selected Poems*
*Brontës, The. *Selected Poems*
*Browning, Robert. *Men and Women and other poems*
*Burns, Robert. *The Kilmarnock Poems*
*Chaucer, Geoffrey. *Canterbury Tales*
*Clare, John. *Selected Poems*
*Coleridge, Samuel Taylor. *Poems*
*Donne, John. *The Complete English Poems*
*Elizabethan Sonnets
*English Moral Interludes
*Everyman and Medieval Miracle Plays
*Everyman's Book of Evergreen Verse
*Gay, John. *The Beggar's Opera and other eighteenth-century
 plays*
*The Golden Treasury of Longer Poems
*Hardy, Thomas. *Selected Poems*
*Herbert, George. *The English Poems*
*Hopkins, Gerard Manley. *The Major Poems*
 Ibsen, Henrik
    A Doll's House; The Wild Duck; The Lady from the Sea
    Hedda Gabler; The Master Builder; John Gabriel Borkman

*Keats, John. *Poems*
*Langland, William. *The Vision of Piers Plowman*
*Marlowe, Christopher. *Complete Plays and Poems*
*Marvell, Andrew. *Complete Poetry*
*Milton, John. *Complete Poems*
*Middleton, Thomas. *Three Plays*
*Palgrave's Golden Treasury
*Pearl, Patience, Cleanness, and Sir Gawain and the Green Knight
*Poems of the Second World War
*Pope, Alexander. *Collected Poems*
*Restoration Plays
*The Rubáiyát of Omar Khayyám and other Persian poems
*Shelley, Percy Bysshe. *Selected Poems*
*Six Middle English Romances
*Spenser, Edmund. *The Faerie Queene: a selection*
*The Stuffed Owl
*Synge, J.M. *Plays, Poems and Prose*
*Tennyson, Alfred. *In Memoriam, Maud and other poems*
  Thomas, Dylan
    **Collected Poems*, 1934–1952*
    **The Poems*
    **Under Milk Wood*
*Wilde, Oscar. *Plays, Prose Writings and Poems*
*Wordsworth, William. *Selected Poems*

RELIGION AND PHILOSOPHY

---

*Bacon, Francis. *The Advancement of Learning*
*Berkeley, George. *Philosophical Works including the works on
    vision*
*The Buddha's Philosophy of Man
*Chinese Philosophy in Classical Times
*Descartes, René. *A Discourse on Method*
*Hindu Scriptures
*Kant, Immanuel. *A Critique of Pure Reason*
*The Koran
*Leibniz, Gottfried Wilhelm. *Philosophical Writings*
*Locke, John. *An Essay Concerning Human Understanding
    (abridgment)*

*More, Thomas. *Utopia*
Pascal, Blaise. *Pensées*
Plato. *The Trial and Death of Socrates*
*The Ramayana and Mahábhárata

SCIENCES: POLITICAL AND GENERAL

Aristotle. *Ethics*
*Castiglione, Baldassare. *The Book of the Courtier*
*Coleridge, Samuel Taylor. *On the Constitution of the Church
    and State*
*Darwin, Charles. *The Origin of Species*
Derry, John. *English Politics and the American Revolution*
Harvey, William. *The Circulation of the Blood and other
    writings*
*Hobbes, Thomas. *Leviathan*
*Locke, John. *Two Treatises of Government*
*Machiavelli, Niccolò. *The Prince and other political writings*
*Malthus, Thomas. *An Essay on the Principle of Population*
*Mill, J.S. *Utilitarianism; On Liberty; Representative
    Government*
*Plato. *The Republic*
*Ricardo, David. *The Principles of Political Economy and
    Taxation*
Rousseau, J.-J.
    Emile
    The Social Contract and *Discourses*
*Wollstonecraft, Mary. *A Vindication of the Rights of Woman*

TRAVEL AND TOPOGRAPHY

Boswell, James. *The Journal of a Tour to the Hebrides*
*Darwin, Charles. *The Voyage of the 'Beagle'*
*Hudson, W.H. *Idle Days in Patagonia*
*Stevenson, R.L. *An Inland Voyage; Travels with a Donkey; The
    Silverado Squatters*
*Thomas, Edward. *The South Country*
*Travels of Marco Polo
*White, Gilbert. *The Natural History of Selborne*